The Indefatigable

Bob Evans

First Published 2005 by Countyvise Limited, 14 Appin Road, Birkenhead, Wirral CH41 9HH.

The author has made every reasonable effort to contact all copyright holders. Any errors/omissions that may have occurred are inadvertent and regretted, and anyone who, for any reason, has not been contacted is invited to write to the publishers so that full acknowledgement may be made in subsequent editions of this work.

British Library Cataloguing in Publication Data.
A catalogue record for this book is available from the British Library.

ISBN 1 901231 53 4

The Story of Indefatigable
1864 - 1995

H.M.S. Indefatigable

Indefatigable Memorial Window
St. Mary's Church, Llanfair Pwll

This book is dedicated to
The Inde Lads

'*And all I ask is a merry yarn from a laughing fellow rover,*
And a quiet sleep and a sweet dream when the long trick's over'

Sea Fever .... John Masefield

Foreword

I commend and congratulate the author on his painstaking research and the production of such an interesting and informative history of the United Kingdom's first and last Training Ship establishment for boys wishing to make a career, essentially in the Merchant Navy, covering its 131 years, 1864 to 1995.

The many extracts from former boys epitomise, not only the training received but life in general and the exemplary standards when at Indefatigable. Also the author notes the involvement, particularly of the Bibby Shipping Line and of many others in the leadership of the shipping industry and of the Maritime and Civic life of Merseyside.

It is worth recounting the following. At the Centenary Celebrations in 1964 when the Ship's principal patron, H.R.H. the Duke of Edinburgh, at the School said: "Any boy going through a School like this is trained for leadership."

At the beginning the Founding Fathers asked the question "What is to be done about the many orphans whose only crime was they were the sons of seamen?" So Indefatigable was set up for 'the training of orphans and boys in poor circumstances'.

1989 saw the final evolution of the School with an up-dating of facilities and a redefining of its objectives to ensure the young men being a success in their chosen careers.

It was an honour to be asked to dedicate the Memorial Window given pride of place at St. Mary's Church at Llanfair PwIl in Anglesey and to read in the Liverpool Post of June, 1999 that we had immortalised in glass the Indefatigable Spirit.

I have been privileged to have been involved since joining the Committee in 1961 and to have been President of the School when it closed in 1995 and now to be President of the O.B.A.

I am delighted that Bob Evans has added the Indefatigable story to our proud maritime history.

H. Lionel Storrs
President of the O.B.A.
Hoylake 2005

Preface

The unofficial motto of the Indefatigable lads is 'Get stuck in and get it done'. That's the Inde Way! Steve Humphries, the secretary of the Old Boys' Association suggested that I do just that ... and his assistance was immeasurable. This book had to be written before time runs out. Patrick Purser, a onetime staff member of the ship, was wise enough to launch a News Letter and these have collated a century of stories. There is no better source for an author. Happily I had already produced an outline of the history in my book The Training Ships of Liverpool and that was the start. Some editing was essential as much material was repetitive with obvious references to food, the lack of, and how tough they had to be to survive, compared to those who came after them. Where possible I have acknowledged in the script all ownership. As ever, photographs have been kept over the years with little if any details of names or dates so many have just been produced into limbo. This preface could be a list of the names of those who readily have given their assistance, but you know who you are and your thanks must be the book itself. There is one exception. The President of the Old Boys' Association, Lionel Storrs, J.P., has ever been a vital player in the survival of Indefatigable, over a number of years and I thank him for his Foreword. We have known each other for over half of our lifetimes and his encouragement, friendship and good humour have been a joy to me.

I am grateful to Jean and John Emmerson of Countyvise Limited for their immense help in the printing and publishing ... they are good friends. However, there will be blemishes, mistakes and omissions and with apologies they can be only attributed to me.

I would like to record the support, patience and skills of my family in the production of this book. I make demands and with a smile they respond!

The Indefatigable lads are all out in the world now, some made their contribution and are no longer with us, others continue to carry the torch which is theirs and as long as they remain, the memories will flourish.

This book is dedicated to them ... the INDE LADS.

The James J. Bibby

This book is sponsored by the Old Boys Association and by the Mersey Mission to Seafarers. All the profits are for nautical charities. Many Old Boys made private donations.

Ann Lyon - In memory of Uncle Edgar 1920/22

Roger Astley 1945/46

Jim Taylor 1946

Ken Hedges 1947/48

Edward Tomlinson 1950/51

Walter Price-Roberts 1952/53

Roger Jones 1953/56

Alan Meadows 1954/55

Iori Williams 1957/58 - In memory of Elfed Jones 1957/58

Spencer Bell 1958

Ian Patterson 1960/65

Martin Bell 1962

Charlie Claridge 1962/63

Tom Keyes 1962/64

Norman Walker 1963/65

Gary Gray 1965/66

Nigel Firman 1967/68

Steve Copley 1973/75

Mike Green 1974/75

Bill O'Leary 1974/76

Steve Humphries 1975/76

Tony Eastham 1975/76

Steve Paris 1976/78

David Levey 1983/86

John Tranmer (Staff) 1983/87 - In memory of Peter Burrell (Staff) 1973/95

Tim Ames 1986/89

Gareth Jones

All Members of the Indefatigable OBA.

Lady Bibby also contributed.

The Indefatigable

Number One was a third rate of 64 guns built at Bucklers Hard in 1784, reduced to 38 guns in 1795 and broken up at Sheerness in 1816. In 1795 she was commanded by Sir Edward Pellew (Admiral Sir Edward Pellew, Bart., Viscount Exmouth, 1775 - 1833).

Number Two was a 16-gun ship, purchased in 1804 and sold in 1805. Little is known of her purpose or history.

Number Three never really existed! She was to have been a 50-gun fourth rate, ordered in 1832 from Woolwich Dockyard, but was cancelled before completion in March 1834.

Number Four was another 50-gun fourth rate, built in Devonport in 1848. She was of 2,626 tons with twenty eight 8-inch guns and twenty two 32-pounders. On the 3rd of January, 1865, she was loaned as a training ship and came to Liverpool; she was sold for breaking up on 26th March, 1914.

Number Five was launched on the 12th March 1891 by the London and Glasgow Shipyard as a second class cruiser of 6,300 tons with two 6-inch guns, six 4.7-inch guns and thirteen 6-pounders. In January 1910 she was renamed Melpomene and sold off in October 1913.

Number Six needed the name change of its predecessor and was a battle cruiser of 19,200 tons. She was completed at Devonport in October

1909, but probably not commissioned until early 1910. She was sunk at the Battle of Jutland.

Number Seven was one of the Illustrious Class Aircraft Carriers of 26,000 tons, built by John Brown on Clydebank and launched on the 8th of December, 1942. She was in the Home Fleet in 1944 and in the Pacific Fleet in 1945. She survived the war, was then used as part of the training squadron and was eventually broken up at Dalmuir in November 1956.

Number eight was H.M.S. PHAETON of 4,300 tons was built by Napiers in 1883. Originally built with ten 6-inch guns, but was sold in 1913 as the Training Ship INDEFATIGABLE and was renamed on the 1st of January, 1914. She remained under this name until 1941, when, requisitioned by the Admiralty she was renamed CARRICK II, served as a store ship on the Clyde throughout the war, and was finally broken up by Wards of Preston in January 1947. It is a puzzle as to why she was called CARRICK II. CARRICK I at that time was the R.N.V.R. Drill Ship in Glasgow and was used during the war as an accommodation ship. She also came to an end in 1947.

Meanwhile, due to the Luftwaffe blitzes on Merseyside, temporary accommodation for INDEFATIGABLE was found at Clwydd Newydd in North Wales before moving to its final home at Plas Llanfair on Anglesey in 1944.

H.M.S. Phaeton

ℭhe Ship's ℭrest

Deo Adjuvante

The ship's crest was adopted from the Coat of Arms of Admiral Sir Edward Pellew, who commanded the first INDEFATIGABLE during the Napoleonic Wars. He earned his title after the destruction of the French Ship-of-the-Line, DROITS DE L'HOMME, in 1797.

The official description of the badge: 'Through a wreath Laurel proper, a Lion penant gardant gold'.

His Motto was also adopted … Deo Adjuvante … 'With God's Help' or 'God Being My Helper'.

But the School had its own translation (that is a loose use of the word), quoted by so many of the boys as they ignored 'Deo Adjuvante'.

'The Inde Way, get stuck in and get it done.'

The Ship's Bell

The Bell was important to the Inde Boys. Most of the Inde boys spent much time cleaning and polishing the Bell, whether they liked it or not!

Dave Wilson wrote in 1985: 'Yoda Burrell was the one who generally caught us talking, but when it was his watch it was a blessing to stand under the Bell, rather than get 'the Keys'! Was it a waste of time? I normally deserved the choice … Bell or Keys … and it helped me adopt the Inde way, get stuck in and get it done.'

There is some confusion as to which Bell is meant … the Ship's Bell was positioned outside near the mast, but another brass fire bell was situated in the main corridor and yet another brass bell was hung in the messdeck!

The Bell was cast at the Rainhill foundry of Utley Ltd. to the order of a Mr. Robinson of Knowsley. It was cast in 1912 and was the next bell to be created after the TITANIC. It was presented to the replacement INDEFATIGABLE in 1913. The Bell was used to indicate the ship's position during fog, as a fire alarm because there was no other sound signalling device and, of course, to summon the faithful to Divine Service on Sunday.

When the School closed, the Bell was auctioned off with all the other artefacts. The OBA was in attendance along with the indomitable Patrick Purser who raised his hand and kept it up, indicating to all that he was going to have that Bell! The bidding ended in the region of £1,300 and we had expected the sale to reach £350. "We had a whip round for the deposit. Luckily a friend of the OBA and of INDEFATIGABLE, Pat Moran, had come to purchase one of the school boats, without success. With further help from Captain Bob Youngman, the Bell was acquired."

Because of fifty years of diligent cleaning, the name was re-cut. Marc Hardman secured the expertise of an ex-employee of Utleys, and in due time the Bell and the Trophies were placed into the safe keeping of Colonel Nichols, Commander of the Joint Services Mountain Training Centre, INDEFATIGABLE.

Bell and trophies presented (on loan), to J.S.M.T.C. Indefatigable at Plas Llanfair 1998

The Ship's Figurehead

The wooden figurehead was carved for H.M.S. INDEFATIGABLE in 1848 (number four on the list of ships) in the image of the Duke of Clarence, who became King William IV.

It was transferred to the new INDEFATIGABLE and eventually ended in the School at Plas Llanfair. It now has pride of place in Liverpool's Maritime Museum after complete restoration by Old Boys of the School.

That restoration uncovered the fact that the entire core of the figurehead had rotted away, necessitating complete renewal of the inner carcass. The Old Boys obtained 100-year old pitch pine salvaged from the old Liverpool Princes Landing Stage to renew that inner core.

To ascertain the correct colour of the Order of the Bath sash, Jack Harrison (1941-1943) wrote to Clarence House asking for the required information. Jack received a length of the Order of the Bath ribbon and best wishes from the Queen Mother.

Two time capsules were incorporated into the figurehead, one in the base containing copies of the INDEFATIGABLE Old Boys Association Newsletters and local newspapers, containing articles regarding the work done on the figurehead.

The second capsule, constructed behind the brass back plate, contains a complete list of all the boys who trained on INEFATIGABLE from its inception in 1864 to the last boy in 1995. Also the names of those who helped in the restoration, a complete set of the 1995 coins of the realm, two complete sets of war medals of the Old Boys from both world wars and photographs of the two ships, along with photographs of interest.

Contents

The Indefatigable

Chapter 1
The Beginning
1864

The name is a proud one ... there were a number of ships bearing it in the Royal Navy. Two of them became schools for the training of boys for the Royal Navy and the Merchant Navy. Many thousands of young men were to learn their trade in INDEFATIGABLE.

One hundred years after the School was founded in 1864, the Centenary Celebrations were honoured by the presence of the ship's principal patron, H.R.H. the Duke of Edinburgh, who said: "Any boy going through a school like this is trained for leadership." No-one can question the importance of community living and outdoor activities in encouraging integrity, self-reliance and those other qualities of character that create leaders.

This is the INDEFATIGABLE story.

All those years ago, there was no compulsory education in Britain. There was no government control or even much interest in educating the young. That did not start until 1872. However, there had been Charity Schools for the poor boys since the Sixteenth Century and even before. Most were Church foundations. In Liverpool we had the famous Bluecoat School, founded in 1708 by Bryan Blundell, another wealthy shipowner, "... to teach poor children to read, write, ... cast accounts ... and to be instructed in the Principles and Doctrines of the Established Church ..."

The City of Liverpool contained many orphans, children of seafaring men. Life was cheap at sea and far too many were lost to watery graves, yet the city was growing rich at a sad cost of human suffering and neglect. Most ports and towns let the public guardians take charge of the poor and needy. Liverpool was different. Badly behaved youngsters were sent to the reformatory •ships (AKBAR and CLARENCE) and were generally treated far better than the lads left behind on the streets. Their only fault was that they were poor. An attempt to obtain government aid was not successful. So the decision to 'go it alone' was made.

In 1863, a Liverpool seaman and ship owner, Captain John Clint, conceived the idea of providing means of training the sons and orphans of seamen and other boys of good character in the ways of the sea. He was concerned about the orphans and poor boys in the city. Clint was an enthusiast. With his friends and the help of the Mayor (Mr. C. Mozley) a public meeting was called at the Town Hall in the September of 1863 and an immediate subscription list was opened to produce the required monies.

Clint set about the task of persuading the 'Liverpool Fathers' to foot the bill for each boy. His intention was to take the willing orphans, to teach them a seafaring trade, and to save them from falling into a life of crime. There were thousands to choose from!

John Clint was a remarkable man. He was born at South Shields in 1787 and at the age of twelve he went to sea in a coaster, sailing between the Tyne and the Thames. Six years later he was engaged as Second Mate on a voyage to The Honduras and on the return journey his ship almost foundered and with a desperate struggle managed to reach Bermuda. There the ship was declared unseaworthy. His ships must have been armed as he mentions that they carried 'letters of Marque' entitling them to a bit of official 'piracy'. Very quickly at the age of twenty John Clint received his first command, the ELIZABETH, sailing for Jamaica from Liverpool.

His life at sea had been full of drama, but in 1822 with his second wife he came to Liverpool at the age of 35 and began his career as a ship owner. In his autobiography John Clint says, 'I bought shares in several ships and made some valuable friends.'

His fortunes rose and he became a respected member of Liverpool's shipping circles. He had his finger in many pies and this resulted in his increasing awareness of the needs of sailors who had helped to create his wealth.

His great friend was John Cropper, who proved to be a motivating influence on Clint, and this friendship resulted in turning Clint's mind to good causes. James Cropper had worked well to abolish the slave trade, and his son John, together with John Clint, were prime movers in establishing the AKBAR, the Protestant Reform Ship off Rock Ferry. Much more was to follow. Clint helped found the Liverpool Shipowners' Association in 1839 and was appointed deputy chairman. Next came the Pilots' Committee, the Dock and Harbour Company, the first Steam Tug Company, the Liverpool Sailors' Home, the Northern Hospital and, above all the Training Ships on the Mersey ... in particular the AKBAR (the Protestant Reform Ship), H.M.S. CONWAY (for Merchant Navy Officer training) and the INDEFATIGABLE. He was the prime mover in all these organisations. But he is on record stating that he regarded the founding of the Training Ship INDEFATIGABLE as his crowning achievement and he devoted his declining years to ensure the success of that venture.

John Clint had asked a question. 'What could be done about the many orphans whose only crime was that they were the sons of seamen?' He was the first to take positive action. He would organise the care of these boys, he stated, as long as they were trained as seamen for Liverpool ships.

The first annual report of the INDEFATIGABLE contained a significant paragraph. 'To the unceasing and benevolent exertions of our townsman, Mr. John Clint, the institution mainly owes its origin.' Of almost equal importance was the first executive committee with well-known shipowners to the fore ... T.H. Ismay and William Inman with James J. Bibby in the chair. If John Clint is regarded as a prime mover, it was to the generosity of the Bibby family that INDEFATIGABLE

James J. Bibby

was to owe its future and survival. The Bibby contribution to the success of INDEFATIGABLE was to prove to be immeasureable.

Having conceived his vision, Clint met a number of gentlemen at a private meeting on the 12th September, 1864, at the rooms of the Mercantile Marine Association. There a provisional committee was formed. A resolution passed, moved by Mr. Francis A. Clint and seconded by Mr. Robert Rankin, that 'a deputation be appointed to wait upon his Worship the Mayor, and request him to call a meeting with a view to ascertaining if sufficient support can be obtained to establish and maintain the proposed new Ship.'

That first committee decided that boys of all denominations and faiths should be accepted for training, although there should be 'daily readings of the Bible and morning and evening services in the form of the Church of England'.

In 1863 Clint applied to Sir James Graham, First Lord of the Admiralty, assisted by Captain Alfred Ryder, R.N., then a member of a Commission of Enquiry into the state of Navigation Schools, asking for a smart, neat, masted ship-of-war for the Mersey.

The Admiralty agreed to loan INDEFATIGABLE, a fifty-gun frigate, built at the Royal Dockyard in Devonport and launched in 1848. The shipowner, James J. Bibby, contributed £5,000 to transform her from warship to training ship. This was a vast sum of money and a remarkable gift.

INDEFATIGABLE had cruised in the Channel for some time and then was sent to the West Indies, under the command of Captain Robert Smart, K.H., and remained there for some time. In 1851 she was fitted out for Mediterranean service, where she was employed until 1853. She was next commissioned as the flag-ship of Admiral Sir W.J. Hope Johnstone, K.C.B., Commander-in-Chief on the South American station and remained there until she was brought back to be paid off at Devonport in 1857.

The length of the upper deck was 190 feet; of her main deck, 186 feet; and of her lower deck, 177 feet. The height between decks was 7 feet 3 inches.

Back home in 1857 she joined the Reserve Fleet in Devonport. It was the time when sailing ships were being converted to engine power and most were to end their days as floating barracks or store hulks. In 1864 INDEFATIGABLE came to the Sloyne, off Rock Ferry, and the work of INDEFATIGABLE started. She was to remain there until she was broken up in Birkenhead in 1914.

Chapter 2
The Early Years
1864 - 1913

Right from the start it was made clear that in no way was INDEFATIGABLE to be a reformatory ship, but was to be used for the training of 'orphans and boys in poor circumstances'.

Her main deck became a classroom, a tailor's shop and quarters for the Captain and his wife. The first master was Captain Groom assisted by his Chief Officer, Mr. Davis; it was part of the scheme for training boys that there should be a maternal influence and so Mrs. Groom joined her husband on board. Their cabin, its ports decked with plants and flowers, became a familiar and homely sight to passing ships and a haven to which boys could come with the kind of problems on which only a mother could advise.

The portholes in the lower deck were enlarged to provide better living conditions for the 200 boys that the ship was intended to accommodate. The lower deck also provided classrooms. The lower hold became the practice room for the band and the upper deck was used as a drill space and for a galley and a hospital.

It was a brave sight of wooden-walled ships ... INDEFATIGABLE, H.M.S. CONWAY, CLARENCE and AKBAR. Another famous old ship, the giant GREAT EASTERN, was also moored off Rock Ferry as a show ship. The GREAT EASTERN's compass was removed and housed aboard INDEFATIGABLE and used for instruction.

At the end of the first year in 1865, just forty-eight boys had been accommodated, but slowly the numbers grew as money was obtained. The aim was still for 200 lads, although the ship could actually house 300. It was estimated that £20 a year would cover the maintenance, the education and the apprenticeship of each boy.

The first boys to join INDEFATIGABLE on the Mersey did so on the 28th August, 1864. Amongst them was Maurice Abrahams. His entry record reads as follows:

Age, 14 years; Complexion dark; Hair brown; Eyes brown.
Height 4 ft 6 ¾ inches; Weight 77 lbs.
Where born: Poulton, Somersetshire.
Last school: Christ Church, Liverpool.
Last employment: Watchmakery.
Father's name: Isaac Abrahams (deserted).
Father's occupation: Pawnbroker.
Mother's name: Ann Abrahams. Character: Good.
Mother's occupation: Housekeeper.
Residence: 45, Clayton Street, Liverpool.
Date of Leaving: 4th October, 1866. Bound Apprentice to Messrs Clint and Co., for 4 years, and joined ship GANGES for Calcutta. £30. (This to last for four years!)
Character on Leaving: Very Good.
Height on Leaving: 4ft 7½ inches.
Report after leaving Ship: September 12th, 1870, left his first employ, but doing very well as Able Seaman.
1876: Drowned at sea.

Incidentally, the very last boy to be entered in the Ship's Book of INDEFATIGABLE was David Reay who joined on the 24th April, 1995, aged 13 years. David lived at Little Sutton, South Wirral. Sadly his time at the School was very short.

This book is the story of the Inde Boys ... starting with Maurice in 1865 and ending with David in 1995.

The Illustrated London News carried an article of note on May 5th

1866. Also printed was a drawing of a 'Divine Service on Board', (the sketch was drawn by Mr W. Woods of Liverpool and the details of the article were taken from Liverpool's Daily Courier.).

'The INDEFATIGABLE is a fine vessel, and she has been fitted up with the greatest regard for utility, combined with comfort. Prayers are read morning and evening by Captain Groom, and the services of the Church of England conducted on Sundays by the same gentleman.'

In 1873 INDEFATIGABLE broke her moorings and was badly damaged. The dock repairs took eight months. No new boys could be accepted. However, back on station, the work continued with the launch of a floating bath for the use of the boys who were able to combine sport with cleanliness. There were 149 boys aboard with the Captain, a Chief Officer, a carpenter, a cook, two schoolmasters and four seamen instructors. There was no aid from the State, but the venture was viable with voluntary support sufficient to meet expenditure.

The Annual General Meeting in 1875 concerned itself about the needs of the boys aboard. Mr. Shallcross, a shipowner, proposed that the lads

should leave INDEFATIGABLE and take apprenticeships aboard vessels. Mr. Bushell, whilst agreeing in principle, thought that it would not be possible until better wages could be paid. The fact was that boys were placed in vessels when they left INDEFATIGABLE, but remained for one voyage only because they could receive better wages elsewhere as ordinary seamen. 'While an apprentice boy received perhaps £40 in four years, boys who went out as ordinary seamen found that they could obtain £1 a month, and in about twelve months were able to ship for £2 10s or even £3 a month. Apprentices receiving only £6 or £8 in their second year therefore became dissatisfied, though the committee pointed out to them that, probably at the end of five years, they would find themselves in a better position than boys who went out at first as ordinary seamen.'

A letter was then read to the Meeting.

'My conviction is that some decided action must before long be taken to maintain the standard of our British seamen, otherwise they will most certainly cease to exist. The rapid deterioration in the quality of our sailors I attribute to the following causes:
1. The best of them settled in California and Australia between the years 1849 and 1860.

2.   *The abandonment of compulsory apprenticeships.*
3.   *The loss of the best of all schools for training seamen ... the coal
     trade on our east and west coasts ... it being now chiefly carried
     on by steam in lieu of sailing vessels.*
4.   *The increased demand for boys in the iron ship building and boiler
     yards of the country, which hold out greater inducements to them
     pecuniarily, than going to sea.*
*Hence, unless better pay is given to apprentices ... as suggested by Mr.
William Inman ... and the system made once more compulsory, I can see
but a gloomy future for the efficient manning of our ships.'*

William Gregson entered INDEFATIGABLE on the 24th August, 1880,
and left on the 17th November, 1882, for Hamburg to join the barque
SCOTTISH CHIEF, owned by Messrs. Tomlinson and Hodgetts, as an
apprentice at £30 for three years. In August 1931 a letter was received
by the ship.

*'A strange address to you.
R1 - Box 387, Fort Worth Tex.
Commander of the INDEFATIGABLE Training Ship for Boys.
Dear Sir and Friend,*

*Anybody would be a friend of mine who had charge of the old tub as she
was called in the year 1880, at which time I was one of the boys and my
number was 19. The greatest pleasure was to do something and get by
the petty officer - also Mr. Carmickle our officer and Mr. Lewis another
and Mr. Smith the bandmaster, a man I will never forget. I was in the
band - or I should say learning to be a band boy. The bandmaster had
a bad habit, or at least I thought it was so, that was rapping the boys
on the knuckles if they did not hold their instruments high enough. On
one occasion I took all that I could stand and like the tortured worm, I
turned. I was leaning on the cornet and on this occasion of which I
write, I brought the bell of the cornet heavily across the bridge of Mr.
Smith's nose - right then he lost what might have been the makings of a
good musician, but I had decided never no more.*
    *'Captain Groom was in command in them days and I will say God
Bless him and his good wife. I am of a turn to do all kinds of fancy rope*

work and twine and Mrs. Groom showed me what became the foundation of my continuing the same. Today my place of business is full of fancy rope work, as you can tell by the cut from our daily paper. (Sadly lost.) Officer Lewis and I were good friends and to make a few pennies, and being of a business idea, chewing tobacco was a best seller, so I would bring aboard about half a pound, and sell that chew for a penny - but the big thing was to get past the gangway with it. The reason I went on shore so much, the Captain's wife had me appointed cabin boy shore messenger. I will state here that it was very seldom that I was caught, yet being searched pretty well, and for the last eight months of my time I was never caught, being told by the Captain's wife if I was caught again, no more shore. I still took a chance at the tobacco business.

'This letter got started to you on account of seeing the picture of the boat race which was printed in the Liverpool Weekly Post of July 11th, 1931. I wonder do they still put up a good meal at the petty officers end of mess table and leave boys at the other end with almost nothing, especially Duff-Day Thursday. I was certainly glad when I reversed ends. I often thought there should be a sign over each mess - do unto others, as you would like to be done by.

'Well for this time will say - give my best regards to the boys and the same for yourself and family.

> *Yours respectfully,*
> *Wm. Gregson.*
> *Rope Cable Splicer and Fancy Rope Worker.*
> *Please answer.'*

Actually the newspaper cutting has been preserved, but no title or date is evident.

OLD SAILOR, FAR INLAND, MAKING SEA-FARING KNOTS.

'Bo'sn William Gregson, seaman on a British windjammer in the days of iron men and wooden ships, is still making knots - while he keeps a weather eye out for customers at his little filling station on the Grapevine Road.

'This far inland, and even on the sea, now that ropes and hawsers have given way to cables of steel, he finds little use for the intricate knots he learned during his eleven years as a sailor. So he has turned to fancy work in ropes, making trees and houses and similar articles from bright-coloured rope strands.

'The talk of the grizzled seaman, 66, who shipped before the mast from a little Lancashire village when he was 14, still has the salty twang of the sea. With a deft twist he fashions a complicated jury masthead knot and explains its use.

' "Your masts have been carried away by the blow," he says. "You cut them away with an axe and set up the jury spar, nailing four cleats at the bottom." Then, grasping the four ends of the knot he has tied, "You slip on the jury masthead knot. One end goes to the bowsprit, one to the right rail, one to the left, and the training ends are the back guys. You run up a little cloth to hold her steady, else you wallow in the trough of the seas, shipping water on one side and emptying on the other."

'Three times Gregson went around the world as boatswain and acting second officer of the British barque, SCOTTISH CHIEF. Seven times he rounded Cape Horn and five times the Cape of Good Hope. He quit the sea to take a job on a freighter on the Great Lakes, having been told it was easier than the life on an ocean-going vessel. But loading lumber and standing watch in 24 hour shifts was not to his liking and he drifted to the oil-fields as a cable splicer. The activity in the oil fields about Beaumont first brought him to Texas and he came to Fort Worth in 1908.

'Since then he has been rigging boss for several structural steel companies and at the helium plant north of the city. But an old man cannot climb. "You see, when a man gets old, his brain turns to water," he explains. "When he gets aloft and the water goes off balance, he thinks he is going to fall ... and he does!"

'So he sticks to running his filling station, busying himself with his knots and his fancy rope work between customers.'

It has been a rare opportunity to follow the career of yet another Inde boy who 'made it good' in the wide, wide world across the pond.

Twenty years after the beginning of the school in INDEFATIGABLE, the main theme at the 1885 Annual General Meeting was 'care of the boys'. The Honorary Secretary, Mr. Charles J. Bushell, reported that, in spite of the intensity of the commercial depression, INDEFATIGABLE was prospering. Describing the boys, he stated that 79 of the lads aboard had lost both parents, 93 had no fathers, 19 had been deserted and only 31 had fathers living. Sadly the numbers shipped as apprentices had slumped to eleven. Again the problem of training was discussed and pin-pointed by the Mayor in his address. 51 lads became ordinary seamen and 15 of them joined the Royal Naval Reserve, 8 were sent to sea as stewards, 1 entered the Royal Navy, 13 were sent to occupations on shore. The grand total of boys on board on the 31st December, 1885, was 222. Captain Miller, R.N., thought the vessel was beautifully clean, and the boys seemed healthy and happy, and were neat, tidy and respectable wherever one happened to meet them. This statement was greeted with applause!

On the 7th June, 1887, a young lad named Henry George Kendall joined INDEFATIGABLE aged thirteen years and remained on board for three years. In the December of 1890 he was placed in the S.S. CITY OF BERLIN as an ordinary seaman. He was 4 feet 6 inches on joining and weighed 74 pounds. On completion of training in INDEFATIGABLE he was 5 feet in height and weighed 102 pounds. In July 1898 he passed for Mate. In January 1900 he passed for Master and in April 1902 he passed for Extra Master.

Why is this information of note?

He was involved with the Crippen affair. As Master of the S.S. MONTROSE he instigated the radio message on the 22nd July 1910, that led to the arrest of Doctor Crippen and his accomplice. Four years later in May 1914, Captain Kendall took command of the EMPRESS OF IRELAND, which was lost in one of world's worst seafaring disasters. Whilst steaming down the St. Lawrence river on 29th May, 1914, she was struck amidships in dense fog by the heavily laden collier, STORSTAD, and the EMPRESS OF IRELAND sank within fifteen minutes with the loss of over 1,000 lives. Her crew were mostly from Liverpool. At the subsequent inquiry, Lord Mersey absolved Captain Kendall from all blame, and found the STORSTAD entirely responsible for the collision.

Captain Henry Kendall, like many of INDEFATIGABLE's Old Boys, served with distinction both in war and in peace for his country and shipowners.

Jack Harrison, 1941-1942, provided the details of that story for Newsletter 2000.

The Liverpool Review published an article headed 'Making Men of Them' on January 21st 1888 and it gives a remarkably detailed picture of life aboard at that time.

'I was crossing to the INDEFATIGABLE by the mid-day boat from the New Ferry stage. A raw, easterly wind was sweeping down the Sloyne, and ever and anon the choppy water splashed over the boat's side as the lads bent vigorously to their work. There were ten of them at the oars - clean, healthy looking, fairly robust, - and seemingly happy as they smiled back to their coxwain's repeated 'Give it to her boys.' Presently we passed under the frigate's stern, and I noticed that the cabin windows were adorned by a collection of plants, among them being a number of newly-shooted hyacinths.

'I found that we had 'landed' on the main deck of the old frigate, and my first feeling was one of blank astonishment. I had no conception of her possessing such a magnificent main-deck as that upon which I stood. Its planks were as clean as a laundress' table top. As I afterwards learnt, its length is about 186 feet, and its breadth 54 feet, and over its entire length and breadth disported the major portion of the 226 youths who make up her company. They were enjoying their half hour recreation after dinner. It was play time. They failed to agree as to whether I was one of Her Majesty's Inspectors, a City Councillor, or a visitor.

'At 1.30 work was resumed for the afternoon. Briefly the routine aboard is this. The boys are divided into two watches, the port and the starboard. From 9 a.m. to 12 noon one set are engaged in ordinary school duties, going through a systematic course of reading, spelling, writing, geography, arithmetic, dictation and scripture. The other set are meanwhile pursuing a course of technical instruction at the opposite side of the main-deck, and are divided from the former by a long canvas screen running nearly the length of the deck. The second set of lads are engaged in making clothes, learning to knot and splice, to make hammocks and mats, and when the weather permits are initiated into the practical duties of a sailor's life. In the summer they are accustomed to going aloft, to setting and reefing sails, sending up and down masts and yards, and, generally, are taught as much practical navigation as can be imparted upon a training ship in berth. At 12 o'clock dinner is prepared. By 1 p.m. it has been disposed of and the lads have half an hour liberty. At 1.30 p.m. instruction is resumed and continues until 4 p.m. Much of their time in the evening is devoted to reading and voluntary studies. Navigation being an extra branch of learning is largely studied by them during the evening hours.

'In the tailoring class, two of them were soon busily stitching away with sewing machines at serge garments. In the splicing and knotting class, a rope was fixed horizontally about five feet from the floor, around which were looped a number of short lengths of thinner rope by means of which a dozen youngsters were mastering the technicalities of knot, noose, and 'hitch', under the supervision of an ancient mariner. Further forward another dozen were busy manufacturing new hammocks, and still further another set were making rope door-mats. Two wringing machines stood 'amidships.' These were occasionally used by lads, who, as if upon the duty of stewardship intent, suddenly appeared from undiscoverable quarters, and wringing such articles as they bore, as suddenly disappeared.

'On Sundays, service is regularly held upon the main deck. One of the most conspicuous articles upon it is a beautiful Connoisseur organ, which the ship's company would not part with for a gold mine. When the strains of that organ are blended with the voices of the 226 INDEFATIGABLE lads ... well! ... I know of Liverpool church choirs of repute which, in comparison, are thrown very far into the background. Stand on New Ferry stage some genial Sunday morning in the Spring, reader, and listen to the music of organ and voices as they float across the water, and say if you do not endorse this opinion.

'Below is the lower or sleeping deck, where in the day time, the only conspicuous feature is vacuity, space, emptiness. The deck is 177 feet long, and in the days when INDEFATIGABLE was in commission it housed some 450 of Her Majesty's tars. In the morning the hammocks are unslung and are stowed away out of sight. At night they are slung and the lads turn in, watch being kept on the lower deck under the superintendence of a petty officer.

'The ship is heated throughout by means of steam pipes supplied from a vertical boiler in the kitchen or 'galley' upon the upper deck forward. By means of steam from the same boiler the greater part of the ship's cooking is done, a separate fire range being, however, provided for roasting purposes. The prepared food is placed in vessels upon the shelves of a cage that descends and ascends by means of a hoist, to the main deck upon which the meals are taken.

'On the upper deck, too, is placed the hospital. This is a roomy and cheerful apartment, for which happily there is no great demand. It had two inmates on the occasion of my visit, neither of whom presented a serious case. The walls were hung with pictures and motto-verses, one of which struck me forcibly. The words were these:
> Guarding the weak, and
> Loving the right,
> Be each British boy
> As a Christian knight.

I thought the words were very simple, very unsentimental, but very 'anglice', very appropriate.

'Sufficient knowledge is imparted to qualify for a second mate's ticket as far as theoretical navigation is concerned. In accordance, however, with the Board of Trade requirement, it is necessary for a boy to serve four years as a practical seaman before obtaining an officer's certificate.'

So ended this rather remarkable article in the Liverpool Review.

The Lancashire Merchant and Ship Canal News contained an article on INDEFATIGABLE in its December 1st edition, 1888.

'The demand for trained seamen continues to increase, and no difficulty is experienced in obtaining situations for the boys. The value of their training is well understood, and they never enter into a seafaring life without a very fair prospect before them. It was recently stated on authority that there were in the British service 200,000 seamen, and that of this number 20,000 were foreigners.

'Every comfort is enjoyed by the lads. They are given a good general education. Captain Groom is to the lads what a kind sympathetic father is to his children. Of course, with so many human beings on board, sickness and accidents must occasionally occur and for these cases a pretty well ventilated hospital is provided. It contains six beds, but very seldom more than two are occupied, for the health of the lads is well looked after, and the dietary scale, which we give below, shows they are provided with wholesome and nourishing food, and consequently enjoy better health than many lads at home whose stomachs are pampered and spoiled with sweetmeats.

SUNDAY
	Breakfast	Cocoa, Bread and Butter.
	Dinner	Roast Beef, Suet Pudding.
	Tea	Tea, Bread and Butter.

MONDAY
	Breakfast	Cocoa and biscuit.
	Dinner	Beef, Potatoes, Vegetable Soup.
	Tea	Tea and biscuit.

TUESDAY
	Breakfast	Oatmeal Porridge and Syrup.
	Dinner	Beef, Potatoes and Vegetable Soup.
	Tea	Tea and Biscuit.

WEDNESDAY
	Breakfast	Cocoa and Biscuit.
	Dinner	Pork and Pea Soup.
	Tea	Tea and Biscuit.

THURSDAY
	Breakfast	Porridge and Syrup.
	Dinner	Beef and Suet Pudding.
	Tea	Tea, Bread and Butter.

FRIDAY

Breakfast	Cocoa and Biscuit.
Dinner	Beef, Potatoes and Soup.
Tea	Tea and Biscuit.

SATURDAY

Breakfast	Porridge and Syrup
Dinner	Beef, Potatoes and Soup,
Tea	Tea and Biscuit.

The article continued.

'It is a red letter day for the lads when the time comes for them to be sent out, which they are, first in small bodies to the Captain of a vessel who may require a hand, and selects the one he thinks the most suitable. The lad then returns to INDEFATIGABLE for his kit and credentials, and his pride may surely be pardoned as he steps aboard, saluting the officer with, 'I'm shipped, sir.' His face is a true index of his heart and mind, as he relates to his companions his account of the vessel he is engaged on.

"And how much a month will tha' have, Jack?" is about the first question asked.

"Thirty shillings to start with and after this voyage something more."

"Where are you going to first?"

"The West Indies."

The lads bid him goodbye, and the more thoughtful determine to push on with their studies.

'Captain John Groom is a man of great experience, and as would be expected, during his travels has collected some rare and beautiful plants, which now help to adorn his room. The steward's apartments are in the fore part of the vessel, and during his twenty four years he has been on her, or since the vessel was placed in the Mersey, he has turned out many efficient cooks. The other officers are provided for as becomes their position, and taken altogether, the greatest harmony and peace prevails aboard, which is saying a good deal, when we remember that 250 of them are lads. with only about five or six men to look after them.'

Whilst we may consider the conditions on board, the monotonous food and firm discipline to be entirely unacceptable today, we must remember that on the streets of Liverpool young urchins were starving, unwanted and facing a life of crime with little chance for survival. Life was hard and cheap.

In November 1888, the Lord Bishop of the Diocese held a confirmation on board the ship, when 26 boys were presented. They had been prepared by the Chaplain, the Reverend John Bridger.

The Lancashire Merchant and Ship Canal News carried a report of interest, 22nd December, 1888.
'At a meeting of the Council of the Mercantile Marine Service Association, held in their rooms, Tower Buildings, Liverpool, a presentation in the shape of an illuminated address was made to Captain Groome.'

The spelling of the good captain's name varies from account to account, but the value of his twenty-four years service in INDEFATIGABLE was never in doubt. The foundations for the years ahead were firmly fixed. The Captain and Mrs. Groom were to receive a number of illuminated addresses!

The Annual Report of 1889 is worthy of note:
The boys on board on 1st January, 1988, were   224
Received during the year   104
Total   328

Sent to sea as	apprentices	22
	ordinary seamen	50
	stewards	15
Sent to occupation on shore		19
Died		1

Boys on board 31st December 1888   221

It was reported in 1890 that 200 boys off INDEFATIGABLE were taken in the armed cruiser TEUTONIC to witness the Spithead naval review. The Mayor at the Annual General Meeting noted that there was an urgent need in the country for the training of boys in practical seamanship and that the advent of steam had dramatically reduced the apparent need for every ship to carry apprentices. This truly was a recurrent theme. It was also noted that Captain and Mrs Groom, after twenty-four years in command, had retired and that they were 'presented with an illuminated address and a handsome gong from the Officers, and a silver-plated crumb scoop from the boys.' Captain A. Bremner and his wife assumed command.

The 27th Annual General Meeting was held on the 22nd March, 1892, in Liverpool Town Hall and the Mayor, Mr. James de Bels Adam, presided. It was reported that the number of boys aboard at the end of 1890 was 231 and an extra 94 arrived in

1891, making the total compliment of 325. 31 had been sent to sea as apprentices, 30 as ordinary seamen, 14 as cabin boys, 4 into the Royal Navy, 9 to occupation ashore, and 2 had died, leaving on board at the end of 1891, 235. Of this number 111 were fatherless, 11 motherless, and 62 without either father or mother; only 28 had both parents living.

The sailing tender JAMES J. BIBBY was presented to the INDEFATIGABLE by Mr Frank Bibby in memory of his father. She was built for the task at the Garston Graving Dock and Shipping Co. Ltd. in 1902 by Grayson and Company. The vessel was an iron brigantine with a rather high to'gallant fo'castle to copy that of a normal deep-water sailing vessel. For twelve years she served as a sea-going tender, making regular deep-water cruises with a crew of a sailing master and sixty boys. Actually the ship was to make a number of voyages, calling annually at Ramsey in the Isle of Man and she also went on training cruises in the Irish Sea and to various ports in Spain. She was obviously a good sea boat.

In 1914 the JAMES J. BIBBY was taken over by the Government to take an active part in the war. In 1917 she was given twin screw auxiliary engines and, and after being renamed PEGGY of London, she was sent to sea as a decoy vessel (a Q ship). Patrolling off the Shetlands and Orkneys she was armed and carried various names, apart from PEGGY she was sometimes called DARGLE or GRABBIT. Several times she was attacked and was credited with having a hand in the destruction of two U-boats. Certainly on one occasion, when stopped by a U-boat, she so damaged the submarine by her gunfire that it surrendered to an armed trawler off the Tyne. She came through the war safely.

Jack Harrison in Newsletter 2000 adds to the story.
On 9th March, 1920, she was decommissioned and returned to Birkenhead and was laid up in Morpeth Dock. According to the Bibby Line archivist, Mrs Christine Spencer, the ship was then bought by someone called A.M. Anderson who in 1921 sold her to a Lieutenant-Commander Sir Warden Chilcott, who renamed her REVERIE. In 1923 she was anchored in the Hamble River, Southampton and became the yacht DOLPHIN. In 1925 she was lengthened by six feet to accommodate new 2 by 4 cylinders and two single acting Bolinder diesels.

The story gets rather confused and cannot be confirmed by me, but in 1935 she was sold to an Italian owner. During the Second World War the vessel was in the Mediterranean and was used by Mr. Chamberlain and Mussolini for the signing of the Mediterranean Pact. At the outbreak of war when Italy entered the conflict, the vessel was seized as a prize and shortly afterwards bombed and sunk by British forces. Eventually, she was salvaged and sold for scrap ... or was she?

The old JAMES J. BIBBY emerges again in 1948 owned by a company called Bianchi & A. Petronelli. From 1948 she continued with the name DOLPHIN until in 1985 she became the DOLPHIN CESARANO. Sometime in 1985-86 the vessel disappears off the Lloyds Register.

Her end is unknown but the ship had a fascinating history from 1902 and the story has still to be completed!

Back to INDEFATIGABLE.

In 1912 an Inspecting Officer of Training Ships confirmed what was already obvious. 'The ship is worn out and unsuitable for further service.'

School Work

Chapter 3
The First Steel Training Ship
1913 - 1939

At the 48th Annual Meeting of the Liverpool Training Ship INDEFATIGABLE, held in March 1913, it was stated that negotiations were under way to obtain a new ship and that PHAETON was available. The Captain Superintendent of the INDEFATIGABLE had served in ARETHUSA, and considered her sister, PHAETON, as being in every way suitable for use as a training ship.

The Admiralty was not in a generous mood. The bare hull of H.M.S. PHAETON, thirty years old, was available for £15,000. The PHAETON was a second-class steel cruiser, not on loan this time, but for sale. The sum was considered too high and negotiations were spread over a considerable period. Again the Bibby family came to the rescue, not only buying the vessel but providing the money for the refit. Out of commission, she had been lying in Devonport for some time and after the removal of her engines and boilers, sailed for her new home on 11th September 1913, in tow of two tugs generously lent by the Alexandra Towing Company of Liverpool.

H.M.S. PHAETON had three sisters ... AMPHION, ARETHUSA, and LEANDER. They were intended for the protection of commerce in foreign waters. She was laid down at the Govan yard of Messrs. Robert Napier and Son on June 14th, 1880, and PHAETON took to the water on 27th February, 1883. She was towed to H.M. Dockyard, Chatham, for completion, having cost over £15,000 for hull, engines and 'incidental charges'. The dimensions were 300 feet by 46 feet and 20 feet 6 inches, which gave her a displacement of 4,300 tons. The engines were a source of great trouble at first and, fitted with twin screws, she was expected to attain 17 knots. Her bunker capacity of 1,000 tons of coal enabled her to steam for 44 days at an economical speed of 10 knots, giving a range of about 11,000 sea miles. Under forced draught she actually topped 18 knots in later years.

She was a model of symmetry, barqentine rigged, two buff funnels between the fore and main masts, having a black hull with white superstructure, she conformed with the practice of the day. The main armament consisted of ten 6-inch Q.F. (quick firing) guns and these were supported by two 14-inch torpedo tubes on the lower deck forward and two aft.

PHAETON was unarmoured, speed being paramount, although the machinery and magazines were protected by a steel deck 1½ inches thick. The coal bunkers gave protection against hits on the water line and water tight compartments would materially help if she was holed.

PHEATON was commissioned in March 1886, under the command of Captain Robert H. Boyle, R.N. Her trials involved two engine failures, a gun accident, a steam steering gear breakdown, screw trouble and a snapped piston rod! Happily by the November of that year all was well and she was to be reported as 'one of the most valuable types on the Navy List'.

She served on the Mediterranean Station, where, on Thursday, 22nd June, 1893, whilst exercising with the Fleet she was 'tail end charlie' in a two column formation preparing to anchor off Tripoli. The two Flagships, CAMPERDOWN and PRINCESS VICTORIA headed each column. The Commander-in-Chief, Admiral Trion, in the VICTORIA ordered each column to turn 180 degrees inwards to reverse course before anchoring. To all captains present, the distance between the columns would not allow for such a manoeuvre, so they decided to wait and see what the Admiral would do. The VICTORIA started the turn and came into collision with the CAMPERDOWN. Within minutes the VICTORIA went down, taking her Admiral with her. Now follows an extract from the log of PHAETON:-

2.25 pm   Formed divisions in line ahead.

2.55 pm   Man fell overboard. Picked up.

3.40 pm   In turning inwards 161 degrees, the two flagships, VICTORIA and CAMPERDOWN came into collision. Stopped.

4.00 pm   VICTORIA went down. Sent boats away to pick up survivors. Picked up Fleet Paymaster Richard, Sub. Lt. Gillett, 1st Class C.P.O. J. Wheel, Ed Lane A.B., Wm. Martin O.S., and Albert Hillier R.M.A.. Up Boats. Fleet reorganised. Took station and proceeded to anchor.

PHAETON, one of the last Naval vessels also to carry sail, served in the Pacific with the China Squadron, which included taking part in the Boxer Rebellion. She was then stationed with the Pacific Fleet at Vancouver where she took part in the abortive search for H.M.S. CONDOR, which disappeared on a passage between Vancouver and Honolulu. Many months later boat's wreckage, believed to have belonged to CONDOR, was washed up on Prince Albert Island. PHAETON then sailed through the Panama Canal to serve with the South American Squadron. After an overseas commission of more than two and a half years, during which time she had covered 4,495 miles, she sighted Eddystone on the 31st March, 1903, and arrived at Devonport to be paid off. There she was maintained as a parent hulk for destroyers, and then a training ship for stokers until paid off for disposal.

She departed from Devonport on the 11th September, 1913. Towed to the Mersey, she was fitted out at Birkenhead by Messrs. H. and C. Grayson. She had been rigged as a barquentine, but the yards and booms had long gone, together with the engines and boilers. There were two funnels left as reminders of her past. The vessel was renamed INDEFATIGABLE … the first steel training ship in commission. For a while both the old and new INDEFATIGABLES lay side by side until on Wednesday, 15th January 1914 the new ship was towed by the tugs, GLADSTONE and HUSKINSON, into the river to take up the moorings recently occupied by the old wooden frigate. The old INDEFATIGABLE was broken up in West Float.

The Last Voyage of Indefatigable.

W. Newton, 1916-1918, wrote in the Spring 1985 Newsletter.

'The date was 3rd May, 1916. My first thought on leaving home was of great excitement on becoming a sailor. My first impression was of the smartness and cleanliness of the boat's crew and I pictured myself becoming one of them as I stamped up the gangway. Shortly after, I was taken to the Quarter Deck and formally welcomed on board by Captain Butterworth. As I went round the ship, I marvelled at the young boys dashing round in bare feet, which I did not fancy at all, but I soon found it was the custom and slowly got used to it.

'I soon settled down to the school work which was of quite a high standard and I was keen to learn. As I expected, being tall for my age, I soon got into the cutter's crew which I found was quite a tough job as sometimes the River Mersey plays tricks and there were some really high, fast tides, often very rough. But, only as a last resort did we have to call upon the motor boat for a tow or we would have finished up near New Brighton. The Captain's galley was a much lighter boat and did not ship in as much water, but even that was better on a nice calm day. I think I had the edge on some things as I had been in the Boys' Brigade for a year or so and I had learned the morse code and signals in general, also a few knots, so I was able to keep up with the older boys.

'In time as a Chief Petty Officer, I took over the Captain's galley and saw a lot of Sharky (Mr. Patton), the Deck Officer. The old Chief Mate (Mr. Pierce) suffered from asthma and always had a stone jar of haricot beans in the galley store for his use, on medical advice, I think! We had races on the river in the cutters and I was delighted to win a couple of medals in the 1st Division boat. The cook was a Swede who spoke very poor English and the parson on board made no impression on me and I do not remember his name. I was very proud to be a C.P.O. and always tried to be fair in my dealings with the younger lads and always kept an eye on the new boys as I could not stand bullies, having clashed with them before in my school days.

'When I left to join DERBYSHIRE in July, 1918, I found my training in INDEFATIGABLE invaluable, especially signals and navigation and geography, which was an asset and set me up for my new venture afloat.'

P.J. Lunt, 1917-1919, enclosed some notes for the Newsletter, Autumn 1987.

The New Arrival

... as regards memories of life on the INDEFATIGABLE, I was always ready to eat due to war rationing ... two slices of bread and margarine with a mug of cocoa or tea for breakfast and supper; and a bowl of stew for dinner. Rule breaking was punished by standing on deck with a hammock over the shoulder for one hour. After 9 p.m. it was 'lights out', and we were up at 5 a.m. on the top deck hauling buckets of coal from the bunker to feed the boiler room. Rope's end was used on rear end before ship's Company for serious offences.

'In 1917, the American destroyers anchored off Rock Ferry by us. They were a wild bunch and caused riots in Scotland Road, Liverpool, bragging about how they had come to win the war for us. I remember the Liverpool Territorials, marching to war. Over 2,000 never came back. I remember the CONWAY as they rescued a couple of Inde boys who fell overboard on the ebb tide.

'I escaped the Spanish 'flu that laid most of the boys up in their hammocks in 1918. I, and others on their feet, went around with 'Condes fluid' for them to gargle.

'When I left in 1919 to join the OXFORDSHIRE at the Pier Head, I got one day's leave. We three boys, as Ordinary Seamen worked four on and four off except in port. We had to hoist the flags for International code, and handle the morse light at night. We had 1,200 soldiers of the Queen's Regiment, and left them at Quatara on the Suez Canal. Took a shipload of Australians, who had been fighting the Turks, to Australia via Colombo where we 'coaled up'. Made another voyage in her to Rangoon when she was laid up to fit out with diesel engines.

'I worked ashore for a few months with a general contractor. I then made a number of trips in Harrison boats ... one round Africa, and then to Brazil and North America. I left in New Orleans in 1922 and I made three voyages in American ships as Quartermaster, two to England and one to Europe.

'I have made quite a few visits home between 1955 and 1973, to my cousin in Old Colwyn. I have had a full and happy life with a lovely wife of 60 years come August 20th ... five children, three boys and two girls ... 10 grandchildren and 8 great grandchildren.'

Those were grand memories of an Inde boy.

Mike Clark, 1919-21, has left some memoirs.

'I joined T.S. INDEFATIGABLE on 10th July, 1919, aged thirteen and a quarter. The only officers I can recall were Mr. Unwin and Mr. Grant. The brigantine, JAMES J. BIBBY, provided first class training in the working of all types of sails. She was square rigged on the foremast, fore and aft rigged on the main and had the usual jibs and staysails. This was a wonderful break from the normal life in INDEFATIGABLE, which I can assure you was rather tough.

'One of our activities ... on the lighter side ... was to take part in what were called "Blue Water Evenings". These were inter-Training Ship and Establishment competitions which were held in Liverpool. I was lucky enough to be a member of the Hornpipe team when we won First Prize. This was in the last competition before I left the ship and I also won a Second Prize for Signalling.

'On 18th November, 1921, I left INDEFATIGABLE to join the Royal Navy at H.M.S. GANGES, the Boys' Training Establishment.'

Mike Clark remained in the Royal Navy and in 1936 became a submariner. He served in CACHELOT and SEALION in which he survived severe depth charging, but was medically pronounced as 'unfit for sea'. For the remainder of the war he was an instructor in H.M.S. MERCURY. He left the Service in 1946, disabled and pensioned. Then he became a civilian Clerical Officer in H.M.S. ST. VINCENT until 1969 and was then seconded to Haslar until full retirement in 1971, aged 65. INDEFATIGABLE had ensured a full lifetime connection with the sea.

In the much loved magazine, Sea Breezes, Arthur Plumridge wrote two articles in November, 1985, about his days in INDEFATIGABLE just after the First World War. The Spartan conditions, uninteresting food, control of pocket money and censorship of letters, which he records, have to be judged against the background of the times. Every word is worth reading as he paints a vivid canvas of childhood memories.

'I arrived at New Ferry, Birkenhead, where a stage hand made the recognised eight bell signal to the ship and a cutter came across and I was on my way. My mother came with me to New Ferry but she was, of course, left at the landing stage. The parting was rather poignant.

'Once on board, I thought, 'Well, here I am for better or worse'. The main deck I thought looked very austere and bare looking, but the planked deck was nice and clean. I later found out how this was made so.

'Of inevitable interest to a growing lad is food and therefore away to the galley. It was quite spacious and equipped with a coal-burning range. There were also two enormous cauldrons, possibly originally used for boiling intrusive missionaries in the more backward countries, but now used in the less drastic operation of making stews and beverages. These cauldrons were heated by steam from the boiler room via a steam jacket.

'This little kingdom was ruled by the cook, one Murphy, (inevitably Spud) who furnished the best example of an expressionless face I have ever seen. I never saw his expression change no matter what circumstances. He had two boys to assist in his labours; I often wondered whether they grew up to be as equally dour as their mentor.

'Our meals were taken at bare wooden tables, 10 or 12 of us to a table, all seated on long forms and the practically unvarying menu was as follows.

'Breakfast consisted of a slice of bread some four inches or so square by a fraction over one inch thick which was adorned by a knob of margarine (known to all us boys as 'spottom') stuck in the middle; in cold weather this was impossible to spread. This delicate piece of tempting food was placed on a bare table opposite one's allotted space, by a cook of the mess, which exalted chore was undertaken by most of us on a rota basis.

'To assist in the assimilation of the food, we were issued with one of Spud's beverages which we dubbed 'cocoa flush' and which had been prepared in the galley by the dropping of solid slabs of cocoa, unsweetened I may add, into one of the cauldrons I have mentioned, this having been previously filled with boiling water. A couple of tins of milk (we never saw fresh milk) were tipped into the cocoa and water, together with a very meagre quantity of sugar. The mixture was then drawn off into kettles, utensils similar in shape and size to a large domestic wash bucket (the mop bucket type) prior to being dropped by the hoist to the mess deck, there to be rationed out using basins as balers. These basins were used as drinking vessels too, cups being completely non-existent.

'Dinner for each day except Fridays and Sundays consisted of 'buzz'. Spud Murphy concocted several kinds of 'buzz'. There was 'pea buzz', 'Irish buzz', 'mystery buzz' and another variety which I have forgotten, although at the time, I never thought it would be possible. These 'buzzes' were neither soups nor stews, but partook of the characteristics of both and were served in those same basins as was our 'cocoa flush'.

'A small pile of broken ship's biscuits was put beside each basin at table and sometimes these were quite palatable, especially to hungry boys, when a new sack had been opened, but if allowed to go stale, they turned soggy and tastelessly horrible, under which circumstances the ever present sea birds benefited. The biscuits were circular, three inches in diameter and about half an inch thick and bore the name 'Ixion'.

'I have since learned that there was a character in Greek mythology bearing the same name who for his sins was bound to a flaming wheel to roll across the heavens for ever. If he'd anything to do with those biscuits than all I can say is that he deserved all he got!

'Dinner on Fridays was usually boiled cod, served on a plate, with the usual biscuits, but on Sundays Spud really triumphed. On this high day we had two slices of roast beef and a couple of boiled potatoes, also on a plate, with 'duff' for 'afters'. This latter Murphy Special was of a dark brown hue, but had the texture of cheddar cheese and contained the occasional lonely currant and raisin. This had to be eaten all the way, but we were all blessed with a good set of grinders. Each portion was about four inches by three and just under an inch thick and was 'served' by being dropped on to the bare table, as we had used the plates for the beef and potatoes. To drink, we had water obtained from a tank on the main deck.

'For tea, we had the usual square of bread - we called it 'tack' but in place of the breakfast margarine, we had a small dollop of jam spooned on to the middle of the piece of 'tack'.

'Sometimes in winter, we had a slight addition to the foregoing menu; breakfast, for instance, would be varied by the serving up of a thick porridge known as 'burgoo'. A small quantity of sugar was added in the making, but we had no milk. On the whole it was not a popular dish.

Occasionally, we would be issued with boiled rice for dinner. This, scantily spotted with raisins, was also not popular.

'Our cutlery, knife, fork and spoon, was lodged in a locker with our kit-bag and carried to the mess deck when the bugle summoned us to a meal. Except for the Sunday beef, knife and fork were superfluous and the spoon was the only tool necessary.

'When a new boy arrived, it was usually in the afternoon before tea. When he was introduced to the mess deck and faced with a lump of bread with a jam stain in the middle of it, and on a bare wooden table, he, having come from a good home, no doubt, and with tender memories of that home fresh in his youthful mind, would quickly lose any appetite he may have had, whereupon the other boys, like hungry vultures, would ask him for his unwanted bread, and this having been handed over, it would quickly disappear. It took a few days for a 'new chum' to come into line, although it was never very long before he too became a fully accredited vulture.

'All the time I was in INDEFATIGABLE, I never saw eggs, fresh milk, fruit, vegetables (other than potatoes), bacon or anything other than

what I have mentioned; there were dried peas and such for the 'mystery buzz', but it remains a great mystery to me how we boys maintained our health and strength on this Spartan diet!

'We did have occasional 'treats' though, for instance if one missed dinner through being adrift in a boat on some exercise or other, we should then find that Spud, on our return, was ready with a round of 'tack' which he would dip in beef dripping, of which he seemed to have an inexhaustible supply. This delicious piece of fat-soaked bread would be carted off like a dog with a bone, to some secluded corner to be devoured away from covetous eyes.

'Our cook had the luxury of his own cabin, on the main deck, and here he kept all his stores, including the 'kettle' full of dripping. Occasionally Spud would relax and stand gazing out of his cabin with a stare that went right through one in an apparently unseeing manner. But I can see him now, wearing a white apron, with a cigarette drooping from the corner of his mouth decorated with a pencil thin, horizontal and carefully-waxed moustache.

'In charge of the boiler room was one 'Tubby' Woodcock, a large man with a comprehensive vocabulary to match his stature. He was, I believe, an ex-RN stoker which probably accounts for much. He it was who discovered that any irregularity in the temperamental boiler feed pump could immediately be rectified by giving the casing a substantial blow with a booted foot. A bunker full of ready-use coal and a few fire-tools completed the equipment of that room.

'On Saturdays, both watches would clean ship and what has remained in my mind in the connection with this particular chore is the novel way in which the decks were cleaned. The upper deck was first scrubbed with brooms and deck scrubbers, then thoroughly washed down and left to dry which was the normal procedure, but the main and lower deck were given much different treatment. After being scrubbed down with brooms as was the upper deck, half-a-dozen lads with trousers rolled for action and each equiped with a piece of old blanket, would kneel in a row like somewhat oddly clad Muslims at prayer.

'These lads would then proceed to wipe down the deck with a piece of blanket each until the material was saturated, whereupon it would be pitched out front in the direction of a lad who would wring it out in a bucket and 'return to sender'. This was a tedious job as was washing paintwork, especially when it was done on the insides of cutters and galleys. Being clinker-built they were a mass of ribs and stringers - all marvellously designed to entrap the dirt in the most effective manner.

'On Sunday mornings there was an inspection by the Captain. This was called Divisions and the whole ship's company would assemble in its four divisions on the main deck. The lads would then, clad in their best gear, be subject to a searching inspection, both 'fore and aft'. This routine was changed every fourth Sunday however when a system known as 'Open List' was used. In this, the whole ship's company would be formed into four long lines facing aft. At the head of these columns and a couple of paces ahead of that position, a circle some two feet in diameter would be drawn in chalk. The Captain and his entourage would then take up position a couple of yards away, and at a nod from the former, a lad would step smartly into the chalked circle at the same time removing his cap to his side. A quick appraisal from the 'Old Man' and the first boy would step out of the circle to be replaced by the second and so on.

'One unwelcome chore for us boys was coaling ship. The coal was taken from a lighter moored alongside and this operation came around once a year. All hands would be employed. The coal was raised with the aid of baskets and a block and tackle. This was an unpleasant task as we and everything else got filthy. After the lighter shoved off, all hands would have to clean the ship and themselves. As usual there wasn't an abundance of either soap or hot water and a rather miserable time was had by all.

'The daily supply of coal for the boiler had to be raised from the bunkers twice a day and this chore was allotted to wrong-doers as a form of punishment, but more of this later.

'The ship's complement of boys was divided into two watches and four divisions, first and third in the starboard and second and fourth in the port watch. Each day, Mondays to Fridays, one watch would be on deck learning seamanship and attending to routine duties, while the other would be in school doing normal lessons as in shore schools, but in addition navigation in the top classes, so that one week a boy would spend two days in school and three days the following week.

'Punishment would vary from being placed on a coaling party for one, two or three weeks for minor offences, loss of leave, strokes of the cane and what was considered to be the most disgraceful of all - 'canvas'. The unlucky recipient of this had to wear a white canvas jumper for the period of his sentence, so that his shame and disgrace would be apparent to all, much in the manner in which a 'dunce's cap' was once used in schools.

'One particular punishment which to me seemed more fitting for the 18th century was meted out (and probably concocted by) a certain officer whom we all disliked intensely. This ill-disposed man would patrol the lower deck at 9.15 p.m. and would examine hammocks for any faults such as crossed nettles or an untidy rope in which case he would bellow 'Carry your hammock on deck' and at the same time roughly shaking the foot lanyard, whereupon the unfortunate boy, nicely tucked up, would have to leave his warm but short-lived comfort to stand on the main deck carrying his hammock and associated gear on his back, in which cold and draughty position he would remain for an hour.

'Washing clothes was a problem. We used to spread flannel shirts on the washroom floor and with a ration of soap about half the size of a packet of ten cigarettes and with a bit of luck and hot water, we rubbed away. Afterwards each garment was inspected by an officer and one's name ticked off on a slate.

'No work was done on Sundays, apart from such essentials as galley and boiler room duties and boat work. A Church Service was held in the school room where there was a hand-cranked organ. Unfortunately, this instrument was the subject of some vandalism because on one occasion when it refused to function, careful examination revealed that its 'innards' had been stuffed with paper and rags and even the peel from an orange.

'On nice Sundays in Summer, I liked to squat on the platform of the main mast crosstrees and survey the world from that elevated vantage point. There was much going to and fro, and the Manchester Ship Canal's entrance not being far away, there would sometimes be quite a procession of ships: Clan, Prince, Manchester Liners, Federal, Elders and Fyffes and tramps of all sorts.

'The INDEFATIGABLE boys naturally had their share of physical exercise and the upper deck was used for this purpose. Apart from drill proper, the officer in charge (without malice) amused himself by introducing a form of exercise which, apparently, he had invented in an idle moment. In this case only a slight tardiness on the part of any boy attracted the punishment of a rope's end around his backside on the completion of the exercise. That exercise consisted of a mad scramble on the part of the assembled class, all in bare feet I might add, up the ratlines of the starboard rigging of the mainmast, over the crosstrees and down the other side. The last boy down got the afore-mentioned rope's end.

'The ship had several boats, consisting of three cutters, two galleys, the motor boat and a small gig, all of which were under strict naval discipline and I consider it a marvel that the massive cutter oars were handled by some quite small boys. The cutter, for instance, was manned by thirteen boys including the coxswain and was used to transport the less important people, as well as carrying necessary stores from New Ferry landing stage to the ship.

'When coming alongside, the oars would be 'tossed', that is, with the blade upright in the fore and aft position. Then would come the order 'boat your oars', and woe betide anyone unfortunate enough to have his hand in the direct line of a quickly descending oar! There was no 'excuse me' or 'beg your pardon' tactics shown at any level.

'Another hazard occurred if and when a new chum was so inexperienced as to 'catch a crab'. The whole rowing sequence would become disorganised and the fellow in front of him would receive a pretty heavy crack to the back of his head.

'The River Mersey has a large tidal range and at springs it would be as much as 31 feet. This makes a quickly flowing stream and with wind and tide together a cutter would often not be able to make headway. I have seen a loaded boat going to New Ferry with a church party battling against the flood tide with a north-west wind for good measure, trying to make the landing stage. After shoving off from the side of the ship, the tide and wind would sweep them down past the landing stage. The trick then was to head close inshore where there was much less force in the stream and head painfully northwards towards the stage. The boat's oars in conditions like this would be 'double banked', that is, two boys on each oar. These oars made of tough ash would bend like an archer's bow. Not infrequently an oar would break and become a candidate for a position in the cook house.

'The other pulling boat was the galley, a clinker-built craft, rather more sleek than the cutter and with a crew of six. She was used mainly for the conveyance of the Captain, Mrs Butterworth or the Chaplain. She had cushions for passengers and was steered by yokelines.

'The motor boat was used mainly to ferry fresh water from New Ferry to the ship. She was an ex-naval launch and at times became a tug to rescue a boat adrift and at leave times to take boys ashore. She had a crew of four ... bow man, stern man, an engineer and the coxswain.

'Shore excursions for the boys were rare. I think I once went to play football and twice for swimming lessons at the local baths. One of the ship's rules was that a boy was not allowed to go on leave or even ashore, until he had completed three months aboard.

'What did upset us quite a bit was the fact that all our letters and parcels had to be censored. It was a scandalous and completely unjustifiable practice which should have been long abolished. We were apprentices, not criminals. It was not just censorship as such, but it meant that during the process any cash which turned up was immediately abstracted and put in the 'ship's bank'!

'One of the memorable occurrences during my time in INDEFATIGABLE was the formation of a band. Its beginnings were very modest, although I shall never forget the circumstances. The port watch was on deck and for the starboard watch it was 'school day', which meant that I, being starboard watch, was at school.

'To a greater or lesser extent immersed in our studies, we were surprised by the dramatic appearance, from the deck above, of our respected schoolmaster in a state of some excitement. Nor was our surprise in any measure lessened when he enquired without any waste of words, as to whether any boy would like to join the band. For a moment there was profound silence as this was so unexpected. Then one or two hands were raised, albeit a trifle hesitantly. For my part my hand was aloft as soon as I realised what was going forward. About twelve of us had our names taken and we learned later that a similar number had been taken from port watch.

'The following morning, we potential members of the new band were ordered to muster on the main deck. We fell in in front of a stack of ironmongery and then Mr. Williams made a rapid appraisal. The drums and E flat basses went to the 'big 'uns' and by gradually diminishing progression through euphoniums and trombones to cornets for the 'little 'uns'. By chance it worked well. Mr. Williams was quickly renamed 'Bandy'.

'Even when we had become proficient enough to play in public, there were times, perhaps during a march, when the baritones faltered or the cornets would waver and good old Bandy would come to the rescue.

'We did concentrate on the more serious side of music-making and it is interesting to record that we eventually rose to the exalted heights of a public appearance or two in Liverpool and I remember we played 'God bless the Prince of Wales' for that popular member of the Royal Family, when he visited Liverpool. We also played at a garden party held by Lord Leverhulme at Port Sunlight and, of course, we usually played the National Anthem at hoisting the ensign.

'Looking back over the years, it was a great time; we all worked hard, but we had youth on our side and enthusiasm and Bandy's guidance. It was all worth while when we heard someone call to a friend, "Oh! Listen to the band." Then we knew that we had made good.

'It cannot be denied that every boy in the INDEFATIGABLE was longing for the day when he could leave and any indication of that possibility was constantly looked out for. Usually it went as follows.

'The cutter would be called to New Ferry landing stage by the striking of eight bells on the stage's bell. This would be for items such as ship's stores like bread and meat, which was bought in Liverpool. It was for ordinary traffic.

'But when it was a matter of special importance, the ship would be signalled by striking eight bells followed, after a pause, by a further two bells. This ten bell signal was for the galley to be despatched as it was designated an urgent call. This meant one of three or four things, for example, the imminent arrival of the Captain or his wife, some important visitor or, and this was the most important of all for us, a telegram to be delivered.

'If one of the shipping companies required another crew member, they would apply to the ship by telegram, so it can well be imagined that when ten bells were heard, there was considerable excitement amongst the older boys as this could be their chance to get away to sea.

'On another occasion, a different aspect of the establishment came to light through the appearance of a very nice looking brigantine ... a surprising sight as she passed very close to us looking very pretty with her gleaming white hull. She was being towed up river, eventually coming to anchor three or four cables further up from us. This was the JAMES J. BIBBY and she was destined to become part of the INDEFATIGABLE Training School.

'When it became known that she was to be crewed by us, of course everyone wanted to go, but only twenty or thirty boys were selected and I counted myself fortunate in being one of that number.

'When it became time for us to shift our berth, we fell in with our hammocks and gear near the gangway. As far as I could see, there appeared to be only two men aboard. The Captain was Captain Cole (who sported a wooden leg) and the other man was a Scandanavian, Mr. Peterson, who turned out to be the cook.

'So there we were, in fresh surroundings and full of hope for this adventure. You might judge my dismay when I found that the most important and pressing job seemed to be that of holystoning the deck.

'The tools used were flat, hand-held stones and larger ones with long handles, the former used on the knees. There was hand scouring of the deck, which entailed a scattering of sand on the chosen area, not for the performance of the 'sand dance'. With a small section of canvas fire hose over one's hand, glove fashion, one could scrub away until the deck itself gleamed nearly as white as the hull. Nor was this the end. After the prolonged scrubbing, we enjoyed some slight relaxation by washing down the whole lot by hose (man-pumped from the river) and mopped dry.

'I must say it all looked very nice, but must also say that we didn't particularly care for the doing of it. Still with our Captain Cole, a white deck fanatic, there wasn't any choice for us; and if we didn't get a lot of instruction in any other department, we certainly got a lot in cleaning ship.

'Although we were anxious to get away, there was absolutely no wind at all, so no chance of moving. We had no auxiliary power. After a day or two, the galley duty rota came round to me. This turned out to be mainly washing pots and pans, but I'm afraid this didn't last very long as I got 'discharged with ignominy' and worse.

'Actually, zeal for work was my undoing as I must now explain to clear my honour, as it were. On the stove in the galley was a saucepan containing a doubtful liquid strongly resembling brown, muddy looking water, which I quickly consigned to the river, where it became indistinguishable from the general content of Liverpool's lifeline.

'Industriously I cleaned the saucepan and stowed it away in its appointed place, mentally patting myself on the back for my keenness and assiduity. Shortly afterwards in came the cook, Mr. Peterson, apparently in search of this pan of muck, and when I told him what a good little boy I had been in heaving it overboard and washing and stowing the pan afterwards, he began to exhibit the most alarming symptoms of wrath and indignation and came at me brandishing a knife, with which instrument he indicated that he would perform some surgical operation on me which would considerably affect any of my life that I might have left after he had finished with me. I beat a hasty retreat in a rather undignified way; after all, these foreigners have some nasty ways at times.

'Later I discovered that the horrid brew I'd inwittingly consigned to the deep was mainly made up of hops which he had left to simmer and it had some connection with breadmaking, although under adverse circumstances I considered further research inadvisable.

'There was still no wind. We did at last unfurl the square sails but apart from the exercise, it was quite pointless as they just hung there like clothes in front of a kitchen fire.

'However we continued to increase our proficiency at cleaning paintwork and the abominable holystoning of decks. In the end the weather remaining dead calm and warm, we were very disappointed at being ordered to return to INDEFATIGABLE. I never saw that brigantine put to sea during the whole of my apprenticeship.

'My main complaint about the boy's treatment was the very poor clothes washing facilities which were instrumental in the boys not using such things as long-john underpants, which were kept clean ready for kit inspection, and boots and socks which were the source of 'coaling party' punishment on account of their being wet (designated dirty). Then, of course, there was the food which I should think was as bad or worse than that given in the poorest institutions of Dickens's days. The boys really suffered in winter through being scantily clothed.

'On completing my training and finally leaving the ship, I was fitted out with quite a huge kitbag full of clothes complete with a suit of oilskins ... and a pair of seaboots tied outside. I was given a Bible by the Chaplain (the one with the handlebar moustache had gone and a more likeable Mr. Saunderson had taken his place) and I still have this in my possession.

'So aboard the ferry and off to Liverpool, which is as good a starting place as any, to join my ship which could be the start of another story.

'Apart from being a member of the band, I cannot recall any happy times I had aboard the Training Ship INDEFATIGABLE.'

That was a sad, but fascinating picture, remembered in much detail.

Arthur Plumridge did return to Merseyside and visited New Ferry in 1940. The Inde was still there with her topmasts gone, leaving her looking like a hulk. The New Ferry pier had almost disappeared, having been partially demolished by a steamer in the early 1920's. He did not have the heart to visit her, but he did wonder if the boys had heard of buzzes and IXION biscuits.

Incidentally, Arthur Plumridge, 1920-1922, died in 1985 and had done much work on his memories of the Inde. In the Spring of 1985, he sent an article for inclusion in that year's Newsletter entitled, 'My introduction to becoming a professional seaman'.
'I, in company with an opposite number, left T.S. INDEFATIGABLE stationed at New Ferry on the Mersey after a period of training, in early spring some years before the Second World War. We were given our tickets via the ferry from New Ferry to Liverpool. Arriving at the Landing Stage in ecstasy and feeling of great importance, we had to laboriously find our way to the dock where our ship was lying.

'When we left INDEFATIGABLE we were given a huge kit bag filled with a complete outfit of clothes, shoe brushes, etc. and a pair of sea boots tied to the neck of the bag and hanging outside. This was in the month of March and the ground was covered with snow. My friend was a little heftier than me, but I was by no means a big 'un and that kit bag was about as much as I could manage. As you can imagine, I was much relieved when we arrived at the ship, a Bibby liner. She was flying 'P' and about to sail for the Far East.

'The pair of us staggered up the gangway to be received by the quartermaster who directed us to our cabin. This tiny appartment was situated at the fore end of the fore well deck, just underneath the forecastle. We boys took alternate watches of four hours each, but as normal changed by two hour watches of the dog watch. Our station was mainly on the bridge.

'We sailed that night and about thirty hours later had entered the notorious Bay of Biscay. Although I have since seen the Bay as calm as a boating lake, my first experience of her was the opposite. She was certainly not in a tranquil mood. I went down to rouse my mate for the 8 to 12 forenoon watch and what a mess I found. The cabin floor was running in water which had leaked through an improperly closed port. The enamelled teapot was rolling about the floor, the contents from the previous meal splashed all over the place. A half pound of butter on a plate was upside down and a sodden half loaf of bread was keeping it company together with some jam. All these things should, of course, have been properly stowed after the meal. On top of this I wasn't feeling very well ... mal de mer having taken charge. I felt I had to have a drink of water and seeing a tap attached to an alley-way bulkhead, I got my head down under the tap and let the water trickle down my gullet. That finished it - the water was salt!

'That was my first lesson in why you should respect the sea.'

Thank you Arthur Plumridge.

Charles Land has also written at length about his much more happy days in INDEFATIGABLE. He joined in 1920 and left in 1923 to sail in the S.S. MINNIE DE LARRINAGA.

'Turning to me, the Chief Officer said, 'Land, isn't it?' I nodded. Whereupon he barked out, 'You must say, Sir, when you answer an officer.' And with this he moved off, bidding me follow him.

'We descended into the after-flats, where his cabin was situated. Drawing up a chair to his desk, he opened a ledger of gigantic proportions, and in it he entered my name and address and also the date of joining the ship. Then turning to a file, produced my indentures to see if they tallied with the information I had given him. Closing the ledger he turned to me and gave me a short lecture.

'You will find the life you have come to is totally different to the life you have led on shore,' he said kindly. 'Bear this in mind. Obey your superior officers and give as little trouble as possible, and apply yourself to your studies, and there's no reason why we shouldn't train you to become an efficient officer.' He finished the short lecture with 'Should you find yourself at any time in difficulty or trouble - come and see me, and I will do my best to help you out.' I appreciated this last bit, for though he possessed a formidable appearance and somewhat abrupt manner, his bark was worse than his bite. Then, pressing a bell, he summoned one of the boys and told him to show me the ropes, and make me generally acquainted with the ship. This apprentice was aptly named Beam, and he afterwards became my bunser (pal). I was to be measured for my uniform the next day. Until so-adorned, I could not consider myself a fully-fledged member of the ship's company. This is the mode of life I was to lead during the next three years.

'To the strains of the bugle, I awoke next morning and slowly crept out of my hammock. With clumsy fingers I managed to lash it up, and stow it, then descended into the bowels of the ship to shiveringly perform my ablutions. This being done - and having had my breakfast - I was summoned to the Captain's quarters, which occupied the whole of the aft part of the ship at main deck level. He used the poop as his promenade deck.. In I went to that awesome presence. It proved to be no ordeal, but just a pleasant chat. I was gazetted to the fourth division and at last I was a fully-fledged member of the ship's company.

'I soon dropped into the ship's routine, and everything went smoothly. Came Saturday morning and I was told off to join a party that had to clean the main and upper decks. This was the routine. Shoes and socks were discarded, and trousers rolled above the knees. We were supplied with a long-handled deck scrubber apiece. Led by an officer, we all trooped to the upper deck. The officer wore thigh-boots, and wielding a hose, he commenced to wet the deck while a line of us trailed behind him and scrubbed with right good will. Perchance he took his eyes off us, and we all started to scrounge, using the scrubber as a prop and gazing soulfully into space. His attention being drawn to our slacking, he turned the hose on us, but being salt-water it soon dried off. The decks were soon cleaned, and after dinner we got ready to go ashore and play soccer. Usually one of the divisions played the other. On Sunday the routine differed somewhat. Instead of rising at six, we had an extra half hour. Discipline was relaxed on the Sabbath, and we were not slow to take advantage of this.

' "Rise and shine. Show a leg there, the sun's scorching your eyes out," roared Jimmy Unwin, the officer on watch. Should some slothful miscreant pull the blankets over his head in vain endeavouring to snatch a few extra minutes, the bed-clothes were ripped off him and his hammock was let down with a bump, but it was all very good-humoured.

'Everything had to be made spick and span for the Captain's tour of inspection, and woe betide the officer who accompanied him if Henry's (the Captain) eagle-eye alighted on the slightest particle of dust. He'd receive the sharp end of Henry's tongue and he could be very sarcastic.

'Henry was the Captain's nick-name, as each member of the ship's staff appears on the stage he will be introduced by his nick-name. Ruling supreme came Henry. His birth certificate endorsed Henry Butterworth. Henry was a bit on the short side, but carried himself like a ramrod. His jaw was like the Rock of Gibraltar, but he could be classed as a good old stick. Henry took the senior boys in 'navigay' (navigation), and made them tremble with the awful sounds of Longitude by Chronometer and Equation of Time. His wife lived on board too, and mostly acted as his secretary. Second in command was 'The Flamer', Mr. Pattern. He got this name by frequently using the adjective 'Flame it', if everything was not going to plan. But 'The Flamer' was quite decent in his own grim way. The most popular officer on the ship was 'Joe Richie', Mr. Joseph Richardson. Next came 'Dennie', Mr. Dennier, the ship's tailor. Running 'Joe Richie' a close second in popularity was Paddy Grant, unkindly called 'Fender Belly' on account of his outsize girth, but the term was used affectionately. Paddy was in charge of the sick bay, and well versed in the arts of quackdom. Pay special attention to this gentleman, Mr. Ellis - 'Little Dick' for short; he stood five feet nothing in his stocking-feet. Anyone would tell you, 'He had a beady eye, and a large red nose, and was always cracking jokes, but cross him in anything and he's as hard as flint!' Leading my own division was Jimmy Unwin, expert in Morse and semaphore. He was blue-jowled and of a nervy disposition, but a decent sort. 'Tubby' the electrician was fat and short-tempered, whilst 'Chippy', the carpenter, was long and cadaverous. 'Spud' Murphy, the cook, was famous for his Irish stew and his immaculate white apron. Mr. Williams was the bandmaster, 'Bandy' for short.

'Bandy' Williams

'Joe Richie, being well-versed in the arts of physical culture, took us for P.T. Standing six-foot tall, he weighed a generous eighteen stone. A somewhat podgy, good-looking face was enhanced by a perpetual smile. Full of bonhomie, the boys adored him. I kept in touch with him for a few years after I left INDEFATIGABLE and was pleased to hear he was eventually made Chief Officer when 'The Flamer' retired, a position he well deserved.

'Whittam, the headmaster, used to run a tuckshop. His counter was a grand piano. One could buy chocolate and most of the popular brands of sweets, only for cash, there was no credit or free gifts where Whittam was concerned. His prices were the same as the average sweet shop, and he made enough to keep himself in pipe tobacco. Whittam was so stingy!

'Paddy Grant formed a minstrel troupe; he was a self-taught musician, and could play both the piano and banjo excellently. I was roped in to perform. My voice was in the process of breaking, and it wobbled between a screeching treble and a scraping basso-profundo ... not so musical, I'm afraid. There were seven of us, and we practised in the schoolroom. Five had to do a solo turn; the remaining two, being humorous, were cornermen. I gave a song and then broke into what was to be an exhibition of the horn-pipe. It was an exhibition alright, but not the way I intended it to be. I put so much energy and enthusiasm into it that I got my feet all tangled up and fell to the deck in an ungainly heap, and nearly broke my neck in the process. The concert party was a roaring success, and we were all invited to dine with the skipper, a singular honour indeed.

'Every Sunday evening, scouts were told off to perform different fatigues during the week. For this a small remuneration would be paid, ranging from sixpence to a shilling. Thus, one boy had to look after the lamp locker; another boy would do duty on the ship's gangway; a cutter's and galley crew would be told off for the week. The galley was a five-oared boat used exclusively by Henry the skipper, when he went ashore to his club in Liverpool. It had to be kept as clean as a new pin, and God help the cox'n if so much as a smudge of dirt sullied the white paint. The first time I was selected for the cutter's crew was a momentous one. Acting as bow, I made a maiden passage to New Ferry. As we came alongside my oar fouled the stage, and the blade snapped like a piece of cardboard. I was a passenger during the return journey, and on boarding, received three of the best for my carelessness, and was unable to sit down for the rest of the day.

'All petty officers were exempt from fatigues, but were put in charge of a party and made responsible for the tasks being performed properly. One act of a P.O., named Jess New, deserves mentioning. Seeing one of the boys overbalance and fall into the swiftly-moving ebb tide, he made a spectacular dive from the upper deck, and with powerful strokes overtook the unfortunate youth, who began to struggle. Hitting him smartly on the point of the jaw to quieten him, he kept him afloat until the cutter picked them up. In recognition of his deed he received a gold medal with his name and the act of bravery inscribed upon it.

'The night watchman, who was there when I first joined the INDEFATIGABLE, was an old shellback. He used to spend the night talking and muttering to himself. If you tried to enter into a conversation with him he would take umbrage and chase you round the deck waving a belaying-pin. We used to call him 'Bungalow' because, obviously, he had nothing upstairs!

'There occurred two hullabaloos during the term preceeding Christmas. William, Duke of Clarence, whose effigy adorned the poop-head, was the cause of all the trouble. At night when we retired he was O.K. But when we awoke next morning someone had tarred and feathered the poor old son-of-a-gun! One eye had escaped, and leered his displeasure, the rest of him was sheer nightmare. To make matters worse it was Trafalgar Day, and we were due for an admiralty inspection. With superhuman energy, 'The Flamer' set some of the boys to work to clean and repaint the figurehead. His toilet was completed in record time, and the business of tracking down the miscreants commenced, but the wily malefactors were of the super class, and not a scrap of evidence could be discovered to convict anybody. Henry nearly went off his nut and threatened dire punishment to the culprits should they be found. However, the officers were baffled and Scotland Yard was not called in, and the fuss gradually died down.

'No less person than the admiral himself was the next victim! After inspecting the ship's company he descended into the bowels of the ship. In order to get there he had to negotiate a companionway with iron tips. Some bright genius greased the tips and when Henry led the way, the admiral followed, at a much quicker pace and in a most undignified position, on his backside. Careering down at an alarming pace, with his sword rattling on the tips like an old tin can, and overtaking Henry, he cannoned into the latter's stern and brought him to earth.. Picking themselves up, they beat a hasty retreat schoolroomwards, mumbling the while, 'Sorry, I slipped.' Oh joy of joys, neither of them suspected that their downfall had been caused with deliberate intent, but 'The Flamer' did. No one could be found to put the blame on, resulting in the whole ship's company being punished. All week-end leave was stopped!

'Every so often we paraded through the streets of Liverpool. Headed by Henry, all togged up in his best uniform, plus his sword dangling by his side, we kept pace to the sound of the drum, nearly jumping out of our skins when the band blared forth in discord. Shortly before Christmas the whole ship's company went on one of these frolics. I managed to get out of it as I was cox'n of the cutter.

'About two in the afternoon 'The Flamer' told me to take the cutter to bring some stores off from New Ferry. We made a quick passage and got the stores on board. Just then, two girls whom I knew came off the ferry boat. I hailed them, and we commenced to converse. Time flies, and glancing at my watch I saw to my consternation it was three-thirty. I hastily took leave of the girls and descended into the cutter. I was greeted with scowls, the poor devils had been sitting there for an hour. 'Let go forrard, back port, give way starboard, round she goes, now then fours, put your back into it and no slacking.' So the return journey commenced. We got clear of the stage, but that was about all. A tremendous ebb tide was running, and for about ten minutes we could make no headway. I put the tiller hard over and sent the cutter further inshore, but it was no use, we lost way and began to drift astern. I tried my best to infuse fresh energy into the crew - but they were dog-tired, and we had now drifted a good mile down the river. Noticing a buoy belonging to one of the fishing smacks - I steered the cutter towards it - warning bows to get his boat-hook ready. We grated alongside the buoy, and oars were shipped, and willing hands hung on. Determined to stay there until the tide slackened, I ordered the painter to be made fast. It was three hours before the ebb exhausted itself, and practically half past-seven when we got on board. 'The Flamer' played merry England. I tried to make the excuse of being held up by the ebb flow, but he would have none of it, and literally snarled, 'If you had not dawdled on the stage you could have returned before the ebb commenced.' He told me to report to him immediately I had had my tea. The least I expected was to be disrated. Imagine my astonishment when all he said was, 'Oh, it's alright, Land, carry on.' At the time I was puzzled at what he said, but afterwards found out that he had just become a grandfather on that particular day, and he was as chuffed as a dog with two tails.

'Three years had elapsed since I had joined the INDEFATIGABLE, and I began to think it was time to look around for a shipping company to serve my apprenticeship at sea. The opportunity arrived unexpectedly. One evening 'The Flamer' called me to his cabin. "Get ready to leave the ship first thing in the morning, Land", he said. "A wire has come through from Larrinaga's, they have a berth for you on the MINNIE DE LARRINAGA and they want you to call at their office tomorrow".

'Next morning I shook hands with all the officers, and a great many of my shipmates. It was rather a sad occasion leaving many friends, having always been a good mixer, many of them were as close or perhaps even closer to me than brothers. I had to see Henry before I left, and walked into his quarters. How different it was to when I had joined INDEFATIGABLE, then it was in fear and trembling I had approached the feet of the master. He laid down his pen and told me to be seated. He handed me a reference which he had just completed. "Just a testimony as to your character," he remarked. "Personally, I think you will become a good officer." I had the singular honour of travelling in the galley with Henry, and taking the tiller for the journey to New Ferry. There we boarded the ferry-boat for Liverpool. One to go to his Club, to browse over a copy of the Times. He was in the autumn of his years, and life had nothing new for him. Myself, in the first full springtide of youth, with adventure ahead, and opportunity racing to meet me!'

Charles Land was a perfect example of a young man who thrived on his INDEFATIGABLE years and made good in his career. They had been for him happy and formative years. For so many others life had been cruel from the start, a battle for survival on the streets, but even for them INDEFATIGABLE proved to be a lifeline and equally formative for their future. Boys became men.

Steve Humphries recalls details of his 'Uncle Edgar', 14th January, 1920 - 14th October, 1922. Edgar's elder sister is still alive at the grand age of 95
'Lawrence Edgar Hanley was born in Everton, Liverpool, on the 2nd October, 1906. His parents were comfortably off, living really on the outskirts of Liverpool with a farm at the end of the road! His mother's family, however, fell on hard times and they lost 'nearly all their money' when 'Bad Uncle George' engaged in some dubious financial dealings and was at risk of going to gaol for fraud. More significantly for Edgar's future career his mother's elder brother, George Holme, was an engineer with White Star Line. In the Second World War, George became Lieutenant Commander (E), R.N.R., when his ship, LAURENTIC, was requisitioned as an Armed Merchant Cruiser and, when George was aged sixty, his ship was sunk by Otto Kretschmer's U-boat. Edgar's father died in 1916 and the family was in desperate straits. His mother worked in a uniform factory and then in the sewing room of a munitions factory.

'So Edgar joined INDEFATIGABLE on the 14th of January 1920, aged thirteen and three months. His mother's occupation was given as 'margarine works' and under 'Father' there was just one word, 'Dead'. Why INDEFATIGABLE? Aunty Rene, a formidable spinster lady, once declared that Edgar was getting into bad company and needed a better start in life. After all, one Uncle was a ship's engineer and another had been a ship's carpenter. Edgar was duly recommended by the Reverend W.J. Elsey of St. Anne's Church, Stanley, and departed from St. Anne's School. He was 5 feet tall and weighed 6 stone 11 pounds, but on his discharge the records stated that he had mysteriously lost half an inch, but had gained 7 pounds in weight.

'Edgar must have flourished in Inde because he became a Petty Officer Boy and was the Ismay Prize winner for 1922. He also accumulated some useful savings. When he received his bank book on 3rd June 1926, it contained the princely sum of £15 3s 11d.'

Edgar Hanley joined the S.S. REGINA and was given apprenticeship indentures in November 1924. By the 1930s he had his Master's Ticket, was a Second Officer with Pacific Steam Navigation in a ship at Falmouth and was 'going steady' with a Falmouth girl named Marjorie.

Steve tells us that only one Edgar story has come down in the family. 'Once home on leave he decided to make himself useful by scrubbing the kitchen floor. Rene appeared, and always inclined to bossiness, she started telling him that he was doing it all wrong! Wherupon he emptied the bucket of water over her. Well, fancy telling an INDEFATIGABLE boy that he didn't know how to scrub a floor!!!'

Thank you Steve Humphries.

Peter Robinson at the grand age of 92 recalled a few odd tales for his son-in-law, Martin Southwood. Peter remembers joining INDEFATIGABLE in 1920 ... but not too sure of the precise date! May we all reach 92 and have such a memory!
'Peter remembers travelling from Euston to Liverpool at the age of 14 and being met by Joe Richardson, the Second Officer. The ship's commander was Captain Butterworth, who lived on board with his wife who was always known as 'Ma B'. When formal occasions demanded, the Commander would don No. 1 uniform, which was still a fore and aft cocked hat and frock coat with sword. Peter recalled being taken by ferry to Rock Ferry where the ship's boat met them on the pontoon.

This pontoon had chocolate machines where one could obtain a chocolate bar for one penny ... in later times it could be operated without any money!

'The ship was moored to a single buoy about halfway between Rock Ferry and New Ferry, but the former pier was then normally in use as a tanker had run through the approach span of New Ferry pier. The duty 'Big Boat's Crew' was called out on an emergency. It was a ship's cutter or 'galley'. On one occasion, the commander and his wife were ashore possibly at the theatre, and the duty boat's crew were briefed to pick them up from the Ferry at 2300 hours. On these sort of occasions it was normal for the Commander to have some food left out for him and his wife in the galley. A roast chicken had been left in the galley oven with strict instructions to the senior cadet to inspect the galley every ten minutes to ensure that no hungry young rascal pinched the food. Peter remembered religiously doing this until it was time to take the boat for the rendezvous. On returning to the ship, the Commander instructed him as senior boat hand to bring him the platter. When this was done and the soup tureen type cover was removed, imagine his horror when he looked and found the chicken had gone and a rather ancient looking jelly fish had been left in its place!

'To make life less harsh, parents were allowed to deposit some money with the Purser so that the cadets could have six pence a week pocket money. This certainly didn't go far and other arrangements were made. His parents sent him a monthly detective magazine of the time, 'Nelson Lee', but far more important than the stories was the one shilling taped to the centre of the magazine! This was often used to buy the forbidden cigarettes which were smuggled on board in various different ways. Some could be hidden in bell bottoms, some behind the cap badge and even some behind a loosely stitched petty officer's badge. In desperate circumstances when no cigarettes were available, recourse was made to trying dried out tea leaves in a roll up or even portions of the cricket net which had been donated by James Bibby. Next cricket season it was discovered that the net had mysteriously developed holes which were put down to rats!

'The ship had originally been the light cruiser PHAETON, but the engines had been removed and the resulting large space amidships was used, among other things, for Church Services. Peter and fifteen others were Catholics and were thus excused, but had to muster in a certain part of the ship during these services. This was a particular corner where a large door was in a nearby bulkhead. It did not take young minds long to wonder what lay behind that door and what skulduggery could be brought into play.

'It was soon discovered that this led to the battery room which didn't help them much, but then someone noticed a sliding hatchway in the deck head and of course this had to be explored. After much surreptitious labour, the hatch was slid away to reveal that it opened into the funnel space. What a wonderful place to skive off, if it could be made suitably habitable. As it was above the battery room, electric power was only a little problem to young minds. Various bedcovers and towels mysteriously disappeared during the washing process, only to end up in their hideaway in the funnel space. One problem that needed to be addressed was that the ship had the type of edging to the top of the funnel that certain old Orient Line ships had (giving the appearance of a hat), and it was expected that the light that they had appropriated would shine through the ventilation ducting and give them away. An ingenious shade therefore had to be made and, strange to say, the Schoolmaster's Homberg hat disappeared at about the same time!

'Just in case they were ever discovered, it was considered prudent to see if a means of escape could be provided by a different route. It so happened that the ship had been in action and a shell had passed right through the funnel without exploding. The resulting hole had been patched up with oval plates on both sides; they were not welded but only bolted to studs on the outside of the funnel. Again, over a time, strenuous efforts were made to free up rusted bolts so that they could readily be undone. Peter tells that it was never discovered in his time aboard, but he did hear that in later years it was all uncovered.

'Once in his two years and five months on board, they were towed downstream to the Clover Clacton drydock in Birkenhead for bottom cleaning. He reckons there were barnacles fifteen inches long on the hull.

'The cadets were organised into two watches, red and green, and each watch into two divisions. Approximately twice a year, leave was granted to each watch in turn, normally two weeks at a time.

'One abiding memory is being permanently hungry. Any opportunity for extra food was instantly taken up. Smoking was also indulged in although banned. If caught, punishment meant a disrating of one level of promotion, such as First Class Petty Officer back to Second Class. This was usually for three months and then you were made up again. In extreme cases, such as proven theft, the culprit was made to wear a white suit of overalls with the word, THIEF, emblazoned, even on days when visitors were on board. Various ways to obtain and hide the illicit cigarettes were discovered. On some occasions, a duty boat would be sent ashore to get some sand for holy stoning. There was always fear and trepidation when returning to the ship in case an officer wanted the sand tipped out because this would have immediately revealed quantities of cigarettes within the sand bags. This was nearly given away at times with the number of cadets taking an avid interest in the return of the sand gathering expedition!

'In their own slang cadets would be recognised among themselves as either 'dashers' or 'scallywags', the former, while by no means angels, endeavoured to get on and keep out of trouble, while the latter made little attempt to get on. He remembers that some dashers occasionally represented the ship at functions, including his own case at the funeral of a prominent member of the Bibby family.

'Towards the end of his time, while waiting for his sixteenth birthday to arrive in April 1924, he won the annual Ismay Prize, which was apparently awarded by popular vote among fellow cadets. The financial reward of this allowed him to be taken to Bakers in Liverpool to be kittted out for his apprenticeship ready to join his first ship, the RAY CASTLE, which was ex-FALKENFELS, a German war reparation vessel.'

Thank you Martin Southwood for those precious memoirs of your father-in-law.

It was a happy chance in 1996 that I met an old seafarer who told me of his time as a boy in INDEFATIGABLE ... his name was Billy Maclean. Billy was born in 1911 and when I met him he was 85, living alone in a spotless flat and he was obviously delighted to find someone interested in his past.

'I first came across INDEFATIGABLE when with two mates I called in the office in Victoria Street - on the glass door it said Training Ship INDEFATIGABLE. The man talked to us. "Are you hungry?" There was only one answer to that. "Do you want a wash?" I explained that we went into the park and always had a good wash every day in the lake. "Where do you sleep?" At that time we had found an old church and that was fine for us. I must have been about ten at that time and there was nothing at home. We lived in a hovel, my Mam and four children. It wasn't much and we ate what we could find. My Dad was long gone! The best place was Great Homer Street Market. If you helped with hand-carts, you got an apple. Everyone I knew was poor!'

Details were taken in the office and Billy thought that nothing more would happen because he was too young. His life of fighting for survival on the streets of Liverpool continued in the same old way ... but he had not been forgotten.

That Chaplain, who had spoken to Billy, made contact with his mother and on the 5th November, 1925, the indentures were signed by the Commander of INDEFATIGABLE, by Billy and by Elizabeth Maclean, his mother. Billy was thirteen and a half years old. He continued with his tale as we sipped our coffee.

'There seemed to be about three hundred lads aboard. Along with the other new boys, I stripped naked and washed myself in half a barrel of cold water and carbolic soap. I had my own tooth-brush and was given powder on a piece of paper ... it was great to clean my teeth! We sat at tables, six lads on either side with a top boy with a cane at the end. I'd never come across Grace at meals before, but I still remember it now.

We present at the table, Lord,
Let manna to our souls be given,
From bread sent down from heaven.

We all gave a loud *Amen* and sat down. The food was horrible; I shut my eyes to eat it, but I was always hungry.

'The bugle went at six. We slept in hammocks which were great; tucked in the hammock was the only private place aboard the ship. I felt safe in mine. The light was very poor in the ship and because we were for ever scrubbing, it was always damp. But we lads were healthy, so it must have been all right. It was a sad-faced place, but we were fed, safe and warm. Remember we were just street urchins.

'They tried to make us seamen, but I don't think it worked. I did learn how to splice. After three months, I was allowed to go home to see my Mam for two hours and then had to report back to Rock Ferry. We rang the large bell and the cutter came to get us. We all learned how to pull an oar; that was the only fun that I can remember.

'The Chaplain was a good man. He talked to us and opened all our parcels and divided any food amongst us all. Punishment was three or six cuts over the vaulting horse with a half inch cane ... most of it was for nothing much! Into our hammocks at seven and emergency lights only.

'Never saw the Captain or his wife or his dog. We never troubled each other! We were just a bunch of strays. Another punishment was to stand under the clock with your hammock on your shoulders for two hours. That was hard.

'One day I was sent for and told 'You're leaving!' I jumped into the tub, then received my kit and was told to join Bibby's LEICESTERSHIRE as a bridge boy. There was no time to go home to tell my Mam or wish her good-bye.

'I spent two years in the INDEFATIGABLE and thirty years at sea. It did me no harm and did teach me to respect God.'

Billy was a quiet, courteous gentleman. Like so many old seafarers, he knew that most people were not in the least interested in his years at sea and, even if they were, did not know how to ask the right questions. Taking him back in memory to his INDEFATIGABLE days had made his eyes dance and shine. It had been a wonderful conversation and I shall ever remember him.

A few months after recording these memories, I was privileged to see Billy 'over the side' for his final voyage and was able to retell his story. INDEFATIGABLE had truly rescued Billy Maclean and yet another boy became a man.

W. Hodgson, 1925-1927, wrote in the Spring 1985 Newsletter.
'I have a photograph that was taken on Exchange Flags on Trafalgar Day, 1926 or 1927. It shows Mr. Williams, the bandmaster, and about five members of the band, including myself on the side drum. As a member of the band I had the privilege of playing to King George V and Queen Mary on the GALATEA, at the Liverpool Landing Stage when they opened the Gladstone Dock. She was followed by the White Star liner, ADRIATIC, and the boys of the various training establishments lined the rails along the foredeck. They were then entertained to what was called 'Big Eats' aboard the ship. As we, the members of the band, were stationed on the landing stage, we were given either two or four days extra leave in lieu of the 'Big Eats'! On a number of occasions we were given trips in the North Wales steamer, ST. TUDNO, and we played for the passengers. Usually the hat was taken around by the passengers and Mr. Sanderson, the Padre, used it for various benefits, like games, football kits, etc. There was also a Civic Week held in Liverpool and we used to play each day at Pier Head.'

The Sixtieth Annual Report, 1925, produced a table of daily work.
6 a.m.   Rouse out, stow hammocks, wash.
7   Breakfast.
7.20   Clear up decks, wash clothes (Mon., Tues., and Fri.)
8   Physical exercises.

8.30   Inspection by Divisions.
8.45   Prayers.
9   Roll Call.
10.45   Stand easy.
10.55   Resume classes.
12.15pm   Dinner.
1 - 3.30 Classes.
4   Wash ˆ
5 - 7   Tea and recreation.
7   Stand by hammocks.
8.15   Prayers.
8.30   Turn in.
Weather permitting, boys land for recreation on Wednesday and
Saturday afternoons.

And as a result of these regular hours and reasonable discipline the boys
are taught - to quote from a boy's own letter to his people - 'self control,
obedience, and cleanliness.'

Will Bramhill, 1926, was born in Liverpool in 1913 and after his time
in the Inde he served with T. & J. Harrison, Elder Dempster and
MacAndrews and worked his way from seaman to Navigating Officer.
His story appeared in the Newsletter of 1997 and is taken from his local
newspaper.
'During the Second World War he saw action in the Atlantic and Indian
Oceans and in the Mediterranean. In 1941 he was commended by
Winston Churchill for his brave conduct in the firing on a U-boat which
surfaced next to his ship. As with great difficulty he angled his
Oerlikon gun at the conning tower, a couple of seamen pelted the sub
with peeled potatoes from the galley, hurling Scouse insults at the
Germans.

'Later in the war, Bramhill was serving on the merchant vessel,
EMPIRE NEWTON, at Juno and Gold beaches immediately after D-
Day.

'In1946 Bramhill moved to Harwich, joining the L.N.E.R. fleet, later

Sealink, and won his Master's Certificate. He first sailed as Master in the late 1950's.

'In 1953 Captain William Bramhill showed great heroism one foggy night. In the early hours of May 6th, DUKE OF YORK, the Harwich ferry, was enroute to Holland with 500 passengers on board. Suddenly the American troopship, HAITI VICTORY, loomed out of the murk. Bramhill, then a Second Mate, was on watch as the ship crashed into the DUKE OF YORK forward of the bridge, slicing her in two. Bramhill and an officer from HAITI VICTORY, Howard Ridenor, sprang into action, working chest-deep in the sinking forward section, hacking and cutting with knives and axes to free the trapped passengers, of which there were many. The collision caused eight deaths, there would have been far more but for the presence of a sailor with the experience, skill and courage of Will Bramhill.'

Another Inde boy!

Sydney Beaumont joined the Inde in February 1927 and was discharged into shore employment in September 1929. Actually, he did not leave the ship immediately as he was apprenticed to a firm of Marine Engineers who were engaged in refitting the electrical equipment on board. He finally left in March 1930. All his working life he was an engineer and has recorded his memories for the Spring 1984 Newsletter. The Captain Superintendent was Rear Admiral Stanley Miller, R.N., (Rtd.).
'Officially our food was described as 'ample and varied', but I can say truthfully that, throughout my time on the ship, our weekday breakfast and tea consisted invariably of two rounds each of bread and dripping or margarine washed down with 'lune', which was the word used for sweet tea or cocoa.

'I have a very clear recollection of one day when we were having our midday meal. We were eating macaroni pudding when a vessel, which had been moored in the river, dragged its anchor. It drifted up stream on the flood tide and collided with our starboard bow. The INDEFATIGABLE took an alarming list to port and our macaroni pudding went everywhere, while all hands rushed to the ports to get a better view. Tugs came from all directions: Cock, Alexandra, Lamey, all intent on rendering assistance and, eventually, we were towed into Vittoria Dock at Birkenhead for the necessary repairs to be carried out while we boys set to, scaling and painting the ship's sides. The work was done fairly quickly and we were soon back in the river off Rock Ferry.

'It was customary for us to receive 'Scout's Pay' for doing such duties as motor boat's crew, band boy, galley boy, heads boy, chippy's mate and engineer's mate. This pay amounted to eight pence a month and, as we had no place to spend it, we would pass it to Mr. Sanderson, the Chaplain, to mind for us until we were going on leave. He was kind enough to let us use his cabin for our club room and it was there we would gather during the winter evenings to converse and write our letters. In summer time we spent much of our leisure on deck, up in the cross-trees watching the Eastham Ferry boats sail by or engaging in inter-divisional races in the cutters. I still possess the silver award that I received in 1928 when 1st Division cutter's crew won the Captain's Cup and some photographs, including one of our winning football team taken on the boat deck with H.M.S. CONWAY in the background.

'They were happy days, but there were some sad ones too. It is with profound sorrow that I recall the death from meningitis of my friend, George Edward Major, who is buried in Public Grave No. K347 at Bebington Cemetery. The funeral took place on Tuesday, 23rd October, 1928, and No. 23 Jones and I marched from Rock Ferry with our bugles to sound the Last Post at the graveside.

'Blad Brooks was another boy who died during his service in Inde. He is interred in Smithdown Road Cemetery and it would be remiss of me were I not to mention that but for Blad's heroism I would not be writing this letter today. It was a stormy, tempestuous day, when, whilst attempting to board the cutter, I received a blow on the head which knocked me unconscious and caused me to fall into the river. Blad and another boy, Walker, realising my predicament, came in after me and supported me until we were picked up by the motor boat.

Unquestionably, they saved my life that day and they both received bronze medals in recognition of their bravery. I contracted a mastoidal ear infection as a result of my immersion and was operated on at Birkenhead Hospital. My hearing was severely impaired and this was the reason I did not become a seafarer.

'I put in twenty-one years Territorial Service with the Royal Corps of Transport and the Kings Regiment, Liverpool, before my retirement.'

Thank you, Sydney Beaumont.

Danger was ever present and could lead to tragedy. This is reflected in the headline of the Liverpool Daily Post on 9th April 1929.

BOY MISSING FROM TRAINING SHIP
Feared Fall Overboard into Mersey

'John Brown, an apprentice on the Training Ship INDEFATIGABLE, anchored in the Sloyne of the Mersey, disappeared from the vessel yesterday afternoon and has not been discovered. It is feared that he fell overboard, but there is hope that he might have swum ashore.

'Brown was last seen on the ship at half-past one and failing to muster shortly afterwards, a search of the vessel was made. No trace of the boy could be found, and his disappearance was reported to the police.'

Could this be Ginger?

Of passing interest we note that the ship's mascot around 1929 was an old 'seadog' called Ginger, a wire-haired terrier. The dog knew the ship's routine well and apparently, as befits an animal with a dog collar, he attended church every morning and also recognised all the bugle calls and appropriate following actions!

The hard and difficult financial years of the early thirties are reflected in the minutes of an Executive Committee held on the 14th May, 1931, at 26, Chapel Street. Here are a few extracts. The number of boys on board was 125.

'As requested at the last Meeting, Admiral Miller now submitted a report bearing upon the salaries including emoluments, as paid to the whole of the officers aboard. In a concluding note he wrote: 'In no case do I consider these salaries to be excessive, and submit that no reduction should be made'. The report was discussed, and apart from instructing the Secretary to ascertain the origination of subsistence allowance as paid to the School teachers during holidays, the matter was allowed to drop.

'Following upon suggestions which Mr Harold Bibby had previously put forward with a view to encouraging the boys aboard to extend the wear of their clothes, Admiral Miller now submitted a scheme under which each boy would be given a shilling per month to defer the issue of a new suit. Although it was not possible to calculate what saving would be effected, Admiral Miller added that no loss would be entailed. It was decided to give the scheme a trial.

'In his report Admiral Miller also stated that the stock of hammocks was hardly sufficient for the present number of boys, and that some were in a very poor worn condition. He was now authorised to make further enquiry as to how the cost of making them aboard would compare with the ready-made article.'

Hard times!

There is a record stating that in July 1931 ... for the first time ... INDEFATIGABLE and CONWAY competed against each other in a boat race with 10-oared cutters. INDEFATIGABLE won!

Another extract from Committee notes dated September of that year (actually the date is almost undecipherable and might be wrong) must be noted.

'Admiral Miller reported that he had accepted an offer of £25 by the Heswall Nautical School (ex-AKBAR) for our band instruments.

'Mr. Fernie voiced his own and colleagues grateful thanks to the Bibby Line, by whose generosity the lost motor-boat had been so suitably and economically replaced.

'In referring to the recent visit to Merseyside of H.R.H. the Prince of Wales, Admiral Miller stated that in addition to steaming around the INDEFATIGABLE His Royal Highness also inspected the boys on the Rock Ferry Pier. Mr. Arthur Bibby had since received a telegram in the following terms: 'I was so sorry not to see you yesterday, but was very interested in seeing the boys of the INDEFATIGABLE, whom I inspected on the Pier at Rock Ferry. Please accept my best wishes.'

'Attention was drawn to the apparently excessive quantity of potatoes which had been supplied to the ship at a time (during September) when prices were very high.'

The minutes of another meeting in 1931 record five applications for admission.
1. Orphan's Pension 5 shillings per week.   Accepted
2. Orphan's Pension 5 shillings per week.   Rejected
3. 3 shillings per week towards maintenance per Liverpool Public Assistance Committee.   Accepted
4. £35 per annum and Sea outfit per The Officers'Association, London.   Accepted
5. £31. 4s per annum from Liverpool Public Assistance Committee. Rejected, colour bar.

The minutes continued: 'The latter application, which was declined on account of colour bar, raised a discussion on the question of procedure regarding future applications of a similar nature, and a definite ruling given.' That matter was happily resolved.

Problems were ever present, the main item usually being finance. 1934 was no different. The Board of Education Grants depended upon the number of boys leaving each year and those numbers were not easy to control. Two factors were dominant ... the numbers on board were below average and the severe depression in the shipping world created difficulties in finding seagoing posts for the boys.

It was reported in 1934 that an Old Boys Association had been formed and the long term plan was to enroll every Old Boy. Mr. A.W. Bibby was the Patron and Mr. A. Harold Bibby was the President. Members met on the last Wednesday of each month at 7.30 in their Clubroom in the Sailors' Home, Canning Place.

On October 21st, Trafalgar Day, and on May 5th, Empire Day, the boys as usual paraded on Exchange Flags, behind Liverpool's Town Hall. On Empire Day the boys gave an exhibition of Morse Signalling and were afterwards entertained to lunch by Sir F.C. Bowring.

Another event recorded in 1934 was a number of trips to Menai Straits and the owners and the Captain of S.S. ST. TUDNO were suitably thanked.

Money was the subject of the A.G.M. The cost of running the ship amounted to approximately £7,000 and that worked out at a cost of about £72 per annum per boy. The maintenance received was £20 per boy for the year. As the normal compliment was 120, there was an annual shortfall of cash of £6,240. INDEFATIGABLE depended upon the charity of its supporters. They really were hard times.

Newsletter, Series 4, Volume 5, of the Liverpool Retired Merchant Seafarers, Spring 2003. The article is written by Bill Smith, 1936-1937. 'It cost by the hour to lie at the Landing Stage in Liverpool, so the early boat to Douglas would anchor at the Sloyne overnight. On a bank holiday weekend, sometimes five Isle of Mann boats would be anchored off Rock Ferry.

'The Inde had a passenger launch called by the lads the Stinker, which was contracted to run the crews to and from Rock Ferry. Bill Smith was often the 'skipper'. Early in the morning, after a breakfast of burgoo and a bowl of tea, Bill and his crew would start ferrying the crews out to the Steam Packets. Hung over and bad tempered passengers were the norm, and if you were lucky, a clout round the ear for 'dropsy'.

'The Mersey is a dangerous river and the Sloyne has its own peculiar hazards. The Rock Ferry stage was anchored to the river bed by huge chains. These chains were a danger to Bill as he had to pick up and land his passengers on the landward or backside of the stage. The wake from a passing ship, ferry, or even a big wave would cause the stage to rise, lifting the chain from the river bed, upsetting any boat crossing over it. It could also land the chain on the boat.

'The biggest hazard of all was the Rubbing Strake on the steamer's hull. This stuck out from the ship's side about 18 inches and was just high enough out of the water for Stinker to get caught underneath it. If any kind of a sea was running, there was a good chance the launch would capsize and a lot of people be inconvenienced, if not lost.

'More frightening for Bill was that whenever Inde's boats were in use, an Officer would be watching through a telescope. All sins were logged and the plum job of skippering the Stinker could be lost for want of a little care in going alongside. There were important perks for the 'Star Turn' in the job, not least of which was access to H.M.S. CONWAY's cake boxes. The Inde boys fed largely on burgoo, bread and jam. The young gentlemen of H.M.S. CONWAY had more refined fare. Boxes of a dozen cakes or sticky buns were delivered by the multitude to Rock Ferry Landing Stage, 'to be collected'. There are thirteen in a Baker's Dozen and Stinker's skippers were very early risers. The removal of one cake from each box had been going on for years, the scam being passed on from skipper to skipper.

'Stinkpot was also used to run 'dancing girls' out to H.M.S. CONWAY, but that's a different story.

'It is to be wondered what the Health and Safety Executive would make of a boy of 14 years running a ferry, full of people, across a turbulent and dangerous river. The kids lost nobody, didn't get drunk, were on time and made some of the best seafarers and shipmates out of Liverpool.'

Arthur Royden Thomas, 1937-1939, Newsletter 2000, 3rd Division, Boy 120. This obituary was written by an old friend Alf Eady, 1943-1944.
'Brought up in a Children's Home, Arthur joined the Inde in February 1937. The Captain was R.E. Jeffreys, a direct descendent of the great Judge Jeffreys. He became the officers' mess boy and received six pence a week pocket money and later was Captain Jeffreys's messenger with a rise in money.

'In the autumn of 1937 an epidemic of paratyphoid broke out, and Arthur was one of the first to go down with it and spent two months in Birkenhead General Hospital. He was convalescent at Seafield House, Santon, I.O.M. until January 1938. On Coronation Day 1937, Arthur was on duty at the Liverpool Cathedral. He summed up his life on INDEFATIGABLE like this, 'Though we did not appreciate it at the time, one has pride at having been on the T.S. INDEFATIGABLE … they taught us to walk tall, and in our uniforms gave us our self-respect.'

Alf Eady continued the story.

'Arthur left the Inde on 24th March, 1939, and joined the S.S. VOLTAIRE, Lamport and Holt, as a chartroom and bridge boy, wages a mere £2 a month. The ship was at Scapa Flow on the 3rd September, 1939, and after the sinking of the ROYAL OAK they took survivors on board in a fearful condition. Arthur was still there when the IRON DUKE was bombed and beached and they received more survivors.

'On the 7th July, 1940, he was sunbathing on the deck of DELAMERE, seven days out of Rio de Janeiro bound for Freetown to meet up with a convoy, when he noticed a ship coming on the port beam. They kept turning away, but in the afternoon the vessel opened fire, hitting them amidships and stopping them. That enemy ship, the THOR, took off the crew and sank DELAMERE. The crew were searched and put below decks. During that next week THOR sank a further four ships and had some 200 prisoners on board. On the 27th July, they were given bread and coffee and were closed down as the ship gathered speed and was in action for four hours with the Armed Merchant Cruiser ALCANTARA, a most terrifying experience. After the action they took off into the South Atlantic and round Cape Horn.

'Arthur recalled that they were allowed on deck at the Horn to see the heavy seas. An Argentine ship helped with the repairs. And then back in the Atlantic, they sank more ships and ended up with more than 400 prisoners. Eventually he was transferred to the RIO GRANDE and on the 14th December arrived at Bordeaux and handed over to the German army, not knowing at the time that their guards were the infamous S.S.

'In the January of 1941, they were moved under heavy guard to Paris and eventually to Drancy Concentration Camp, where the food and conditions were terrible. They were systematically starved. Arthur cut his own wrists and had ten stitches inserted without anaesthetic, being held down by the doctors.

'In late April, 1941, they were given one hour to ready themselves for transfer to N.W. Germany enroute to Sandbostel. He remembered that while marching through Drancy to entrain, some French risked their lives by throwing food and cigarettes, and the German guards opened fire on them to stop them doing so.

'On arrival at Sanbostel they were photographed and finger-printed and given a POW number, his was 89494, then billeted in Lager VI, 24 men to a room, 10 rooms to a hut, which was filthy and stunk. He with others worked on a peat bog, six days a week from dawn to dusk and were deloused once a week in the bath house. Winter 1941-42 was bitterly cold and typhus was rampant in the camp. Some of the guards were ill with it.

'In May 1942 they were transferred to Westertimke Malag und Milug

Nord, working in clay pits, carrying bricks and forestry cleaning. By this time Arthur was far from well, he had pleurisy in 1942 and in January 1944 caught pneumonia. He was then transferred to a place called Elsterhost; his right lung had collapsed and in August 1944 he was recommended for repatriation, but celebrated his 21st birthday in captivity.

'He travelled home to Liverpool from Sassinitz to Trelleborg in Sweden, then to Gothenburg and on the S.S. GRIPSHOLM finally arriving in Liverpool. He was admitted to Fazakerley Sanatorium, receiving treatment for his other lung, which was not a success.

'After a long stay he was finally discharged in October 1948, but it was 1950 before he was found fit for light work and in the April he was employed at the Rushworth Organ Works in Great George Street. He stayed there for nearly forty years.

'Arthur passed away on the 8th August, 2000, and was survived by his wife Jean and two sons, Peter and David. At his funeral there was a large company of friends, Captain Harry Traynor read a passage of scripture, his coffin was draped by the INDEFATIGABLE blue ensign.'

Arthur Royden Thomas was a brave man ... and yet another Inde boy.

Here are the memoirs of Patrick Stuart Bowers (Davis).
'I joined the ship in April 1938 one month after my fourteenth birthday. Other than Commander Jeffreys, I cannot remember the names of a single person aboard, but I was never much good with names.

'The only time we wore boots was to go ashore with the Padre and march to New Ferry. Pictures on a Saturday morning (Wild Bill Hitchcock, etc.), to Port Sunlight's sports ground on a Thursday, football in the winter and cricket in the summer. Quite often we would play against selected celebrity teams. My claim to fame ... I hit Gregory, the then well known Surrey fast bowler, for four. I was clean bowled the next ball!

'We always did very well at the boat races, especially the cutter and galley boats. I think this was because we trained on the River Mersey, most often against the tide, whereas the shore based establishments used to train on the Manchester Ship Canal. Another event that comes to mind was the day of athletics organised by the East Lancs Police, again at Port Sunlight. The great feeling of being rubbed down by the physio! The one year I won the 100 yards.

'Because we were moored out in the Mersey, whenever there was a fog we had to stand a two hour fog watch, ringing the ship's bell. There was always a lot of movement on the river. Daytime someone would bring you a cup of loon (tea). If it were the middle of the night, in the early hours the watchman would bring you a steaming hot cup of cocoa.

'Some of the older boys used to play lots of tricks on the younger, New Cocks as we called them. Lights out at nine o'clock, followed by the Officer of the Watch going round to check that everyone was properly esconced in their hammock. Just when everything was quiet and most boys asleep, you would suddenly hear the thump, one or two or three or four. The head lashings had been released! Another favourite after lights out was to grab an unsuspecting victim and put him in the dumb waiter, then hoist and leave him suspended midway between the galley and the mess deck. Later he was released by the watchman ... no-one was ever caught. Another trick was to take the victim to the boiler house and smother him with oil, especially the hairy parts.

'School was five days, Monday to Friday. Evenings were free, except when you were involved with boxing or exercises in the gymnasium. Some of us were in the Chorus Line and practised the hornpipe and the sailor's gig. These would perform along with other shows at the Liverpool Empire and other venues in Liverpool and in Birkenhead.'
There was much more, but Patricks' recollections were unique ... well done!

Eric Nash,1938-1940, Newsletter 1994.
'In November 1940, I joined the troop-ship ANDES of the Royal Mail Lines, taking troops to Egypt via Freetown, Capetown, Mombasa and

Port Said. I joined the M.V. DARLINGTON COURT of the Court Line, a voyage to New York, Albany and Halifax, Nova Scotia. During the trip to England the ship was torpedoed with the loss of twenty-five of the crew. Only twelve survived. I spent most of the day on a raft and later transferred to a lifeboat. The following day we were picked up by a Dutch rescue ship and taken to Reykjavik in Iceland. After a week in a survivors camp, we were put back on the rescue ship to return to Scotland. During the voyage the ship was bombed and the ship's company and survivors were machine-gunned and I was wounded. I finally returned to Liverpool.'

They were really only boys ... but they were Inde Boys and all were destined to play a major role in World War Two.

Chapter 4
The War Years on the Mersey

Gerald Morgan, Boy 122, Hood Division 1939, has put his thoughts into the Inde Newsletter.

'I joined the Inde in the Mersey on the 16th of January, 1939. Among the 120 boys there were three others besides me from Secondary Schools. We were given a hard time by the officers and the boys, in the class warfare and snobbery of that time. When I finished in the school room, with the Navigation Prize for 1940, I was too young to leave, so was appointed the first 'quartermaster' ever. My duties were to keep a gangway watch and write a daily Inde Log. I never got to leading hand, but on leaving the ship I was cheered away by a crowd at the rail, much to my surprise.

'In 1939 the ship was commanded by Captain Jeffreys, R.N., very impressive and lean. He was seconded by a wonderful Chief Officer Strivens, a stout retired R.N. Petty Officer. There was a fine schoolmaster, Mr. Dixon.

'When war came, the ship's upper decks were soon painted grey and there were other changes. Mr. Strivens went back to the Navy, was commissioned lieutenant and sent to the U.S.A. to do something with friendly neutral ships. Captain Jeffreys went somewhere. In his place came the older Captain Cochrane, who had won a V.C. on a 'Q' ship in 1916. He really was a pain. Even the newly-promoted Chief Officer Mr. Unwin (expert R.N. yeoman of signals at Jutland) remarked on the Captain's unfairness to me. Among other crimes, I was the senior of a dozen Catholic boys, dissident to the R.N. religion of proper Admirals and the King.

'In the summer of 1940, one of the boys escaped by jumping overboard because, although he was about to leave for sea, Captain Cochrane forbade him to go ashore for his sister's wedding. I helped the boy Callaghan to escape. He was sighted and fished out of danger by our boat, quickly sent. Before all hands, he was dismissed in disgrace (but in his very good humour!). I've not heard from him since.

'Mrs. Cochrane was something else. She got our bread ration increased, with cakes too. In the winter 1939-40, historically cold, she got us issued with woollen underpants for the first time. We laughed at them as 'sissie', but they made a difference to our ordeal. Even the Committee refrained from inspecting the 'too cold' ship. Meanwhile, Mr. Dixon stayed on board as our schoolmaster and was a very great help, until he left to join the R.A.F.

'The Inde was important for shipowners; the Committee was headed by the Chairman of Bibby Line. Many boys began their seagoing in Liverpool ships. However, the boys had much to learn, which they had missed because the Inde was run in the Navy style. But the Inde boys had a good name in the Merchant Navy for seamanship and discipline. I never heard of any of them sworn at as a slacker or a 'bolshie'. When I went up for second mate, I answered some questions stupidly, but the examiner let me through. He said, "As you're an INDEFATIGABLE boy you probably know better than you say." Apart from all that, the fact was that so many mates had been drowned or blown up, the shortage was desperate in 1944.

'I had boarded the Inde with the M.N. in mind and greatly enjoyed our benefits of watching all sorts of ships in the river. One of them was the tanker, W.B. WHITE, which bumped the Rock Ferry landing stage one summer evening in 1940. I went aboard her some months later in Trinidad, shortly before she was torpedoed. Leaving the Inde, I was determined never to ship in the R.N. under any circumstances. It was a great day when Captain Bambra came to the Inde from the Merchant

Navy, replacing Captain Cochrane, but I only knew him for a few weeks until the 24th October, 1940, when I departed.'

Gerald Morgan continued his memoirs with a glimpse at his sea career.

'As a deck boy signaller I joined the TRAVELLER of Harrison Line, which even in the 1940's carried a lamp trimmer. It chanced that he, too, was an Inde boy and that made my way easier in the wholly strange life. In my third Caribbean voyage in 1941 in that ship I made as ordinary seaman; the other O.S. was Maurice Aitken, boxing champion of Inde, who had left her before I had. That voyage we came home in convoy HX 133, heavily attacked and for the first time I saw a ship blown sky high under the midnight sun. We stopped to pick up survivors of the NORWEGIAN SOLOY, next ahead of us. I never heard of Maurice later. We both left TRAVELLER and after a week's leave on the new Merchant Navy Pool, I joined LAFIAN for a West Africa voyage. That trip ended when a torpedo hit us homeward bound in September 1941, when convoy SL 87 lost seven ships of eleven. Some of us survivors didn't start home from Gibraltar until December 1941 in convoy HG 76. It was heavily attacked and we lost the aircraft carrier H.M.S. AUDACITY.'

There was more to befall this Inde boy ... bombs off Italy at Christmas 1944, Adriatic and Baltic minefields while short of compass and charts, civil war in Greece and China, revolution in Cuba. He took his Master's ticket in 1953 in London, acquired a B.A. degree on the way and then added a few more degrees. He ended as a full Professor at a Canadian Military College and there was so much more. He was proud to have been in INDEFATIGABLE.

Captain Harry Traynor was the Chairman of the INDEFATIGABLE Old Boys Association for many years and both he and his wife Joyce are personal friends of mine of many decades. At the tender age of thirteen years and two months Harry joined INDEFATIGABLE in May, 1939. He recalls that his parents paid thirteen shillings and six pence a month (half a week's wage) during his time on board.

Harry recalls his early memories.
'I joined Inde in the May and was placed into the 4th Division, No. 139. Our P.O. was Bob Harrison; Bill Owen and Brian Vincent joined about this time. The staff I recall were Captain Jeffreys, his good lady wife and their daughter, Griselle (she was the poor boys equivalent to Rosemary Goddard); Chief Officer Strivens, soon to leave to fit guns to merchant ships; there were four Divisional Officers ... Jimmy Unwin who replaced Strivens as Chief Officer, Charlie Rosevere, Mr. Doodson and Daddy Nash. We were blessed with two schoolmasters ... Mr. Williams (Bandy) so called because he taught music and coached the band and Mr. Dickenson who taught the senior boys and cadets (known as class 6).

'In 1939, compulsory education ended at 14 years of age and few boys were good enough to attain Mr. Dickenson's class 6. Consequently very few boys attended school. We slept in hammocks which we slung up each night and lashed and stowed every morning. There were no life-jackets provided so the hammocks had to be lashed up in such a way that they provided a means of flotation for their owners. This was our first lesson in doing a job correctly!

'Sleeping in a hammock caused a few problems, first learning to stay in the thing, then if a boy was a bit restless and twisted and turned in his sleep, his hammock bounced up and down, this resulted in rows breaking out after lights out with dire consequences. The night watchman, Ted Highway, a survivor from the TITANIC, would scream out (in our case) "Third division, up and over the mast! Larst six down gets six across the harse!" You can imagine the mad scramble as the boys vacated their hammocks and made for the boat deck and the main mast! Our night attire was a long night-shirt which blew above the waist as we raced up the mast ... and race we did. Ted's threat was no idle one. There were so many bare bums on display that the good folk of Rock Ferry must have thought that the Indy was festooned with chinese lanterns.

'The race up the mast is well worth recording. We were supposed to climb the rigging in the usual way, i.e. up the outside of the rigging, over the cross-trees and down the other side. Any boy going that way deserved 'six across the harse'! Our way was to climb until we could leap from the inside of one set of shrouds to the inside of the other. Few went higher than that. Thus most of us avoided Ted's wrath and were safely back in our hammocks, whilst Ted dealt with the laggards.

'Shortly after joining the ship one had to undergo the initiation tests set by the boys, some funny, some not and some dangerous. These tests were done without the knowledge of the officers. One test was to climb the mast to the crosstrees, then shimmy up the remainder of the mast and carve your name into the top of the truck. Another, climb down the hawse pipe, down the anchor chain and dip one's bottom into the river! You had tô return with a wet bottom. If your nerve failed ... your pants were wet with fear anyway.

'The winter of 1939 was a severe one; the upper reaches of the Mersey were frozen and the entire river was covered in ice floes. This gave rise to the very dangerous game of climbing down the anchor cable, jumping onto a suitable ice flow and riding it to the gangway!

'War came to the boys of INDEFATIGABLE early in September 1939. A lookout post was erected on the boat deck, consisting of sandbags placed around the semaphore stand, but not over the top. The lucky lad would sit inside this haven of safety and listen out for the air raid sirens. Should they be heard from the shore, the alarm would be raised by the rapid ringing of the ship's bell. Another use for the bell was in fog. Whilst on the fog watch the duty lad would sound his bell to a strict routine. It went as follows. Rock Ferry landing stage would start the sequence by a rapid ringing of the bell, followed by two distinctive strokes. This was followed by CONWAY with a rapid ringing followed by three strokes on a deep toned bell. In turn these were followed by INDEFATIGABLE rapid ringing and four separate strokes. It was very effective.

'Within days of war being declared, a party of Inde lads were sent to paint the white bands on the CONWAY's shipsides black! Why we Inde lads had to do this job is beyond me, but it must have been a fiddle between the two captains. Some of the working party on CONWAY were Bill Owen, Brian Vincent and myself. Gregory may have been the Petty Officer, but I am not certain. The job took several days and a few adventures to say the least! The buzz was that the CONWAY crowd were in hospital suffering from German measles. One day we were on the boat deck of CONWAY, about lunch time, when the destroyer H.M.S. RATTLESNAKE opened fire on a squadron of aircraft that were over the river. We were clustered near the old gun, sited on the deck, and Captain Goddard ordered us to stand clear in case the aircraft mistook us for one of the gun crews who were firing at them. Good thinking, I thought in later years!

'CONWAY always had one anchor hung off the bow. Two or three of us were sitting painting this anchor, when the word was passed that the Captain's daughter was having a bath. I was disgusted to see how many lads could hang on to a paint pot lanyard without spilling paint all over me. The pay for our work painting this ship was sixpence each (a fair amount of cash for us in those days) and a large tin of fancy biscuits to be shared between the lot of us. This anchor and gun are now at the Maritime Museum, Liverpool.

We got a tin of biscuits for painting the ship

'Our next war work was the rescue of a Fleet Air Arm Swordfish which had force landed on the river. Long after lights out, we heard the cry 'Away seaboats' crew'; shortly after the motorboat was launched (the Stinker she was known as), returning sometime later with the Swordfish in tow with the pilot and observer still on board. The aircraft had run out of fuel. It was from the carrier, H.M.S. COURAGEOUS. Next day I was in a party of boys when we took our water boat to Rock Ferry Stage and picked up some 40-gallon drums of fuel. We returned to the ship and plane and started the long and tedious job of refuelling the plane's tanks with a hand pump! For this we received no pay. Soon after this episode, H.M.S. COURAGEOUS was lost to enemy action and the plane and her crew were probably lost.

'Our boats were hoisted and stowed every night using 'Norwegian' steam. The boats were placed under the davits and the falls hooked on with the hauling party stretched out along the deck. On command, about twenty lads caught hold of the hauling part and ran along the deck as far as possible. Reaching the end of the deck, they let go and ran back and caught hold of the falls again near the davits and ran away yet again. The boats came up as smooth as an electric winch. When the boat reached the davit head, the next order was 'Avast heaving'. All movement stopped and the boat was held suspended under the davit head. Two boys in the boat, one at each end, passed the lifeline around the lifting hook and over the davit head several times. Then they secured the lifeline with a clove hitch. The order 'Lay to' was given and the hauling part of the falls was released. The boat was secure for the night.

'INDEFATIGABLE supplied fresh water to CONWAY on several occasions during 1939, using our own water boat. I believe it was whenever CONWAY's own water boat broke down. Thinking back it seems like Indy was like a Fairy Godmother to CONWAY at times! It would be interesting to put a little note into CONWAY's newsletter and see if any of the Old Boys remember us painting their ship.

'The field gun was a three-pounder, complete with ammunition limber. It was hauled by twelve boys, six each side pulling on two white traces. The boys could dismantle that gun, throw the bits over the wall and reassemble it as good as any naval team. I wonder what happened to it.

'A little about the uniform ... we were told that the flat cap was to hold out to the Officer to receive our pay. Yes, we were paid for our labour! The name tally, we were told, was handy for those boys who could not remember what ship they were from. The black silk around the neck and tied with a bow at the waist was in mourning for the death of Lord Nelson. The blue collar was the colour of the ocean and the three white stripes were in commemoration of Nelson's three great victories ... Nile, Copenhagen and Trafalgar. Bell bottom trousers with the flap front, the sailor's quick release gear should he fall overboard, enabled them to be removed with ease. Finally, the white lanyard was to carry a knife and whistle. Every part of the uniform had a function and a purpose.

'The uniform worn on the ship was a white flannel sailor's shirt, navy blue serge shorts and a sailor's cap. No footwear was permitted except during parade and on visitors day. For shore-going we had the same rig as the band wears now. The field gun's crew and duty boys sported white gaiters.

'We pressed our trousers in a special way so as to have creases to represent each of the four oceans and each of the seven seas. We made our own trouser press with two eight-inch pieces of wood and two six-inch nut and bolts. The trousers were turned inside out so that the creases ran down each side. Soap and water was then applied wherever a crease was wanted. Then each leg was folded like a concertina, one leg placed on top of the other, put into the press and the bolts set tight. After a few days, the trousers had a most wonderful set of creases.

'One had to be punctual from weekend's leave. If the last boat was missed, it was a night on Rock Ferry Stage for the late ones. All boats were crewed by the boys. No officer went along unless it was considered too rough for the boys to be unsupervised.

'The plum job was Mailman. This entailed going to Liverpool to the Sailors' Home to collect any mail from the office. There were perks in the Tailor's Shop and the Cobbler's Shop. Another good job was to be in a boat crew ... the Stinker and the water boat. A very special job was taking the Captain's dog for a walk! This entailed going ashore after breakfast, ambling about town and back for lunch. Working in the galley was a favoured job for some! The ship was painted each year. The masts, the funnels and upperworks were painted by the boys ... we enjoyed this task as it meant that Prize Day was fast approaching. When that great day did arrive, the ship had been painted, the decks holystoned, scrubbed and washed down until they gleamed. The ship was dressed overall and the guests and parents arrived alongside on the passenger boat tender, FLYING BREEZE. All the guests were led on board by Sir Harold Bibby. It was the high point of the year.

'Maybe a good last thought must be the food. The wartime cooking was done by the lads with a chef keeping a sharp watch. And memory tells me that the food was wholesome and the water sweet!'

After only one year and one month in INDEFATIGABLE and aged fourteen and three months, Harry Traynor, in what can only be described as a 'Pier Head jump', joined the Harrison Line's CUSTODIAN with the princely salary of four pounds a month. In no time the ship was at Alexandria and travelled the north coast of Africa dropping off jerry-cans of water for General Wavell's troops in the desert. The next task was to sail to Greece to pick up the 64th Royal Medium Regiment, Royal Artillery remnants which had suffered badly ... they were mostly from Liverpool ... and then they dropped them off on Crete just in time to meet the German paratroops who were to capture the island. It was here that Harry 'enjoyed' his fifteenth birthday! There were many near misses from German and Italian aircraft and sadly, twenty-eight Merchant Ships were lost.

Young Harry Traynor on board Custodian off Greece and on the way to Crete

Coincidence is certainly stranger than fiction. When the CUSTODIAN arrived safely back in Alexandria, almost the first person that Harry met when he came ashore was his father, a cook aboard the troopship ALCANTARA. They had last met at home early in 1940 and Harry's Dad did not know that his young son was at sea.
"What are you doing here, son?"
"Looking for Germans, Dad!"
They were to meet next at the end of 1941. His father was in the Military Hospital, which we now know as the Southport Floral Pavilion.

Of the boys on INDEFATIGABLE during Harry's year, thirty-three were to lose their lives and three became prisoners-of-war … one in Germany and two in Japan.

Captain Harry Traynor became a master in Harrison's and fondly recalls that there were at least a half dozen other Inde boys in command in that Company. They were proud to be Inde lads.

W.N. Owen, 1939-1940.
'After leaving INDEFATIGABLE, I served a further ten years at sea until I swallowed the anchor, during which time I was torpedoed twice in the Mediterranean, off Oran, Algeria. The first time was on the BROWNING of Lamport & Holt. The three deck boys we had were on their first trip. Their names were R. White, D.H. Brown and B. Preston, all of whom were working on deck above where the torpedo hit. White was blown over the side, but managed to hold on to the rails. Preston tried to save him, getting badly burnt in the process, but White could not hold on and he dropped into the sea. The sea was ablaze all round us. White was never seen again, but for his bravery, Preston was mentioned in despatches and later was awarded Lloyds War Medal for Bravery'

The story is enlarged by Edward Molloy, 1935-1938. He served in the S.S. BROWNING and had joined the ship with another Inde boy of his year, William Smith. He writes in the Newsletter, Spring 1985.
'We left Birkenhead for Barrow-in-Furness to load a full cargo of explosives and ammunition. We then sailed to take part in the invasion of North Africa. On November 12th, when in convoy, we were hit by two torpedoes on the starboard forward side.'

Edward then re-tells the story of the three deck boys and of the bravery they showed at such a tender age. His final comment was, 'The ship very shortly afterwards was blown to pieces.'

If you know anything about Liverpool, the ships and the Mersey, the name Derek Whale, his nautical books, and his journalism, will need no explanation. Under the headline 'Yesterday' the fascinating story of this Inde boy was told. This is the true tale of Bert Preston, who was in 1st Division of INDEFATIGABLE, 1941-42.

Happily we have the newspaper cutting about young Bert. As ever, there is no date recorded or any indication of which newspaper ... but it must be in a wartime edition of the Post or Echo!

A Hero Deckboy
'Crazy for the sea' says his father.

Described by his father as a boy "simply crazy for the sea", Bert Preston, the 15 year-old son of Mr and Mrs Preston of 102, Kingsway, Prescot, who regardless of his own safety, and the fact that his torpedoed ship might blow up, attempted to rescue a shipmate, has been awarded Lloyds War Medal for Bravery.

The doomed ship carried a dangerous cargo, and Preston could have jumped to safety, if he had wished, and swum clear. Instead the deckboy, just 15 years and four months at the time, and newly out of the Liverpool Training Ship INDEFATIGABLE, braved smoke and burning oil in an attempt to reach the man he had seen thrown overboard by the torpedo explosion.

The man was struggling close to the ship and, unable to pull him aboard because of the oil which covered both of them, Preston ran through smoke and fire to the foc'sle to fetch a line. His arms were burned, but he returned with the rope, only to find that his shipmate had disappeared.

"Bert was simply crazy for the sea" said his father. "I wanted to make him a toolmaker, sure of a regular job." To that Bert replied: "It's a bit too regular for me - up early in the morning, shut up in a factory all day, home late at night - then bed. It might suit father, but it doesn't suit me. I want to live and see something."

Preston left Whiston Central School at 14, went straight to INDEFATIGABLE and "pestered until we agreed to let him sail with the Merchant Navy at 15 as a deck boy".

"You know the rest. Between voyages he had a week's rest as usual and actually tried for a job on shore to fill in the time. 'We don't want juveniles', was the answer he got. He hadn't the nerve to explain that he was a torpedoed seaman. The only sport he ever went in for was swimming, and it seems to have served him well."

Derek Whale under a headline of 'No Grave but the Sea' fills in the story. Bert and his pal 'Knocker' signed on the Pool and were assigned to S.S BROWNING. Apparently it was Knocker who had been blown over the side and Bert had dashed through burning oil drums. Meanwhile an escorting destroyer was depth-charging the attacking submarine and poor Knocker was washed away. Bert was picked up and taken to a shore hospital where he heard the surgeons discussing the amputation of one of his arms. He absconded and got a passage on the EMPRESS OF CANADA, whose surgeon saved his arm. The Lloyds Medal is the Merchant Navy's highest award. Bert died in 1990.

They were only young lads!

Leon Maurice Jones, 1940-42, wrote in the 1997 Inde Newsletter.
'I joined the Inde on 8th August, 1940, aged 13 years and 10 months. Memories of those first few months! My first meal aboard was tripe with a large slice of bread and marge (I've hated tripe ever since), the second day when I got my kit I felt very homesick, but it was too late to change my mind then. I used to enjoy climbing the mast and sitting on the platform, until one day, I was watching two aeroplanes when a loud voice from below bellowed, "Come down you idiot, don't you know there's a raid on." Needless to say I got a clip around the ear (no good asking to see your lawyer in those days, Ha Ha!).

'Then there was everyone's favourite task, scrubbing decks in bare feet in the middle of winter. Oh! Those chilblains!

'Memories! The night watchman Rough House, I cannot recall his real name. I remember leaving the ship when Liverpool was being heavily bombed and seeing all the firehoses on the way to the Sailors' Home. Having been sent home on leave, I was recalled some weeks later to report to Clywdd Newydd, where I always remember being cold and hungry.'

Leon Maurice Jones, 1940-1942, adds further information about his days at sea after Inde, Newsletter 1999. He was in an Illustrious Class Aircraft Carrier, named INDEFATIGABLE, launched on the 8th December, 1942; the vessel survived the war and was broken up in November 1956.

'I was serving aboard the H.M.S. INDEFATIGABLE in the Pacific during the Second World War. My action station was on the Air Defence Position above the bridge. Watching the Japanese planes attacking the fleet, one peeled off and dived on the deck of the INDEFATIGABLE, hitting her in the base of the island. I believe that quite a lot of damage was done and several of the crew were killed. Despite all that the ship was operational in just a few hours and able to land her own aeroplanes, which in the meantime other carriers had taken on board. I think that the INDEFATIGABLE was the first British ship in the Pacific Fleet to be hit by Kamikaze.'

Captain Peter E.R. Hutchins has some interesting thoughts.
'I joined the ship on the 8th August, 1940, and left on the 12th September, 1941. My number was 35, 1st Division, and my nickname was Major (because my father was) and I never did like it. The first thing that I remember was that they took my shoes and socks away and you had to go over the top on the first day or you would never live it down. I can still dry myself on a hand towel. I think that INDEFATIGABLE was very good for me. I learnt many lessons that were a great help to me through life. I joined the S.S. WANDERER as a deck boy and the pay was £4 a month, plus £3 10s 0d danger pay. Overtime was 5d an hour when it was not classed as 'safety of the ship' and then there was no pay for overtime. I now live in Halifax, Canada.

'There is something that I want to say. Canada has recognised their Merchant Seamen after fifty years. They gave them a medal, as Britain did after the 1914-1918 war, but did not do so after the last war. I have a picture of THE MERCANTILE MARINE WAR MEDAL issued in 1919. Also Canada have awarded their M.N. people between 6,000 and 24,000 dollars depending upon time served.'

It is easier to forget!

Derek Baxter wrote for the Inde Newsletter.
'I was 13 when I joined the INDEFATIGABLE in 1940. I was unable to go home for Christmas as my home was occupied by members of the Foreign Office which had been evacuated to Bletchley Park. It took me

thirty years to find out about the Enigma code-breaking operation. However, staying in Liverpool was no hardship as we had a family friend with a parish in Liverpool. The Reverend Jimmy Knowles and I got along fine and I rather enjoyed the excitement of the three-day blitz. Along with other rubber-neckers, we went to see a landmine hanging by its parachute from the tram lines. If it had fallen it would probably have killed us all! Later I was in disgrace for squandering the fifteen shillings railfare that I should have used to go home. My pocket money was half a crown a month from which I was expected to buy stamps to write home each week. No more pocket money for three months! But by that time there was more bombing, which resulted in us leaving the ship. If I had been older, I would probably have been frightened by the bombing.

'One particular memory is of every Saturday morning spent scrubbing the decks in our bare feet with water straight from the Mersey. By God, it was cold even in the mild weather! During the whole war I can only remember being frightened once. Perhaps anxious would be more appropriate. That was when I was placed in charge of a lifeboat and took the trouble to calculate that we had hardly enough lifeboats for more than about a third of the ship's complement of troops and crew. Sharks the size of miniature submarines in Freetown Harbour did little to encourage me. Following the North African landings, we were subjected to more overnight raids and cover was provided by a smoke screen. I was not alone in subsequently suffering from an ulcerated throat, which discouraged me from smoking. I have never smoked since. So the Germans did some good after all.'

Derek Baxter added further thoughts in the 1998 Newsletter.
'I remember the tripe; I didn't eat it then and I have never eaten it since. There was the lumpy burgoo (porridge), tea drunk from basins and the shout of 'tuppence' if anyone broke a plate. It was all very primitive, but except for it being a ship and all the deck scrubbing, etc., conditions were not too unlike any other boarding school of its time. We saved to buy a proper Royal Navy cap, which were exempt from clothing coupons and we scrubbed our dark blue collars in an effort to lighten them.

'The headmaster of the ship was named Bell. I cannot recall a lesson where he didn't cane someone, not me fortunately. Teaching standards were pretty low, I sometimes wonder why we are so nostalgic about it all.'

D.E.K. Evans has written well about his Inde days. Derek's tale covers time on the Mersey and the transfer of the ship to Ruthin. Here it is verbatim. The date was February 1941 and Liverpool was the last place for safety in wartime. The infamous May Raids were just around the corner.

His memories are recorded in the 1998 Newsletter and he opens his thoughts by recalling his version of the Inde Song.

I was one of the Inde lads
I was one of the boys
We learned our manners
We earned our tanners
We were respected
Wherever we went.

'On a cold, damp, typical February morning the young boy and his widowed mother stepped off their train from Llandudno and out into the busy Liverpool Lime Street, en route to the Sailors' Home in Canning Place as a pre-entry condition to join the T.S. INDEFATIGABLE as a trainee boy seaman.

'On arrival at the Sailors' Home the boy reported in and joined a number of other hopeful and very nervous applicants. There was an aura of trepidation and uncertainty during all the preliminaries and once these were all completed the results were then collated and the unsuccessful candidates were let down as lightly as possible, whilst the successful boys were informed that they were due aboard that very afternooon, much to the surprise of the boy's mother who had an unused return ticket, and a very difficult explanation to make to her mother as to why she had left her grandson in Liverpool. It turned out later that there was a very frosty atmosphere at home for a considerable time.

'Goodbyes were said with a touch of embarassment, as the boy didn't want to appear to be a Mummy's boy, so kisses were kept to a minimum. After all the farewells were made, the 'nozzers' with an escort were tendered out to the Inde, which on first sight appeared very large and very daunting. All the boys aboard the tender were very quiet and very apprehensive about what lay in store, and what the future would hold for them. Could it be a somewhat unusual dream and could we possibly wake up in our beds in the comfort of our homes?

'However the embarkation took place and we went down to the mess deck for tea! No cups or mugs to drink out of, but basins! Never having drunk out of a basin before this was another shock to the system. Thick slabs of bread and marge and some form of bread pudding, which to say the least was very sloppy, and not at all like what mother made. After all the excitement of the day it was very unappetising and definitely not wanted, which suited all the old hands who more than took advantage of the situation and the unexpected food bonus. Our appetites soon recovered, and by the time of the next 'nozzer' intake we were as avaricious as everyone else and tried to take advantage of their queasy stomachs.

'After our meal, we were taken to our part of ship, and shown how to sling our hammocks and as no one had ever slept in a hammock before, this was probably the high spot of the day. We were also shown how to lash and stow in readiness for Reveille and, as this was February, 1941, air raids were very frequent at that time, so all our clothes and footwear had to be placed to hand in case of enemy action and possible evacuation.

'Eventually Pipe Down was sounded and everyone climbed into their hammocks (not without some initial difficulty) and settled down after a most traumatic day. With all these thoughts racing through his mind, the boy had great difficulty in getting to sleep. However, sleep finally came and Reveille sounded, at an unearthly hour, a new day dawned in very strange surroundings with everyone, but for the 'nozzers', knowing what was required and where to go and what to do. Strange loud shouts of 'Lash up and Stow', more ribald shouts of 'Let go your **** and grab your socks' rang out and the first full day of Inde life had begun.

'Breakfast was as exciting as last evening's tea, and then we had a tour of the ship and an introduction to the ship's officers, and then it was discovered ... horror on horror ... that schooldays were not over and there were classrooms and even a school teacher on board. The Captain's name was Bambra and his wife (for ever after known as Madame) was in charge of the sickbay and her alter ego was as a form of Matron. Chief Officer Unwin (Jimmy the One) was in charge of day-to-day running and directly responsible to the Captain for discipline. Charlie Rosevere, 'Daddy' Mash, and 'Bandy' Williams were some of the names the new intake had to remember and it was difficult initially to put a name to a face.

'Another excitement for this day was a visit to the Slop Chest for kitting out. At first nothing seemed to fit but eventually a reasonable compromise was reached. After that, Official Numbers and parts of the ship were allocated and the boy found that he was no longer Derek Evans, but now was to be known as Number 162 of the 4th Division and his part of the ship, for cleaning duties, was the Poop Deck and these duties would take place as from Day 2 onwards. All these rules and regulations took a lot of getting used to; presumably the idea was to keep everyone busy and fully occupied as a form of therapy.

'After this very busy day, whilst in his hammock, which incidentally had turned out to be exceedingly comfortable, a little self doubt crept in and whilst wondering if he had embarked on the right career, thoughts of home intruded, and a few muffled sobs and presumably tears from adjoining hammocks, as homesickness reared its head, and then he really was not sure that he had done the right thing. However, sleep took over and all of a sudden Reveille sounded and a new day had dawned.

'New routines of a daily nature took over and gradually homesickness receded until the first letters from home arrived (plus a parcel) and a big lump in the throat was there for most of the day. Popularity was very apparent until the cake, which had arrived in the parcel, was all gone and then everything returned to normal.

'The older hands were a mine of information, and misinformation at times, about everything and in particular an initiation rite or ceremony which went by the peculiar title of 'so many aboard'. It consisted of a series of punches to the upper arm muscles, one for each month aboard, by any boy senior to the recipient. This could only take place on the anniversary date of coming aboard, so one learned to keep a low profile on these days, but human nature being what it is, we all looked forward to the next entry intake when one would not be a 'nozzer' but at last senior to someone!

'Several of the older boys had what appeared to be good or cushy jobs which carried some kudos. There was the Post Boy who had to go ashore to Rock Ferry most days to take the ship's mail to the Post Office and to collect the incoming mail. This enabled him to do a bit of shopping for essential supplies such as Woodbines or Players Weights. etc. The going rate was at this time one cigarette for a penny, and as the retail price ashore was five for two pence, a thriving business was being conducted except for the difficulty of buying the cigarettes, as they were in short supply due to wartime production and privation. The boys in the stokehold had a well scrubbed shovel and could supply for a penny, a slice of fried bread, which helped to supplement the rations from the mess deck, the difficulty being again the pennies to purchase these delicacies. They were definitely budding entrepreneurs and never missed a trick.

'Lessons, the three 'R's, were conducted daily by 'Bandy' Williams who was in charge of the Drum and Bugle Band, of which organisation the boy soon became a playing member because the Band was in great demand for the various Fundraisers ashore. It was good to be on land for the marches, especially during Warships weeks. Even better these outings often ended with big Eats and they were good runs ashore!

'Other lessons, which were compulsory, were Boat Handling and

General Seamanship and they were a great relief from the three 'R's. It was what it was all about, the main reason for joining the 'lady', not boring old school lessons but Bends and Hitches, Knots and Splices, Anchors and Cables. They all took a lot of mastering, but once mastered they are still remembered to this day.

'Clear Lower Deck was piped one day. All hands fell in on the Main Deck at their stations. Mr. Unwin announced that one of the older boys was having trouble with his personal hygiene and was failing to wash either himself or his clothes and an example was to be made. He was to receive a public scrubbing.

'The water was obtained from the River Mersey, by buckets. A combination of long handled deck scrubbers, disinfectant and soft soap used with vigour, if not expertise by the crew, left the unfortunate boy red raw and very humiliated. The public exhibition had a very salutary effect on everyone who had witnessed it and resulted in everyone being very fussy about their own personal hygiene for quite a considerable time afterwards. When the ship's company fell out, there were many huddles and whispered comments about the harsh discipline aspect, but it was a lesson readily understood and stood the boy in good stead for the rest of his life. Cleanliness is a very necessary requirement in confined spaces like shipboard accommodation. Discipline in the Inde, although hard at times, was generally fair.

'After several days, routine established itself and as time passed homesickness was forgotten. Everything became very ordered with plenty of cleaning ... spit and polish ... plus seamanship lessons and the hated three 'R's and then the business of greeting the new intake of 'nozzers', thus losing the hated title, and trying to behave like 'old hands'.

'A buzz went round the ship one day; one of the boys had been taken ill and was to be moved ashore to hospital. Apparently the first diagnosis was that he had contracted spinal meningitis and was going to have various tests to confirm or deny this. He was placed in an ammunition stretcher and lowered over the side into a waiting tender and thence to hospital. A favourable report was received later, but he never came back on board.

'Shortly after, the Captain's two Coolies ... so called because of the high-collared, buttoned, white mess jackets worn ... were due to be drafted either to the Royal or Merchant Navy and their successors were duly chosen. The boy was ordered aft to report to the Captain and Madame's quarters where he and another boy were to be initiated into the mysteries of domestic life under the eagle eyes of Madame herself. Cleaning and polishing were easily mastered, but cooking for someone capable of burning water was much more difficult. Madame was a very patient lady!

'This job had one great consolation because it meant the 'coolies' ate the same food as the top brass and had a little of the leftovers, which sometimes ended up on the mess deck. This made for a modicum of popularity. Lessons, of course, had to be done but there was no more deck scrubbing which was a blessing because in winter or summer it was always with cold water from the Mersey.

'Liverpool at this time was suffering nightly air raids and, when it was discovered that mines were being dropped ... a magnetic mine had been near the wooden-walled training ship CONWAY ... the Admiralty decided that an evacuation of the INDEFATIGABLE crew be made. Everyone was moved ashore to the 'safety' of the Sailors' Home in Canning Place.

'All the crew was installed in the cabins on the various landings and when the air raids sounded we all went down to the cellars, which doubled as an air raid shelter. During one of these raids the Customs House, which was opposite the Sailors' Home, received a direct hit through its dome. Next morning it was a scene of utter devastation. It had been a fortunate escape. The result was that a decision was taken to send the boys off on extended leave whilst alternative accommodation could be found for the schooling to continue.

'During the stopover at the Sailors' Home, a serious incident occurred.

During a game of cards in the Home, a Lascar seaman suffered a fatal stab wound apparently by one of the card players. This had been witnessed by one of our boys and, if my memory is correct, he had to stay behind as a witness. We never did find out the result of this occurrence as we left the Sailors' Home within a couple of days and with home leave being offered this was a more interesting prospect and even after regrouping nothing was ever heard of this matter.'

After a few weeks all boys were ordered to report to the ex-Merseyside Holiday Camp at Clwydd Newydd, near Ruthin, in North Wales. Derek Evans will continue, in the next chapter. his memoirs with memories of life in the rigours of the hills of Wales where the enemy was not the Luftwaffe, but Welsh weather.

The INDEFATIGABLE was in full use as a training ship until March 1941, when it was decided on Admiralty instructions to evacuate her because the Germans were bombing Merseyside. The boys, as we have heard, were housed in the Sailors' Home. As the air raids were particularly bad and continuous, the Committee considered that it was wise to advance the Easter holidays and disperse the boys to their homes.

Liverpool and Merseyside was bearing the full brunt of the Blitz.

After much thought it was decided not to bring the lads back to the ship. It was fortunate that a Holiday Camp at Clwydd Newydd was vacant and arrangements were immediately made for the boys to assemble there at the start of the summer term. They were well away from the bombing. There was much to be done to prepare that camp for winter!

What of the ship?

She had really reached the stage where ever-increasing repairs were necessary at great cost. If she were left unoccupied there would be much rapid deterioration and even higher costs to bring her back to standard. There was only one solution.

The old ship was sold to Messrs. T. and W. Ward for breaking up and was towed in June 1941 to Preston Slipway, but as her hull was still in remarkably good condition, she was acquired by the Admiralty (not to fight!) for use as a store ship in the Clyde and renamed CARRICK II. After the war she was towed again on the 20th January, 1947, to Preston to be broken up after 64 years at sea.

1941 saw the final departure of the training ships off the Sloyne at Rock Ferry. It was truly the beginning of a new chapter, but certainly not the end of the training of young seafarers. The Merseyside story was to continue in new surroundings, yet the Merseyside interest was not to diminish.

The Last Voyage

Chapter 5
Clwydd Newydd - North Wales

Having found temporary premises at Clwydd Newydd, near Ruthin, very quickly there were misgivings because the site was rather exposed. In fact, in spite of that first cold winter of 1941-42, the health of the boys improved.

For schooling, the boys were grouped in three forms according to their knowledge and ability. All new entrants spent the first three months in school and to help with their grading they were given a grounding in Seamanship and Signalling, subjects new to them. The lack of sea experience away from the Mersey was remedied in part by sending batches to the Outward Bound School at Aberdovey.

It was at this time that steps were taken to amalgamate the INDEFATIGABLE with the Lancashire and National Sea Training Home, which had been situated in Wallasey. Following air raid damage, the Home was temporarily based in Penrith. The negotiations rambled on, held up by legal formalities and Government regulations, for almost two years before amalgamation was effected

We take up Derek Evans' tale again.
'After a few glorious weeks at home, a very unwelcome arrival was received at Sunnymount, 15, Old Road, Llandudno, in the shape of an official-looking envelope containing my recall papers and requiring my presence at 'the holiday camp'. Fortunately I did not have too far to travel, although it did necessitate a couple of trains to reach there.

'The due day arrived and I and my kit left Llandudno Railway Station, changed at Llandudno Junction and eventually arrived at the Railway Station in Ruthin, a town that I had never visited before. I walked up the hill to the Town Square and then made enquiries as to the whereabouts of Clwydd Newydd and the best way to get there. The information that I received suggested that as it was only a short distance to the camp and, as there were no buses running in those days due to petrol and fuel rationing, it would be a little stroll and, as it was a nice day, off I set. As I remember it was about five miles ... Welsh miles are notoriously longer than English miles as they have more bends in them ... so it was a very tired and thirsty and hungry boy who arrived at that Merseyside Holiday Camp. It was the right place because it said so on the notice on the gate.

'At first appearance it all seemed to be uphill or, at least, on the side of a small mountain. In the distance were a lot of what appeared to be long huts or bunkhouses! Just inside and to the left there was a house, which later turned out to be the Captain's quarters and where I would spend a lot of my future time. To the right of the path was what appeared to be a summerhouse and, on the extreme right, a swimming pool.

'Reporting to the Main Office, which was half way up the hill, I think it was Charlie Rosevere, one of the Officers and Instructors, who detailed one of the other boys to guide me up to the Fourth Division hut. Naturally this was even further up the hill. We duly trudged up to the hut.

'My heart sank more than a little as I surveyed the interior. There were double rows of bunks on both sides with wire bases. I don't think I ever counted them, but there appeared to be dozens. I chose a lower bunk towards the far end on the right-hand side and placed my kit on it.

'I was then shown to the galley and the mess deck to find out if there was any food to be had. Nothing changes about growing boys' appetites and whatever was on offer was gratefully received. Curiosity then took over and a tour of the new 'ship' and her amenities was undertaken. Bedding and towels were supplied from the slop chest and my bunk was duly made up. It wasn't going to be as comfortable as a hammock, but with my kit stowed away and everything looking shipshape, the world seemed a little better, even if there was an uncertain air about everything.

'It turned out that the boys who lived nearest Ruthin had been sent for first so that we could be the advance party to smooth things out for the rest of the ship's company, when they were due to arrive over the next weeks.

'After a short settling-down period, routine reared its ugly head and all lessons and duties were resumed, all on a similar basis as a ship's routine. I and my fellow 'coolie' returned to our duties as general factotums to Captain and Mrs. Bambra. The white 'coolie' jackets we wore meant a considerable amount of dhobeying to keep them in pristine condition as Madame could spot a dirty mark from a thousand paces and it was easier to do our washing than have a tongue lashing.

'Some distance from the Captain's Quarters there was a quasi-summerhouse and, whilst on cleaning and polishing duties, there was a great deal of reading done as this bolthole contained a considerable library. I think my love of books and literature probably stems from this period of my life.

'Contact from home and parents was by letter and parcel so the arrival of the Postman on his bicycle each day led to eager anticipation, which was not always realised by the joy of a parcel.

'The farms in the locality supplied us, the Top Table, with hard-to-come-by produce, most of which was on ration. One of our perks was to be sent to fetch a previously-ordered pile of 'goodies'. This was fine until one day I was told to go to a farm to collect eggs. Armed with a wicker shopping basket I made my way. There were three to four dozen eggs, the sun was shining, all was well in the world until in a moment of bravado and folly I decided to swing the basket over my head to prove the existence of centrifugal force. Wales is different. Sod's Law entered the picture. I dropped the basket! Heart in mouth, I rushed back with my budding omelette of broken eggs and confession of having tripped. Madame was very good about it and seemed to accept my 'eggsplanation'.

'There was a very unusual custom which took place every night before lights out. A very large bucket, reminiscent of a coal scuttle, was placed just inside the hut doorway in case anyone needed to go to the 'heads'. Complete blackout was the order of the day and as the heads were some distance away, it was a safety measure in case anyone fell whilst attempting this perilous journey. These buckets were called 'pumpship' buckets for obvious reasons. This proved to be a boon during the winter months as there was no heating in the huts! It was absolutely freezing, so if you could not wait until morning, you did not have to venture outside. Although it was someone's duty come Reveille to empty and prepare for the next night.

'We had a very large night-watchman whose nickname was Roughhouse and it was rumoured that his pre-war occupation was that of an all-in-wrestler. It was his job to patrol the camp and also to give early morning calls to the galley staff and the duty bugler, who had to be up and about to sound Reveille. I can vouch to the Roughhouse title, as he was none too gentle with his waking-up techniques. This 'gentleman' used to roll his own cigarettes and his tobacco was always either Bacco Bryniau or Amlwch Shag, both of which were very strong and had a pungent odour, hence one was always aware of his presence, before he actually arrived.

'In a letter from home, my mother told me that my Auntie Dilys, my father's sister, who lived in Penrhyn Bay, had a relative in Clocaenog, a village a few miles from Clwydd Newydd. So one Saturday with permision I made my way to Clocaenog and to my surprise I found another Inde boy visiting. It turned out that we were related and were second cousins. His name was Ieuan Evans and it is my regret that we never kept in touch after leaving the Inde, so I have no idea if he is still alive. We spent many an afternoon in that cottage.

'Daily routine was Reveille, Ablutions, Breakfast and then Morning Divisions when the Colours were hoisted to sunrise, then lessons ... the three 'R's or Seamanship. However, we 'coolies' had to do our duty to the hierarchy and see their quarters were spick and span after their breakfast was prepared and served. As I remember they always had porridge ... we used to prepare enough for the week and cook it in a Bain Marie. Our days were full and we slept soundly. Part of our seamanship lessons consisted of Boatwork and there was a lake a few miles away where a cutter and a whaler were moored. The arts of pulling and sailing were instilled into our lives. Nearby the lake was a freshwater spring and I swear the water within was the coldest and purest in the Northern Hemisphere. We would march there and back and sometimes in the most inclement weather, so it was not always our most popular outdoor pursuit.

'Warship Weeks were a popular method of getting the public to donate cash to a fund to buy a warship, so the Bugle Band and the ship's company were often called upon to take part in the Parades up and down the North Wales coast, plus some inland towns. Denbigh, Ruthin, Rhyl, Prestatyn, Colwyn Bay and Rhos-on-Sea, Llandudno, Bangor, Mold and Buckley run off the tongue. Often there was food for us and we felt that our war effort was valued.

'One of the local clergymen used to come to the camp to take Sunday Services and Church Parade. It was decided to hold confirmation classes for anyone who wished to become confirmed, so after a number of lessons we, the chosen few, arrived at Derwen Parish Church and were duly 'done' by a visiting Archbishop.

'A generator, which was somewhat temperamental, powered the camp's electricity and the boy whose job it was to supervise this beast had many a bruise to prove how obstinate and hard it was. There was a hook handle, which fitted onto the flywheel and this, when cranked, had a nasty habit of slipping off and cracking him in the ribs. He was probably the best customer in the Sick Bay!

'Summer and autumn led to a winter and that year, 1941, it truly was cold, but being young and fit, plenty of exercise and good food helped to pass that winter by. In the spring it was time to Pass Out and leave the comparitive safety of INDEFATIGABLE to make my way into the wide, wide world and the Royal Navy.

'Overall I had enjoyed my time, both on the ship and at the camp and had achieved some self-confidence, some cooking ability, (thanks to Madame) and a belief in myself, which has stood me in good stead these last fifty-five years.

'As I write, I have in front of me my Apprentice's Indentures, which were signed by me on the 13th February 1941. After this I served in the Royal Navy until being badly wounded after H.M.S. SPARTAN was sunk at the Anzio Beachhead in Italy and was consequently discharged as unfit for further service with a 70% Disability Pension.'

Well done, Derek Evans ... an Inde boy!

Jack Harrison, 1941-42, has written his memories of his Inde days.

'The bombing of Liverpool on 12th August, 1940, being the first bombs on Birkenhead, and in March 1941 magnetic mines dropped by parachute, one falling astern of CONWAY, the Committee following instructions from the Admiralty decided to advance the Easter Holidays and disperse the boys to their homes, those boys without parents or relatives were found accommodation in the Sailors' Home, Canning Place, Liverpool.

'Recall papers were sent out to all the boys at home in May 1941 and all the boys were instructed to report to Derwen Camp, as it was called in peace time. And so the shore establishment of T.S. INDEFATIGABLE came into being.

'Summer saw the boys established in their new quarters with a healthy environment, open country, and plenty of fresh air, the Shore Establishment accepted by staff and boys alike, as well as by the local village, called Melin yr Wig, and the farming community and, of course, by the local traders.

'The day started with Reveille, the night watchman being responsible for the rousing out of the galley staff and bugler. The lads went to ablutions; we never saw bacon or eggs, as far as I recollect, the porridge was mostly lumpy and tasted of the sack from which it came, but all went down with a relish. At home I wouldn't eat greens and was fussy about this and that to eat, well, after a few weeks aboard the Inde I would have eaten the mess deck table. My mother couldn't get over the change in me on my first leave.

'Came the winter, 1942-43, we were installed in the swimming baths. The snow came. Snow two feet deep and frost the like of which we had never seen before. We did PT in shorts and bare feet in the stuff. Eventually, the water tower froze up and as the ablutions required water, the boys (from the shortest to the tallest) chained buckets of the liquid from the baths up to the tower on top of the hill where the officers climbed the ladders and relieved the shortage. We were frozen stiff at the finish ... proverbially brass monkey weather.

'When the good weather returned we had a nice diversion. Warship, War Bonds and National Savings weeks started up and we of the Inde were picked to attend these marches through the towns and villages of Wales: Colwyn Bay, Prestatyn, Bangor, Mold, Ruthin and Buckley. We marched behind the Royal Navy followed by the other Services, always good for the boys as we were treated to a good meal after the parade. We were proud to have taken part.

'Religious services were taken for the C. of E. Boys on Sunday mornings by Captain Superintendent W. Bambra in the mess hall. The boys of R.C. denomination marched to Ruthin to the Catholic Chapel, a distance from the camp of five miles. Amusement was created when passing an Italian P.O.W. Camp on the outskirts of the town, insults and banter were passed by the boys and the prisoners along with rude gestures from both sides, highlight of the day!

'Time rolled on and winter turned to spring. We had a good knowledge of Seamanship and were able to conduct ourselves as the 'Inde' had taught us. Time to leave ... some to the Royal Navy, some to the Merchant Service, others to shore establishments.'

John Dickinson, 1942-43, recalls in 'The Inde' souvenir copy magazine his time in the hills of Wales under Captain W.A. Bambra, the Commanding Officer.

'I will never forget my initial introduction to the camp at Clwydd Newydd after being met at the little railway station in the valley which always seemed so far below our elevated position on the mountain summit. When I stood at the Divisional hut looking out, all compass points were downwards. It was a very scenic and wonderful landscape, even to a child like myself who lived in and knew the countryside. Those early mornings; the crude wooden hut with double-tier bunks lining either side of the duckboarded central aisle and a single door at the far end. I now think how much it all related to the cramped quarters of the Navy's messdecks and flats.'

One can assume that the last writer must have just missed that cruel winter.

Derek Evans in 1997 added a footnote to his excellent memoirs.
'Recently my wife and I took a voyage of rediscovery to Clwydd Newydd and Derwen. We drove to Ruthin and then took the scenic

Cerrigydruidion road and discovered the length of the Welsh mile, if anything, had increased. Signs which read 3 miles found with ease a differential with the car mileometer. When we arrived at Clwydd Newydd I failed to recognise any landmarks, which I thought had been etched into my memories.

'Sadly we traced our way to see St Mary's Church in Derwen. Memories took over. This indeed was the church of my confirmation and where I had taken my first communion back in those long distant days of 1941. I signed the book before we left stating that I was an Inde boy and was there in 1941.

'These memories are of happenings of fifty-six years ago. I wouldn't have missed it and I'll always be proud of being one of the Inde boys.'

Harry Robinson, Jack Harrison, Brian Vincent, Derek Evans and Mac McNeil put it all into verse on their Diamond Jubilee ... 1941-2001.

The time has flown; the years have gone
Since we met in forty one.
We parted friends; we still were young
Our adult lives had just begun.

Our sailor's lives had started then,
We all went different ways again.
We never remet 'til recent years
Fond reminiscence, without the tears.

It's sixty years ago this year
Aboard the Inde - from the pier,
We went aboard - but not for long,
The Mersey mined, 'twas her swan song.

We all went off to a North Wales Camp,
We slept in huts; they were slightly damp.
Friendships made, were made to last.
They still survive, despite the past.

We've greying locks; we've limbs that ache
And through our lives we've made mistakes
But one sure fact beyond all dates
We're awfully glad we're Inde mates

There's Harry and Brian, Derek and Jack,
The Manchester whippet is still called Mac
Whatever the outcome, whatever our ends
I'm proud of the fact that we're all good friends.

Albert Spavin, Boy No 167, 1942, recalls his days in North Wales.
'I joined the Inde in 1942 and no-one ever forgets his number! There was a great deal of bullying and violence among the boys. I vividly remember my first night. In my Division, the Fourth, the first thing the boy Chief Petty Officer, by name of Twist, wanted to know was whether I could fight. Knowing full well that if I refused to fight, I would be kicked around by everyone … I fought! My chosen opponent was a red-headed boy called Adams. I gave a reasonable account of myself and was left alone after that. I made friends with boys of my own age and we found that by joining together against the bullies we were left alone.

'The food was awful by any standards, but we all seemed to thrive. When I went home they all commented as to how well I looked. Breakfast was supposed to be porridge which we called burgo. A great treat was a slice of bread dipped in fat. Almost everyone smoked. Some boys bought cigarettes and sold them for a penny each.

'As winter approached we were moved from our huts into the heated school rooms. Double-tiered bunks were set up for us. It was warm and snug. In spring and summer we had to scrub the wooden floors with huge cobs of Sunlight soap and jars of disinfectant. I had chilblains and the disinfectant caused my fingers to swell badly. My best friend was Archie Holdcroft who came from Wolverhampton. One day Archie removed a few cobs of soap from the soap locker and posted them home to his mother. Soap was in great demand. He was seen by a boy called Shearer who informed on him to the Captain. Archie was given six of the best. However, Archie had received six the week before and was still very raw. He therefore ran away to home. His mother brought him back and he was given another form of punishment. Thereafter Shearer was dubbed Shearer the Snitcher.'

Brian M. Riordan, 1943-1945, Newslettter 2000.
'I joined the Inde at Clwydd Newydd on July 8th, 1943, three days before my fourteenth birthday. My real memory is the time we took the first boat out to the lake on the Cerrig road. We loaded the boat on a truck and off we went. I think Unwin was with us and Dobson. We successfully launched it and in doing so failed to hold on to the line. The blasted boat drifted slowly from the shore with one lad and me on board ... without any oars! You can imagine the faces of Unwin and Dobson and the lads ashore. Me having no sense in those days, stripped off all my clothes and dived into the frigid lake to swim ashore to get a pair of oars. I can tell you it was bloody cold. I tried to dry myself as well as I could and we proceeded to be instructed in the art of oarsmanship.

'No truck to go back to camp, so after a couple of hours we hoofed it back. The next morning I awoke with a hell of a fever and aching from head to toe. There was considerable panic when my temperature was taken ... it was 107. The next thing I remember was the bumpy ride to Ruthin, I had pneumonia! But the reward for this excursion was that I met the girl who was to become my wife. We celebrate our Golden Anniversary next May.

'I had the good fortune to be Chief Petty Officer Boy in 1944 when plans were afoot to move us to Llanfairpwll. For reasons that I am still not able to figure out, Captain Bambra decided that I should accompany him and Madame to inspect our new quarters. I was a bit overawed, first the car ride to Llanfair, then to be confronted with this huge mansion, especially after our wooden huts. We all thought we had gone to heaven when we eventually moved in. The one thing I do remember was the bloody Yanks had filled the pool with sand and concreted it over. You can guess who had to dig it out!'

A very old friend of mine, Ron Wilkinson, spent some time in the new camp and I have recorded his memories. Ron's father had been lost in November 1941 when his ship, NOVA SCOTIA, had been torpedoed off East Africa ... only 14 of the crew were saved out of a total of 114.

'We were interviewed in the old Sailors' Home where 'Bandy' Williams gave about a dozen of us a written exam. They sent us by train to Chester and then on to Ruthin. There was no-one to meet us so we all started walking, but the Captain's wife then appeared with a car and picked a few up at a time. Next day we were kitted-out in our sailors' rig. Life was tough in those huts, rough and ready and very cold. I believe the place had been the Merseyside Children's Holiday Camp. I arrived there in March 1944 and it was no holiday.

'We were divided into four divisions with about 50 in each division. We slept in two-tier bunks and we were so cold. There was no heat in those huts and it was like the Arctic. I kept all my clothes on in bed and acquired as many blankets as I could. When the weather was desperate we all moved into the school room, the mess deck and the swimming area. That was a little better.

'I never forget the food. Breakfast was porridge, chunk of bread and marge and a mug of tea. Lunch was meat of some sort with potatoes and gravy, followed invariably by a sort of 'spotted dick'. Tea was pilchard pie cut into slices, two half-inch chunks of bread and a mug of tea. Supper was a real rock cake and half a mug of milk. We were always starving. One day we refused to eat the stuff and in due course the chef was sacked.

'In one half of the day we did Maths and English and for the other half we worked. The mess deck had to be cleaned, the huts to be sorted, the boiler house supplied with logs ... we called the place the 'bug house'. One lad was in charge of the paint shop and the water boy looked after the pump to get the water up to the huts.

'It was early in 1945 that we moved to Plas Llanfair. Two lorries ferried some of the lads and all the property like the figurehead, the bunk beds and the ropes and that sort of stuff. The job took a week and most of us went by train.

'Llanfair was like a luxury hotel to us! Gone were the oil lamps because we actually had electric light and proper hot water. The food was much better, but I was only there two months because my time was up.'

Ron was to train as an engineer and served at sea from 1950 to 1981. His elder sister, Joyce, was sadly to lose her husband, Ray, in the Piper Alpha disaster when the oil platform was destroyed by fire and explosion on the night of 6th July, 1988. Their mother, Lillie, went to sea in 1946 and spent seven years with Cunard as a stewardess. She recalled her time in the SCYTHIA carrying displaced persons from Cuxhaven to Canada. My contact with this remarkable family was when Lillie volunteered in the early sixties to look after our Ancient Mariners' Club for retired seafarers in Kingston House. We are all much older, but friendship and memories bind us together. Sadly neither Lillie nor Ron are now with us.

J.H. Dickenson, 1943-45, takes up the story.
'I was late joining due to my sister's contagious scarlet fever, the incubation period over-ran the time for the Autumn intake and I arrived three weeks after the main batch. I remember being met by Division 1, Boy Petty Officer at the little Station Halt Cefn y Gader.

'I climbed over the railway fence and up that mountain, and up and up, and as I flagged, he took my case off me with a threatening comment, "Keep your mouth shut; I never did carry this case for you." He threw it back at me before we reached C.N. Of course, today I realise that I climbed 650 feet in less than a mile and a third, at a pace I shall never achieve again except in my turbo car and that will probably overheat.

'Before Inde left that mountain, I could run and climb anything within sight. Only we who lived on that very mountain top, know that going anywhere down was easy, coming back was up ... and shut up! How those muscles were asked for extra effort as so often we had the clock to beat before rollcall and its punishment without question was 'missed teas'. The only times we were excused (after Captain Bambra had checked) was the late bus or, if it was too full, a later return via the train. Like that initial mountain training exercise, 'We Saturday Cinema Party' were put through our paces, but appreciated every last crumb saved off the galley tables. By that time 'Rough' would be up and about, and nobody took the 'mickey' out of him or the minutest suggestion of lip. Or you bit the floor to nurse your wounds and keep stumm, possibly dreading 'Doody's' sharp eye whilst bathing down at the swimming tank, his sharp flexing cane quick to switch to a darkened flesh bruise in attention to any boy's failure to wash or bathe efficiently and in summer you might be caught standing on the edge dithering which encouraged the biting danger of his cane.

'When the move to PG finally came, those grand lads, the Travel Party, threw the lot 'Officer Punishment Canes' over the Swallow Falls Bridge and my punishment had to wait a day or two until Bangor Stores supplied some more. Four strokes for allowing spuds to roll around the galley floor ... warning me twice in two quick visits ... maybe Madame was giving him a hard time upstairs, so he passed it on! But, Chief Officer Unwin was unhappy at going to PG and he applied the cane lightly. Then he went for it when I got six at CN after mother wrote complaining of my behaviour on a leave.

'As Office duty boy both at CN and PG, I often ran extra errands and that must have been a compensation. It also was Chief Officer Unwin who tipped me to return after Christmas with signed 'permission to ship'. I didn't need reminding that the Authority may not notice your birth year (so I made sure and changed the nine to eight) ... much later the income tax people looked more closely.

'Boys will be boys. My Office duties included mail despatch and collection. Some parents sent cigarettes, some packed parcels very well, others used poor paper and needed seamanship lessons in knots and hitches but it did help to ensure that fags fell out before arrival at the Inde Office. Deciding which to let run through and be confiscated was difficult as the more generous parent often sealed the parcel efficiently. This prompted the expectant Tobacco Baron to demand that it be lost on its first port of call (I understand shipping companies used the phrase 'if sufficient inducement' to call at another port), but the Hedgebottom Harbour was prone to pirates and gale damage. Some past illustrious carriers had been trapped by established Custom parcel counting. I always let enough through to be found. Some parcels smelled strongly. I knew the customs rummage gangs were able to find caches simply by following their noses.

'I suppose CN hedgerows were a blessing in autumn, full of cob and hazel nuts and a possible fortune to be made picking rose hips at the expense of thorn-damaged limbs. If I remember correctly, a halfpenny was paid for fourteen pounds and then they had to be clean. The trick was to go towards Clocaenog, send a runner to buy fags, then carry them safely in daylight and stash until evening, as night adventurers and runners frequently got caught by farmers and other night prowlers. We were not the local's favourite cup of tea and the real bottom line was that they were generally afraid of us. On reflection we must have seemed to be a tough bunch. Even today's lads might have wilted from our presence and lifestyles. Of course, Madame Bambra circulated the area in her car, though how she made the petrol spin out must have caused her to coast many miles with the engine shut off. Whilst we were allowed to march up and down, the most looked-forward-to march was for rowing and sail training instruction on a very tiny reservoir on the B5105 west 2.5 miles. The swans were always on guard!

'Another boat was made available from a Yeoward shipwreck which we manhandled on to a lorry; sheer boys' muscle lifted it and counter-balanced it. Going up some steep hills it nearly launched itself for a long run to the sea. It was completely recaulked, painted and when Yeoward came to see our excellent work, he wanted it back! Captain Bambra was furious as he thought it was a gift to the T.S. Shipowners never change!

'Ring Down, Finish Engines, slip the canvas over the Telegraph. It was all a long time ago.'

That camp saved INDEFATIGABLE at a time when every seaman was needed by the country. One suspects that the Welsh wind and rain and cold prepared many a boy for what lay ahead in the Atlantic and Russian waters.

Wartime Postscript

During Battle of the Atlantic Remembrance Service in St George's Hall in Liverpool in 2004, Pastor Peter McGrath (ex-British International Sailors Society) read a graphic summary of those years of survival. So many Inde boys were involved and it seems appropriate to recall Peter's words to mark their contribution and to remind all those who followed after them that we should all be proud of those ' boys who became men' and, in the process, became heroes.

'The Battle of the Atlantic was the most prolonged struggle of World War Two. It was easily the one that came closest to ending the War in Hitler's favour.

'On the day that Britain declared war on Germany, September 3rd, 1939, the British Liner ATHENIA was torpedoed by a German U-Boat, killing one hundred and ten passengers and crewmen. This marked the beginning of the Battle of the Atlantic.

'At the beginning, the Germans underestimated the impact of the U-Boat, but all this was to change. From mid 1940 Britain was led by Winston Churchill. Standing alone against Germany, Britain was entirely dependent upon merchant ships from North America to supply her with much that was needed for daily survival. Without these vital supplies, Britain's armed forces would not have been able to fight.

'Admiral Karl Dönitz believed that the best weapon to use against British merchant shipping was the stealthy submarine, the U-Boat. At first Hitler failed to agree, but after Germany's failed attempt to invade Britain (Operation Sea Lion), he stepped up the U-Boat building programme. Britain was not prepared for anti-submarine warfare and her only recourse was to institute the convoy system.

'A North Atlantic convoy was made up of a group of merchant ships. They would load in America, then assemble in Nova Scotia, Canada. From there they were escorted by Naval vessels to Britain. As the war progressed and more and more ships were sunk, older and slower vessels were called into service. Many that should have retired were pressed into action.

'For the first nine months of the war, the U-Boats operated in British waters and our surface vessels operated in the Atlantic. There were few U-Boats available and not many of them had ocean-going range. The Royal Navy introduced the convoy system, but being short of escort vessels it meant that many ships had to sail independently, without protection. Losses in this category were phenomenal. By the end of 1940, Germany had sunk eight hundred thousand tonnes of shipping.

'The fall of France in 1940 gave Hitler a number of U-Boat bases on the Atlantic coast, thereby increasing their range. The growth of submarine production in 1941 allowed Admiral Dönitz to bring in a system whereby the U-Boats could attack in groups. They became known as 'wolf packs'. They would surface and attack at night. Then they produced a new type of submarine, one that was bigger, better equipped and able to spend a long time at sea.

'In Britain, long-range aircraft were not assigned to convoy protection in sufficient enough numbers to cover the whole crossing before 1943. Consequently there was a huge 'air gap' south of Greenland where most of the battles took place. The area earned itself a number of nicknames including 'Torpedo Alley', 'The Black Pit', and 'The Devil's Gorge'. To make matters worse, the weather along the North Atlantic convoy routes bordered on the hellish and proved to be just as dangerous as the Germans. The storms of 1942 - 43 were the worst to hit the Atlantic in fifty years. It is little wonder that Churchill is reported to have said, "The Battle for the Atlantic was the only thing that ever frightened me."

'In 1940, 1,059 ships were sunk. In 1941 ... 1,328 and in 1942 ... 1,661. The Germans called this phase of the war the 'Happy time'!

'One can hardly imagine what it must have been like to battle the ferocious winter storms and then be hit by a torpedo. A short extract from an account written by a nineteen-year-old boy gives us some idea.

"I was in the mess when Charlie came in from his watch. 'It's freezing out there', he said. 'I'm going to try and get my head down.' He climbed into his bunk. That was where he died. A minute after he climbed in there was a terrific explosion. The ship lurched to one side and water came flooding into the messroom. Instinctively I reached for my life-jacket, but I couldn't find it. I had to get out. I heard the Bosun shouting 'Don't panic!'. He never got off the ship. I struggled up towards the deck, but the force of the water pushed me over. On all fours, I climbed over the coaming when the steel door swung closed crushing my hand and breaking my ankle. With my good·arm I managed to push the door back far enough for me to get out. I headed to the side of the ship. The ship was listing badly as I rolled over the side into the icy sea. I fought to the surface, gasping for breath. It was snowing heavily.

"With my good arm I tried to swim away from the ship. Suddenly a lifeboat arrived and a couple of rough hands grabbed me by the shoulders and heaved me aboard. I was the last one they rescued. There were fourteen of us out of a crew of forty. The convoy was out of sight. It would have been suicide for any ship to stop. They would have been sitting ducks for the U-Boats.

"We spent a long, bitterly cold night under heavy snow. At daybreak we saw a couple of ships at a distance heading our way. We were concerned they might be German surface raiders, known to ram lifeboats or to open fire on survivors. We needn't have worried as thankfully they were ours, a destroyer and a rescue ship. The destroyer circled us while the rescue ship came alongside and dropped a cargo net for us to scramble up. I couldn't manage it. One of the crew came down to help me up.

"The U-Boats had had a good night, the rescue ship was crowded with men pulled out of the icy waters. I was carried to the hospital area where I saw a sight which still horrifies me. Lying on the bed was Stoker; he was in the engine room when the torpedo had struck. A fuel pipe ruptured above his head drenching him with boiling oil. Nobody knows how he got out of the ship, there wasn't an inch of flesh left on his body. Nothing could be done for him. We just hoped and prayed that he would soon be out of his dreadful agony. Later that day we rejoined the convoy and settled in for another long night of terror."

'Such stories could be multiplied a thousand fold.

'Once the ship had been torpedoed the odds of a merchant seafarer surviving and being rescued were very poor. Those who were not killed outright in the explosion were often badly injured. Many were drowned, suffocated by oil, or paralysed by the freezing waters of the North Atlantic. Some managed to reach a life-raft only to face a slow, lingering death by starvation or exposure. Less than half of all merchant seafarers survived the sinking of their ships.

'The Allies were frantic in their search to find ways to stop and defeat the enemy. In the early days the Royal Navy placed a lot of faith in ASDIC, an early form of sonar. Aeroplanes with a longer range were developed, planes were able to penetrate the 'Black Pit' area. New depth charges were developed and fired in patterns to box the enemy in. The 'hedgehog' type proved to be very effective. Intelligence was greatly improved when the 'Enigma' code was broken and by the end of 1943 the tide began to turn in favour of the Allies. Nevertheless, the Battle for the Atlantic, which started on day one of the war finished only when the war was over. It lasted the whole duration.

'The personal price paid by the merchant seafarer cannot be reduced to statistics, but at least knowing some statistics gives a small insight to what it cost them.

'13.5 million tonnes of shipping was sunk in the Atlantic.
Almost three thousand merchant ships were sunk.

The loss of life totalled between thirty and forty thousand British and multi-race seafarers sailing under the Red Duster.

'Often sailing in worn out, outdated, barely-seaworthy ships, these men, although civilians, were at the forefront of the biggest survival battle Britain has ever seen. Men, who if they were fortunate enough to survive the sinking of the ship, had their pay stopped before the ship had settled at the bottom! Men, who after enduring the reality of the U-Boats, mines, air attacks and the might of the German Naval Fleet, not to mention the perils of the Atlantic, were often looked upon with distaste simply because they wore no uniform which would identify them with some branch of the armed services. Such men were just as much in the front line as the guardsman or the fighter pilot to whom they ferried the necessities of combat.'

Such were the young men who stepped on to their first wartime ship and were then transformed from the ordinary to the extra-ordinary.

These men were heroes of the highest calibre.

The Inde produced many thousands of seafarers who served in many conflicts with courage. It is their sacrifice that has given us our today.

The Merchant Navy Memorial, Tower Hill, London bears this inscription.

On all the oceans, White caps flow,
You do not see crosses, Row on Row,
But those who sleep, Beneath the sea,
Rest in Peace, For your country is free.

To the MERCHANT NAVY
Thank you.

This Postscript is dedicated to them.

Chapter 6
Llanfair Pwll on Anglesey

LLANFAIRPWLLGWYNGYLLGOGERYCHWYRNDROBWLLLLANDYSILIOGOGOGOCH
*'Church of St.Mary in a hollow of white hazel, near to a rapid whirlpool
and to St. Tysilio's Church, near to a red cave.'*

The Annual Report of the Lancashire Sea Training School for the year
ending 1945 spells out the problems. 'The properties at Withens Lane,
Wallasey, are still under requisition by the Ministry of War Transport
and the boys are still accommodated at Ravencragg, near Penrith.'
Eventually the two organisations came together in March 1946.
Meanwhile the wooden holiday camp near Ruthin was beginning to fall
apart, and new plans had been made.

Sir Harold Bibby, the then Chairman of the School Governors, wrote to
his uncle, who owned an estate on Anglesey, asking him if there were
any seaside properties. The mansion of Plas Llanfair was owned by
The Marquis of Anglesey and had once been the home of his great
uncle, Admiral Clarence Paget (who built the Nelson statue on the
foreshore of the Menai Strait). During the 1930s it became an hotel,
and was requisitioned by the War Office in 1939 for the use of
American Servicemen training, rumour has it, for clandestine purposes.
In 1944, after de-requisitioning, the estate was leased from The Marquis
by the INDEFATIGABLE; and a year later was purchased outright.

The initiative started two years earlier. The INDEFATIGABLE's
Annual Report in March 1943 stated: 'Because the INDEFATIGABLE

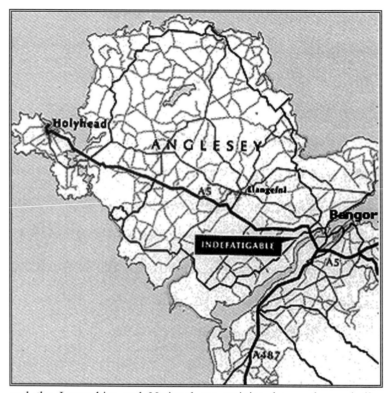

and the Lancashire and National sea training homes have similar objects, an amalgamation of the two institutions would be beneficial.'

The name was changed on 26th March, 1945, to the INDEFATIGABLE and National Sea Training School for Boys. Withens Lane was still under requisition, Plas Llanfair had been de-requisitioned. The Report at the end of March stated: 'After long negotiations, legal and physical difficulties, the boys from Ravencragg are now resident at Plas Llanfair, so all the boys and staff are now under one roof, and the amalgamation is running and working smoothly.'

Norman W. Howell was in the National and Lancashire School, 1941-1943, and has written the story of the school in 'The Makings of

Seamen' (1997). It was a great source of information.

But what really happened when the schools came together?

Derek Darlington, ex-Lancashire and National Sea Training Home at Ravencragg, Penrith.
'When returning from Christmas leave in the January 1945, we were informed that we would be moving to Anglesey to join the Training Ship INDEFATIGABLE. This was a surprise to us all and we found that only Mr. Derrick would be going with us. During the next six to seven weeks we started to pack everything up. The seamanship room and signal room were dismantled and sent on ahead. By the time the move came, all that we had left were our clothes and beds.

'I'm not sure what day we moved, but it was very hectic. After breakfast we had to pack all the beds and stack our kitbags into the removal lorry. We paraded and Captain Denny gave a talk and wished us all the best for the future as he was retiring. So it was hats off and three cheers for the Captain.

'We then marched to Pooley Bridge and boarded a bus to go to the station in Penrith. We were supposed to have a reserved carriage, but it was wartime and the train was absolutely crowded. We had to find seats or standing room as best we could. As I was the Chief Petty Officer Boy I was told by Mr. Derrick to keep walking up and down the train to make sure that the lads were behaving themselves.

'It took four hours to reach Crewe where we had to change to the Holyhead train. It was quite chaotic, getting all the lads off the train and assembled in the station. Mr. Derrick had arranged with the NAAFI on the station for a meal.

'After the meal, we paraded for the Holyhead train. We found out that two of the lads had legged it on to a London train. Seeing the London-bound train and, as both were from London, the temptation was too great.

'Mr. Derrick phoned the police and they were picked up at the next station down the line. They both spent the night in the cells, returning to INDEFATIGABLE the next day for punishment.

'A squad from the INDEFATIGABLE met us and we marched up to the school. This was about nine o'clock at night. When we arrived, we found that the lorry bringing our beds and kit hadn't. We had a very uncomfortable night, most of us sleeping on the floor with what mattresses and blankets the INDEFATIGABLE had spare.

'The next couple of weeks were spent cleaning the school. This meant holystoning all the decks to remove the old polish and dirt, washing all the walls and cleaning all the paintwork. Outside, a football pitch was created by taking all the bushes out and levelling the ground.

'There was no integration! Both schools kept to their dormitories, etc. This carried on for about three weeks until, I think it was a Sunday dinnertime, I don't know how it started, but the mess erupted in one big fight between both schools. Tables were overturned, plates and mugs were thrown, knives and forks were used as weapons. There was no way that the Boy Petty Officers could contain it. I was in the midst of it. Looking around I could see Mr. Derrick and Captain Bambra looking in at the door. The duty officer must have alerted them. It seemed ages before Mr. Derrick intervened and stopped it.

'After a good clean up, we all assembled and then assessed the damage both to ourselves and to the school. A couple of the lads had broken fingers and had to have them set in hospital. A few had to have stitches. A couple of mess tables were broken. I had no idea as to how many plates and mugs were broken.

'Mr. Derrick informed us that there was only one school now and that was the INDEFATIGABLE and National Sea Training School For Boys. We were then given new dormitories and divisions to integrate both schools.'

Plas Llanfair on the Anglesey side of the Menai Straits had been derequisitioned and the Committee were fortunate in buying the remainder of the lease from the tenant and arranging for the option of an extension with the Marquess of Anglesey's Estate. The grounds ran down to safe bathing and boating water on the Straits and the house itself required little alteration for the number of boys.

There is a side note of interest. In 1859, John Clint wrote a letter to the then Secretary to the Admiralty, asking for a training ship. He asked for the frigate SHANNON, which was to be broken up; but without success. He then asked for DRUID. Much later he settled for INDEFATIGABLE. And who was the Secretary to the Admiralty? None other than Lord Clarence Paget, M.P., the eldest son of the Marquess of Anglesey and the owner of Plas Llanfair from 1853! INDEFATIGABLE had indeed 'come home'.

INDEFATIGABLE was in good heart.

The mansion, Plas Llanfair, which had been used by the Americans to train officers, was well adapted to become the new INDEFATIGABLE. It was a wonderful site for training and along with many friends I travelled from Liverpool to enjoy the open days when the boys were put through their paces. I had arrived in Liverpool in 1961 and was appointed as Chaplain Superintendent of the Mersey Mission to Seamen. My contact with the Inde was immediate. On occasions, I was invited to take a Padre's Hour. I talked about the Missions to Seamen overseas, showed them photographs and explained the advantage of having their own club wherever they went. I also met the lads at the start of their time in INDEFATIGABLE when they arrived at the Sailors' Home in Liverpool to be 'kitted-out' under the watchful eye of Bill Hobbs. There were normally some 150 boys, aged between 13 and 16. Many of them were to enter the Services or the Merchant Navy.

Education was always the primary objective and subjects were taken up to the equivalent of G.C.S.E. level, together with Seamanship and General Maritime Knowledge. Uniform was worn at all times and discipline well maintained. The shore base was a vast improvement on the hardships of the old floating vessels and the challenge of that hill

1945

camp. Times had happily changed. There were three cooked meals a day and I suspect that not one lad had ever heard of 'buzzes' and Ixion biscuits and 'burgoo' and 'spottom'! One generous donor presented a 'fives court' for the use of the boys … this was another world indeed.

J.H. Dickinson, 1944-1946, recalled an event in the 1998 Inde Newsletter.

'It was an adventure discovering what the new school contained, as the American Air Force had left its mark both on the building and on a lot of girls around, and frankly we found it difficult to follow in their footsteps, though some of us would have liked to try! Cash was the great down-to-earth controller, nevertheless it created some assembly lectures from Captain Bambra.

'I remember one night we were called to assembly in the dining hall. We knew some lads had gone overboard to meet the girls, so a more ragged roll call was attempted by the boys and, of course, it was not presenting the results wanted. We were ordered outside to the parade ground until we got the message ... freeze or obey. As I remember we only had our flannel on. One or two who were in the grounds or over the walled garden and greenhouses answered the roll call on the check list. There were some still in seventh heaven, but they soon discovered the Captain's wrath and punishment. This steadied us all and frolics had to wait for shore leave in Bangor.'

Maybe it refers to the same episode, but Jim Hollingshead (1946-47) gives us this account.
'I just wondered if you remember the name of the boy who fell off a drainpipe whilst breaking out one night to go and meet one of the village girls in the greenhouses. He badly damaged his left foot, and spent the night in the boiler room, which was lucky, as it was his week for stocking up the boiler. His excuse was that he fell down the boiler room steps - that did not cut much ice with Captain Bambra. There was a lot of "Why do you lie to me, boy, don't you know I will write to your mother and let her know what is going on!"

'On leaving the Inde in July 1947, I followed the well-trodden path to T.& J. Harrisons ... a shipping company that started so many of the Inde Boys on sea-careers. I started as a Cadet, but such things as Mercator and me were like oil and water, but T.& J.'s were kind enough to take me on as a ship's writer, and by the time that I left I was sailing as Purser.'

R. Astley, 1945-1946, has a vivid memory.

'Being hungry seems to be one of the main memories of those days, of food parcels and sneaking out to the village shop (the one with the long name on the roof) to buy bread and something to spread on it, sauce or conny onny (condensed milk), everything else was rationed.

'After a few months I went upstairs to the Captain's Quarters and without doubt with the perks of the job it was the best job in the whole school. I prepared and served the meals. Whatever the sweet was that day, we shared between us after Captain and Madame had finished their meal. We also had the chance to invite a different lad each evening to help us eat it, no shortage of volunteers there. Our reign came to an abrupt end one evening. Wearing my steward's jacket with Bibby Line buttons, I had just returned to the kitchen when Madame called, so back to the dining room. It wasn't just my heart palpitating when she angrily pointed out the Captain's plate. Sitting neatly uncovered amongst the broccoli was the wire wool that somehow Charlie, washing the dishes, had combined into my cooking.

'Next day I was back with Mr. Doodson cobbling boots, Charlie also got his marching orders. Fortunately I was a better seaman than I was a cook.'

James Taylor has made a major contribution to our story. He lives in Frankton, Victoria, Australia. Number 62, 3rd Division, 1946. There was need for very little editing.
'My wish to go to sea in 1945 at fourteen came as a result of WW2 and dying to do my bit, being a sea cadet for over a year, but finding I was too young to be called up. I learned at the Labour Exchange that the only way I could get to sea so young was to go to a Navy Training Ship first. I solicited my parents' support and Mr. Gastall, my headmaster at Claremont Boys Secondary School in Blackpool. He was delighted that I had chosen a career and gave his approval, becoming my referee.

'The morning set for my examination at 0800 at Liverpool for entry to INDEFATIGABLE, (of which I had no knowledge), was too early to catch a train from Blackpool to be in time. Taking an afternoon train the day before, I journeyed to Liverpool on that cold November day in

1945 in a dogbox compartment of an unheated carriage that left me chilled to my frail bones.

'With great trepidation and an anxiety that made my heart tap as if clutched in the talons of a vulture, I stepped into the unknown. Arriving in Liverpool, the scene of blitzed devastation from outside the station shocked me. I set off with my street map to find Canning Place. Most of the buildings between the station and the Sailors' Home and down to the docks were piles of rubble with whole streets of terraced houses gone and only the skeletons of major buildings left standing. India Building, Cunard Building, the Liver Building and the Town Hall miraculously remained.'

At this point James' memory went astray. The Custom House was flattened, not the Sailors' Home as James wrongly recalled. What he went on to describe as a jail was in fact the Sailors' Home! His description is otherwise good.

'The jail had the classic internal construction of the Victorian period, with floor after floor of lace-balconied walk rounds outside the rows of cells, now cubicles, with an open centre for better security surveillance. It was gloomy and foreboding, a temperamental caged lift that constantly clanked and groaned noisily up and down the outside of the balconies gave access to each floor.

'The night I stayed at the Sailors' Home, Canning Place, Liverpool, I lost my youth and commenced my hard journey to manhood. Little did I know what lay ahead in a future fraught with danger and blessed with adventure. I ate at a long trestle table in the ground floor common room with mostly old sailors, mainly drunks and homeless. Eating a meagre meal due to wartime rationing, I listened to the jibes and insults of the sailors informing me that kids that went to sea were nothing but bumboys and as such it was their duty to keep the seamen happy. I was constantly molested, touched up, the common vernacular for it, by one after the other as I passed with my plate to find a vacant seat.

'Catcalls followed me along the line, "Wait till we show you the golden rivet later," and "You'll be a sweet bit of navy cake tonight," made my heart heavy believing I had made a wrong decision if this was to be my lot. But I was determined that I was going to be a tough seaman and hold my own. That night I learned well what they meant and later put the episode into the not-to-be-mentioned basket.

'My entry examination the following morning for the Training Ship INDEFATIGABLE took place on the ground floor in the large room to the right of the entrance. I sat on a straight-backed chair at a wooden desk with an old ink pot and with what looked like a broken nibbed pen. I was an equal distance from the other twenty or so boys and stared blankly at the sheave of exam papers placed on the desk by a tall, thin, hook-nosed man with the fixed stare of the devil, dressed in a dusty old officer's uniform and an indistinguishable badged cap. It all seemed fit to adorn the back room of a pawn shop. Resuming his seat, he coldly informed us we had three hours to complete the examination. "Now start," he informed in a thin throaty voice that did little to inspire.

'Some time later, after I had ink-spotted and dismally blotted my papers, wasted time and left many questions unanswered, the officer wheezed, "Stop!" Papers were collected and we were informed results and acceptance would be forthcoming. "Leave now and go home," he curtly informed us as we stared in awe.

'To this day, I do not believe I achieved a significant pass result. I am sure my acceptance was due to the fact I would be a paying enrolee and not, as I learned later, a boy that made the decision to try to make something of his life, rather than the alternative of going to Borstal for some petty misdemeanour.

'Christmas and New Year behind me I had heard nothing, and then on the 8th January, 1946, I received a cryptic letter informing me to be at Llanfair P.G. railway station at 1600 hours on the 10th January, 1946.

'Some hours after leaving Birkenhead railway station, the old bottle-green steam engine, pulling four dilapidated coaches, progressed down to Wales, crossed the Straits of Anglesey and chuffed to a stop enveloped in clouds of steam at Llanfair P.G. railway station. I alighted with a small battered brown suitcase containing all my worldly possessions to mingle with thirty other bewildered looking boys on the platform. "Fall in!" shouted an authoritative voice, startling the throng. Accustomed to the war and all its tribulations and teachings, we boys knew what to do.

'Excitement hung over the two deep columns of boys in an aura of keen expectation. This was it. This was the start of an adventure of rare dimensions. Now we are men, we thought, soon we would be in sailor's uniform looking for all the world like the brave sailors that had vanquished the German and Italian Navies, and heroes all to be!

'We marched down the Welsh lane away from the station, swinging our arms with pride, moving forward into history. Arriving at a farm gate set in a high hedge, the column entered the Western boundary of the shore-based Training Ship. Marching on down a long incline following the Officer we passed through a stand of giant pine and fir trees. Ahead could be seen a crowd of small boys, dressed in black short pants and dark blue sailors' jumpers. Derisive cries and jeers assailed our ears. "Nozzers, Nozzers," came the chant, "You'll be sorry, can't go back to your mummies now, you'll be sorry!"

'They surrounded us, following us down through the trees to the imposing stable outbuildings and the stately old Mansion, one of the Marquess of Anglesey's homes, loaned to the INDEFATIGABLE as a more substantial training base than the temporary shacks in the Welsh mountains. The jeering lads broke off as we drew up to the parade ground in front of the main entrance and mounted the steps, through the front portal and into the impressive wood-panelled reception area. The walls were covered in brass artefacts and naval memorabilia.

'We lined up, navy fashion, in two rows facing the Officers. Chief Officer Mr. Derrick, a stout, big-chested man with a cruel-looking face and only two fingers on his right hand, was the only one to speak. He introduced Captain Bambra, a small, thin, frail-looking man, and then informed us of the rules, barking out instructions in an aggressive style.

We handed our ration books over, a slip of paper with all our details, and our small suitcases.

' "You will always double across the parade ground and you will obey the bugle commands immediately," barked Mr. Derrick. "You will learn quickly enough from the other boys what you must do and how you must do it. Any break in protocol will result in your name being presented before dinner in the mess hall or at Morning divisions for extra work duties, called Jankers. Your first three months will be on a work party, there will be no shore leave for this first term. You are not to be trusted for you may try to make a break, but fear not, you will be caught and returned for severe punishment I swear. From now on you will be addressed as 'boy' by the Officers, Petty officers and senior boys. When you hear that word aimed at you, you will jump to it right smart or get a clip behind the ear. When your surname is called, it will be called for more specific orders."

'I thought, damn! What have I got myself into here, it sounds like a concentration camp. Our dormitory numbers were read out to us and we were told the other boys would put us straight on what we must do.

"Right turn, dismiss."

An older one-ring Officer, Mr. Williams, herded us out of the room down a hall, out the back to the stables. Many boys in short pants and navy

Captain Bambra & Mr Derrick

jerseys jeered and laughed at us along the way. There was no doubt we would go from quite recently proudly-acquired long trousers to conceal our not-long-found manhood, back to short pants. I was appalled that this would be our dress, even in the Sea Cadets I wore a full navy rating's uniform, surely this is not what I intended to be … a boy again!

'Reaching the stables, we were equipped with our new dress of dark blue serge shorts, matching jersey, navy rating top with the square flap on the back, navy collar, silk, lanyard, long bell-bottoms, round flat-topped cap and INDEFATIGABLE cap ribbon, two pair of long thick socks, a pair of heavy boots and a grey flannel nightshirt with square neck line in the navy fashion, edged in dark blue. Some of us dangled below our nightshirts and although we laughed about it, it did take away one's privacy. We changed quickly as instructed into our shorts, tops, socks and boots, ignoring our nakedness. Our civvy clothes were taken off us and we never saw them again, I suppose as we were still growing. From then on, when we got holidays later, we wore navy dress at all times which gave us all free entrance to cinemas, ballrooms and transport charges that still applied as war measures.

'Following the lead of senior boys we began to pick up the routine, tea in the great hall at 1800 consisted of a dollop of tasteless Shepherd's Pie and a mug of weak, sugarless, stewed tea. Mail was flung to each recipient by Mr. Derrick, having unerring accuracy. This over, he read from a list the names of those who had committed a misdemeanour that day and must report for jankers during the free period. To my surprise my name was called. I mustered with the five other offenders and received my instructions to report to the cook in the kitchen. I asked of Mister Doodson, a senior Officer, what my offence had been and found to my further dismay this was another offence. If I did not know what wrong I had done, I was immediately put on 'jankers' for the next day. Our punishment was to peel potatoes from huge sacks, putting the finished article in a huge oval tub of water until full. I thought we would never fill it. I came to the conclusion that to feed a large number of boys and Officers, potatoes must be peeled in large amounts every day and somebody had to do it outside the normal day's regimented activities, so petty slackness in duties, protocol, rules or general bad behaviour resulted in a report. This could make a boy's life miserable to the extreme. I spent every night of the first three months on 'jankers'. I learned that spuds, lumpy porridge, without milk or sweetener, and two thick slices of not-well-baked bread every morning, (Knockers we called them), meatless stew called potato hash or cottage pie were our main diet. Just before lights out each night we received a mug of dark chocolate scraped from a large block and mixed with hot water. We called it Kai.

'Every Friday afternoon was a special event, much enjoyed by the Officer staff by their looks of glee on beholding the entire school of boys, lined up naked, bum to dick, for shortarm inspection by the local doctor. Eagerness by the boys to get it over resulted in much nudging and horseplay as the line moved forward. Arms out, arms in the air, give a cough! with foreskin drawn back, rotated and bum inspected, then number ticked off to make sure no one dodged the muster, we quickly returned to our clothing. I often wonder what the doctor was looking for amongst a bunch of virgins. Later as seamen at the Merchant Navy Shipping Pool, there were medicals before sailing and, in ports around the world, quarantine doctor's inspection. They, of course, had significance.

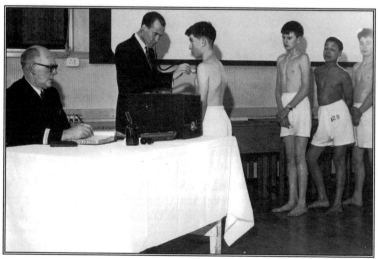

'My group spent that first three months on work party, cutting down giant pine and fir trees at the back of the property, hauling them on a large wagon up wet, slippery, mud slopes, which was murderous work for a start. Then with large cross-cut saws we cut them up into logs for the boiler which provided hot water for the galley, Captain Bambra's rooms and some heating for the Officers quarters.

'Every morning at 0600 we did a two-mile run, followed by one hour scrubbing the hallways and rooms of the building, hurried on by many kicks in the bum and clouts around the head by Mr. Doodson's bunch of large keys, if not scrubbing with vigour. Mr. French's favourite joke was to plant his foot on our rumps and viciously shoot us forward on our noses through the foaming suds. At the next single note of the bugle, we would dash for the showers to prance excitedly under the cold water and then line up outside the Galley to collect our usual fare. Friday was the delegated day of joy for us all, especially during January, February and March, as after our run we would enthusiastically dash naked into the frozen waters of Menai Straits below the Church of St Mary's, near the rapid whirlpool. We would splash around in a frenzy to keep warm for the entertaining delight of cheering passengers hanging out of carriage windows of the express train which passed at this time of day. Strangely this was the one gleeful activity of the training ship the Officers did not join in with us, but they watched enviously from the banks of the Straits. The next event that we equally looked forward to was the Friday morning after-breakfast dose, actually under-diluted overdose, which was 20mls of Epsom salts. The race to the toilets was something to be seen, Roger Bannisters each one of us before the man was even known. I still have the bruises on the inside of my thighs, keeping my legs crossed waiting for my turn at the receiving bowl.

'So the breaking of a boy and the making of a man began. It was a long, hard-fought battle of mind and stamina. The older boys themselves were as tough as the masters and as sadistic. That is those of them that were at the training ship longer than you, for on the monthly anniversary of arriving each and every boy above would grab you tight, and each one in turn would give you a knock to one or the other upper arm. This was done by twisting your arm inward until the bicep was taut, then pushing out the knuckle of their second finger from the rest, they would give you an almighty thump into the muscle which resulted in extreme pain and later bruising compounded on and on until the arm hung limp. Usually we received fifty to sixty knocks in total, but some of the senior boys did not do it. This practise was watched by the officers and condoned; it should have been banned as it can cause permanent damage to the muscles which resulted in weak arms.

'More severe punishments were meted out for certain offences such as smoking or running away. During my first term around March 1946, I was put on notice for association with two boys caught smoking. Only the boys that had punishment by the indoor swimming pool knew how it was. At morning Divisions, names of offenders were read out and then the boys mustered. They were taken down alongside the swimming pool, trembling all the way in silence. The cane was taken out of a locked cupboard on the starboard side of the pool by Mr. French and handed to Mr. Derrick. It was a long stout cane bound round with copper wire, a thicker handle made of black electrical insulation tape to cushion the hand of the flogger. On sight of this terrible instrument of punishment, you were left quaking in your shoes and wetting yourself.

"Boys take off your tunics, drop your pants and right turn," thundered the Chief Officer. "Taylor step forward three paces," he ordered with delight.

'Being naked and eyed by the officers was unsettling and humiliating, but taken by the neck by Mr. French and savagely bent over to tauten your buttocks seemed extreme. An arm was twisted up your back and held firm by neck and body. Mr. Derrick with a sadistic sneer on his face flicked the end of my penis with the tip of the cane, which resulted in bruising, brought my head down lower. Swishing the cane in the air in circles to get the feel of it, making it sing and strike further fear in our hearts, he then pulled it back and round letting it strike with all his might, slicing the flesh of my buttocks like a knife into a ripe peach. The first three strokes were suffered stoically in silence, the ones that followed fetched screams of pain to the joy of the punishers and the fear of those to follow. With each scream Mr. Derrick gained more strength and laid into me with gusto in the true Captain Bligh tradition.

'It took many days for me to sit comfortably as my bottom was criss-crossed with deep cuts. The prime offender, a pretty Welsh boy taken advantage of by some of the senior boys, passed out on his sixth stroke. He was confined to sick bay where we visited him each day for six days, whereupon he was taken to the swimming pool and made to finish his punishment. He disappeared after he recovered, and the rest of us were none the wiser as to what happened to him. Boys did run away, not willing to take the discipline. One boy drowned in the turbulent Menai Straits; another was killed in the tubular tunnel rail bridge when an unexpected train hit him.

'If you were lucky to receive a food parcel of whatever your parents could manage due to severe rationing, the senior boys had the self-imposed right to plunder the parcel. It was common practise to share the rest with your pals. Captain Bambra, his wife and teenage pretty daughter, (much coveted by the boys - in your dreams, lads) ate well together. One of the boys would be assigned as cook in the quarters up the stairs to the left of the front reception room. Luckily this fell to my good friend Roger Astley, who did so much for me, helping me along the way. We are still good friends today, but far apart. Roger would have me and his other pals sneak up the back stairs and he would pass out left-over food which there always seemed to be plenty of. One might ask who took charge of our ration books.

'Saturday afternoon shore leave saw most of us stride out down to Menai Bridge, cross over and make up the road to Bangor to gain the TocH for a rock-hard bun and then to Bangor, taking a girlfriend to the pictures for sixpence each. Arms around your girl, petting and breathing heavily giving the weekly release from the rigour of the training ship until the matinee finished. Then we went for walks along the hill backing the main street of Bangor. At the station with our girlfriends, we would take the tank-engine-drawn train back to Llanfair P.G. with lots more high jinks, especially in the dark, through the tunnel bridge. The girls would return to Bangor later when the tank engine returned.

'There was a lot of bullying by some of the tougher boys and they would make your life miserable. If you stood up for yourself, you were in for a good scrap and I had many.

'In the long hallway from the front reception room to the kitchens at the back there were several small stained glass windows set into the wood panelled alcoves. Each had an old saying. The one that impressed me and has stayed with me says: "How much better is it to weep at joy than to joy at weeping," I buried my homesickness in that alcove. The author is unknown; I have never found a reference.

1945

'After my first term and on leave, I contemplated not returning, but came to the conclusion that having come this far I must continue the second term. Our group were placed in the school to continue our general education under Mr. Williams, a great school teacher and there was another teacher, not friendly at all as he constantly sneered and put us down. I believe he did not like the job at the school and took it out on us. Again, I saw myself on nightly work parties. As the nights were lengthening we worked outside struggling with the dense, botanic, foreign bushes and undergrowth leading down the almost overgrown long path to the sea front. It was extremely hard work and our hands blistered and bled with wrestling with the tenacious, mostly sub-tropical, imported bushes. That term we cleared the entire path and, to this day, it has been kept in pristine condition. We also for the first time concreted the stone driveway up to the main gate under the direction of Mr. Derrick, working us like a slave gang.

'Term three we took to sport, field and track for the coming annual sports day, swimming and boxing. Mr. Derrick gleefully took command of swimming, trussing those who could not swim into a harness rigged to an overhead pulley. By cranking a handle the poor unfortunates were dragged through the water, mostly underneath, to emerge the opposite end almost drowned. Instructions by Mr. Derrick in regard to the boxing event informed us he would not stand any lack of zeal in attempting to down your opponent, leaving us anxious about having to almost do to death, boys you were pals with. Boys were paired off according to weight and matched in the ring for three events, consisting of three two minute rounds per bout. I won my first and second and lost my third, not remembering the first lucky punch that floored me. We had no training or instruction for this, but got into a bloody brawl, egged on by Mr. Derrick informing us we would suffer dire consequences if we flagged. He screamed and bullied each contestant to the very end of each round. During the third term we also went through seamanship training, knots, hitches, splicing, compass and signals with Dad Williams, a kindly man we all liked.

'It was during the summer that the band was ready to play on parade and to march ahead of the rest down the highways and byways of rural Anglesey. As we struck up 'Anchors Away', the boys sang our own Inde song, (sadly I have forgotten the words), to the music. As we marched up the deserted road to Llanfair P.G., door after door of the terraced cottages opened and heads of the villagers popped out and peered in wonder at our band. Falling in behind the boys, the gathering crowd marched with us on a long round tour and back to the main entrance of the training school. Our fame spread to the benefit of the band, for we were invited to play at Church picnics and garden parties all over Anglesey, which resulted in extra tucker for us in the way of buns, cakes and lemonade, a great treat.

'On many summer nights, after lights in the dormitories, we expressed our sexuality and sported with each other. (This aspect of typical public school dormitory behaviour was no different to the best private schools, young boys when together in intimate proximity experiment. It is folly now to deny the INDEFATIGABLE was any different; at the time it was seen as great fun).

'A good pal and I regularly sneaked out of the building, climbing down a drain pipe, slid down a roof, down another drain pipe onto the forecourt and away down to Menai to meet our girlfriends, Bronwyn and Gwyneth, for kisses, cuddles and other experiments to broaden one's knowledge. The boys applauded us, but no others were game to follow our lead.

'I did not compete in the sports day rowing and track events as I caught a severe ear infection from the swimming pool and had to be moved to Bangor Hospital for two weeks. On my return, I found that the coveted position of Petty Officer of number three division I was in line for had gone to another boy and I had secured the Leading Seaman's position. I was well trained, confident, and tough, capable of taking on what life now had in store for me. I showed no fear, I did not panic, I was well disciplined, and they had done a good job on me.

'Mid-October I was suddenly informed to gather my belongings together and prepare to leave the training ship, as I was the next in line to go to sea from the INDEFATIGABLE. This took me by surprise for I believed I would be at the school until I was at least sixteen. Most of the boys went on to H.M.S. GANGES to train for the Royal Navy. Only a few of us elected to go into the Merchant Navy. I never sailed with anyone from the INDEFATIGABLE; ships' Officers I found had a deep respect for Inde lads.

'On arrival in Liverpool I was once again billeted in the Sailors' Home. A mentor of the Training Ship took me under his wing and saw to it I was outfitted for the sea on deck. Down by the India Building, a shop of volunteers made up of caring women provided heavy woollens, all hand knitted. The officials at the Shipping Federation, Cornhill, refused at first to enrol me because I was under sixteen. My mentor found a way around this and I was signed on a Panamanian foreign-registered Esso tanker as deckboy, a captured German vessel named CLIO. After two short trips of six weeks, I walked the docks and acquired a berth on a Liberty ship, S.S. SAMUTA and was given the position of Junior Seaman, nine months before I qualified. We took arms, tanks and trucks to Malaya and Singapore, for some of the Japanese units still fought in the hills of Malaya, Sumatra and Java long after the end of official hostilities. So commenced my eleven years at sea. I believe that I became the youngest A.B. at seventeen due to my shortened terms as deck boy and ordinary seaman. I served most of my time with Alfred Holt's Blue Funnel Line, due to the efforts of my original mentor to get me on the Blue Funnel register at Birkenhead.

'I left the sea in 1957, married my teenage sweetheart (we are still together), and emigrated to Australia with our daughter Susan.

'I firmly believe that the training and comradeship one developed at the INDEFATIGABLE gave me the strength to master all I became involved in and gave me the presence of will and mind to beat all adversity. I know the spirit of the INDEFATIGABLE will go on in the memories of those left from my time and in those from the later years. As much as we may resent some aspects of our training, we cannot deny it did us proud, made men of us so we are able to handle all adversity.'

Thank you James Taylor, No. 62, 3rd Division, 1946. That was a remarkable picture of your time in INDEFATIGABLE.

P.J. Kissane, 1946-47, wrote in the 1997 Inde Newsletter.
'When shore leave was granted on a Saturday afternoon who remembers making a run to the cake shop in Menai? If you didn't get there first, the cakes were gone and all that was left to eat was bread. Mind you, I've eaten many a loaf of bread in the cinema at Menai along with a tin of Blackcurrant Puree to help it go down.

'I think my main concern while I was in Inde was food. I always seemed to be hungry, then somehow my prayers were answered. I became the Captain's Tiger. Now the food upstairs was marvellous, cooked by Madame (Captain Bambra's wife). We helped of course.

'Then I became a Bugler. Perhaps, it was because Buglers received a piece of parkin every week from Madame. I thought it was worth it. I remember four of us Tigers waiting on about forty or fifty guests from all over Anglesey. The Marquess was there, the Mayors of Holyhead and Beaumaris and all our Officers and their wives. Mr. French was the only one to give us a good tip ... good old Mr. French.

'To get back to the afternoon tea, I had never seen so many cakes in all my life. Everything went according to plan. After all the guests had gone, Madame Bambra came back into the room and she said "Just help yourselves, boys" and walked out of the room. We all looked at each other and smiled, then grinned, we could hardly believe our luck. With that, I rolled a four tiered trolley loaded with the most marvellous selection of fancy cakes I had ever seen in my life (remember this was 1947). I ate everything on my trolley, all the other boys had done the same. All that was left was a plate of sandwiches. One of the boys finished off by eating the sugar lumps. What a day that was!

'Then in walked Captain Bambra. "What had happened to all the food?" he asked. We said that Madame had told us to help ourselves. He never said another word, just walked out of the room.

'The Officers from that day and for many days after never had any cakes for tea.'

Bernard Millichamp, 1947-1949, recalled his memories in 'The Inde' Newsletter.
'I joined the Inde on 5th May, 1947. I and the rest of the intake from various parts of the country had to report to the Sailors' Home, Canning Street, Liverpool on the 4th May where we were given a room for the night. The following morning after breakfast we were given a written test (which I don't think anyone ever failed) set for us by one of the

school teachers (Mr. Lake). Needless to say, nobody failed! After that we signed our indentures, boarded a train at Lime Street station to carry us to Llanfair Pwll on Anglesey, where we arrived quite late in the evening.

'The first sight of Inde was quite awe-inspiring. We approached via the back entrance nearest the station. The building loomed out of the gloom looking like Colditz Castle, with just the odd naked bulb glowing in the dark, and from one or two windows bodies would appear dressed in grey nightshirts calling out, "Anyone from Liverpool?", or London, or any other place.

'We assembled in the reception hall where I was allocated the number '109'. So I was now a 'Nozzer'. A 'Nozzer' was a new intake which lasted until the next new intake arrived; then they inherited the title.

'The worst day of the week, in my estimation, was Friday. It started as a usual type of a day - Reveille at 6.45 a.m. - get washed, dressed and bunks made up - and by 7 o'clock we had to be at our allocated tasks. At 8 o'clock we lined up for breakfast as usual; but on Fridays we were treated to a large spoonful of piping-hot Epsom Salts, which you had to drink down in one gulp and give your number afterwards to make sure you had swallowed it! This was followed by breakfast, then a dash to 'the heads' (toilets) to join the queue. Epsom Salts were discontinued during my stay at Inde.

Mike Weller, 1948-1949.
'After that, the morning carried on like any other. Working parties and instruction. Midday was dinner (fish on Friday), followed by kit muster and bath (with the usual cold water). Next was the doctor's muster on the messdeck. Tea was at the normal time; and at 6.30 p.m. we mustered on the messdeck for an evening with the padre (the local vicar). We usually 'plugged' for a singsong starting off with '10 Green Bottles', which we could stretch out to about '500 Green Bottles'! By the time the song was finished, the poor old padre was exhausted, the reason being that he had to pump the harmonium with two foot pedals as he played. If he had been in the 'Tour de France', he'd have worn the

'yellow jersey' for the day! So ended the worst day of the week.'

Mike Weller, 1948-49, goes on to recall his departure from Inde.
'We stood there at attention, in neat lines, just as we had done many times before. We were going on Summer leave and Mr. Derrick was slowly walking up and down the ranks, casting his critical eye over each boy in turn. Closely following him was Mr. Strong, School Secretary and popular Bandmaster. 'Doody', Mr. Doodson in formal terms, stood to the side and was waiting for the call to attend to hair that was too long or a uniform not up to standard and which would result in the culprit being backlisted to a later train.

'For me, this was different from the other times that I had waited for my turn on similar occasions, this was the last time, for I was leaving the Inde and a new exciting world beckoned to me beyond the gates, if only I could get through them!

'At last my turn came, Mr. Derrick stood in front of me, and this time, instead of looking over his shoulder as I would normally have done, I looked him in the eye. To this day I don't know what I saw in them. At other times I had seen anger, kindness and sometimes amusement. This day though the look was inscrutable and after a short moment he moved on. Not given to displays of emotion was the Chief Officer!

'At last the ritual was over and we were marching up past the laundry and the staff houses, over the route we normally took when on domestic duties such as taking boots to the cobbler in the village. The handful of us that were leaving had entered the Inde down the Main Drive, and here we were leaving by the back door!

'When our train arrived at Liverpool, my friend Barry and I said goodbye, he was off to Stricks as a Cadet and I was to join The British Tanker Company of London as an Apprentice. We never saw hide nor hair of each other again. In later years, communicating with various Stricks ships by signal lamp and enquiring after him, no one ever had any news.

'A couple of months later on August 29th, 1949, saw me feeling very conspicuous in my new Apprentice uniform and with all my luggage on the dockside at Falmouth waiting for my first ship to come alongside. She was the BRITISH RESOLUTION, 12,000 tons deadweight and built in 1936. Joining her was one of those moments in life that one never forgets.'

There was much to follow as yet another Inde boy set out on his chosen career.

Chapter 7
Changes Ahead
1949 - 1972

Captain Bambra retired at the end of 1949 after stalwart service during difficult years of survival and was succeeded by Captain G.W. Irvine. Captain W.A. Bambra was to die the following year. He took up command in September 1940 and had steered INDEFATIGABLE from the Mersey, to Clwydd Newydd and finally to Plas Llanfair. He had shown tireless ability and leadership.

Don Griffin, 1948-1949, Spring 1988, Newsletter.
'On my last visit to Inde in 1976 I watched my own son - Petty Officer Boy Robert Griffin, No. 76 - lead the band on parade. As you know Robert was lost during the Falklands Campaign.

'Although I cannot be certain of the words now, I can clearly remember being 'fell in' on the Parade ground and, accompanied by the band, we all sang.

> We are some of the Inde boys,
> Sailors of Britain are we.
> We all know our seamanship,
> We can run a battleship.
> We are respected upon the high seas
> As we go sailing from shore to shore.
> Holds and hatches battened down,
> Then you hear the bosun shout
> Put that ruddy Woodbine out.
> WE ARE THE INDE BOYS.'

Don Griffin's son was Divisional Petty Officer in 1976, and in 1982 Robert was killed on the last day of the Falkland Conflict. Don had served in the Korean War in the Royal Navy at the age of only sixteen. Robert on leaving INDEFATIGABLE joined the Royal Marines. He was in Norway and Northern Ireland and was returning home from the West Indies when he was told that his unit was going to the Falklands. He served on board H.M.S. FEARLESS and was ferrying troops ashore on landing craft FOXTROT FOUR on June 8th, 1982, when it was attacked by an Argentine aircraft. A bomb struck FOXTROT FOUR, killing Robert and five colleagues and wounding other members of the crew. The landing craft was taken in tow, but sank before reaching shore. Robert is therefore buried at sea.

"We will remember them."

Two more houses were built for the staff, the playing fields were extended, and a concrete cricket wicket added to the facilities. By 1950, two new classrooms had been constructed, together with a large library, a quiet room and a well equipped Instrument Room where the boys were taught the use of Navigational Instruments and Meteorology. There was a large Arts and Crafts cellar where all kinds of modelling were taught and once a week the boys were given a cinema night. Incidentally, it was about this time that the old stables were converted into a fine gymnasium. INDEFATIGABLE was entering a new world, although the boys were still responsible for the boiler house!

That same year the Marine Society presented the school with three cutters and a gig. These were of inestimable value to the training and enjoyment of all. At the same time, the Marine Society provided Bursaries for the senior boys to attend courses at the Outward Bound School in Aberdovey. This gave them much confidence before taking up their seagoing careers.

It was with great pride that it was reported in 1952 that His Royal Highness the Duke of Edinburgh had consented to be a Patron of the school. His interest in the sea was obvious, and from that stemmed the need to encourage young men to join the profession. Every entrant was interviewed by the Committee, and only boys who would appear to have the likelihood of making good seamen were accepted. It was no kindness to take a boy and train him if he was unlikely to prove suitable for such a career.

Captain G. W. Irvine

Money was ever a problem and certainly was not helped when in the following year it was discovered that the wiring of the main building had deteriorated to such an extent that it had to be renewed throughout. A further blow was the inadequacy of the laundry facilities and the need to rehouse and rebuild. The Captain's quarters were also appearing on the agenda, and that it where that problem remained for a few years. Mrs Irvine's thoughts have not been recorded!

There are other memories of Liverpool which most Inde boys would have shared in the late 1940's and 50's. I do not know who wrote the words.
'Who can remember the lifeboat school in Salthouse Dock, where we usually took the first certificate of our careers, rowing around the dock to the jeers of the dockers working the ships there. If you managed to pass and get your certificate, the next one you went for was the EDH (Efficient Deck Hand), but you couldn't take that one until you were a certified lifeboatman. The EDH school was in Canning Place above the Seamen's Union Office. It was a ten-day course, but once you passed it you were well on your way.'

John Prestwich, 1952-1954, is especially remembered by his friends at Inde. John went to sea on leaving INDEFATIGABLE in 1955 and soon after that his life changed dramatically. For almost half a century he has been paralysed from below the chin and is entirely dependent, twenty four hours out of every day, on artifical ventilation to keep alive.

Maggie, his wife, hoped that this book would include his story. 'John was a student for twenty months - and Head Boy around 1954. In November 1955 - the week of his 17th birthday - whilst his ship was docked at Corpus Christi, Texas, he was stretchered off board and taken to the Memorial Hospital and put into an iron lung. He had contracted bulbar poliomyelitis.'

John Prestwich's story is remarkable.

Cliff Adamson was a staff member, 1953-57 and wrote in the 1968 Newsletter.

'I recently picked up Vol. 1 'THE ILLUSTRATED WAR' ... on November 28th, 1940, Liverpool had its 200th air raid, the war was only 400 days old! I made enquiries about the Merchant Navy and I accepted entrance into the Wallasey Sea School. The PTI advised us that all the equipment in the gym belonged to the INDEFATIGABLE and ordered us to treat it with respect. I left my sweat on the vaulting box and the parallel bars, and blood on the ropes of the boxing ring.'

He was to join T.& J. Harrison and sailed in the HISTORIAN; he became a member of the gun-crew as No. 7, sight setter, the one that sat next to the breech as it exploded! Eventually, after two interviews, he came to INDEFATIGABLE when Captain Irvine was looking for staff.

'Mr. Derrick was Chief Officer, Mr. Napthene 2nd Officer, Mr. Doodson Stores Officer and Instructors, Messrs Protherch, Firth, Bell and self with Jack Snape Bursar/Secretary and Mr. Roberts Teacher (later Goronwy Owen Jones). Long hours and hard work, never knowing whether I was teaching Signals, Seamanship, classroom or PT. The old vaulting box and parallel bars still had my sweat on them and the first thing I did was to see if I could still do my triple axail some ten years later!

'We were expected to perform a spectacular display for the Annual Prize Giving Open Day, which we did. The first row of guests were filled with Cadets in plaster who forgot to land on their feet after a double somersault over the box. We also gave displays of swinging telegraph poles to music ... and also judo. The director of Naval Training was very impressed and decided to include judo in Naval Training.'

Cliff Adamson also recalled the occasion when the Heswall Nautical School (the old AKBAR, previously on the Mersey) offered their mast to the Inde. He added that Captain Irvine, Mr. Derrick and himself went to Wirral to dismantle and re-erect it. He wonders if it is still the same one on the parade ground.

Signals Class 1955

David Parkes, 1955-56, adds his thoughts.
'In my day the place was run on very strict lines, almost penal! There were a number of categories of boys, fee paying (which I was), orphans

and welfare cases, and those sent for a bit of discipline. I remember one particular incident, when about 2 a.m. we were all aroused from our bunks and ordered on to the parade ground in our pyjamas. Apparently one of the duty Officers had spotted smoke coming up from under the floorboards on the main stairs. It turned out that a boy had deliberately shorted out the electric wiring to start a fire, which could have had devastating consequences.

'We were kept at attention for over two hours, waiting for the guilty boy to own up. He didn't. A few days later a boy did confess, and was ceremoniously 'drummed out' of the school. I shall never forget witnessing that event.

'There were boys who tried to run away, but they were nearly all caught! Whenever we heard that a runaway had made it home we would give a cheer.
'A pleasanter moment was the visit of Wilfred Pickles. I remember we had to sing the Inde song. Can anyone remember the words? Maybe there were various versions.'

INDE BOYS ANTHEM

We are some of the Inde lads,
We are some of the boys,
We know our manners,
We are respected wherever we go.

As we go marching down the King's highway,
Doors and windows open wide,
When we hear that 'Copper' shout,
Put that bloody Woodbine out,
We are the Inde boys.

Joe Earl makes his contribution.
'On 16th January, 1956, at the age of fourteen and a half, my mother put me on board a train for Liverpool ... my instructions were to find the Sailors' Home. Later that day we lads boarded a train en route to

Anglesey. And we arrived at Inde about seven thirty on a dark, cold January night. We filed into the long hallway of this large mansion, were told to place our bags on the deck and proceed to the mess hall.

'We stood to attention by some long tables with painted linoleum forming the top. Placed on this were two slices of bread and a small pat of butter at intervals alongside a plastic mug of very weak orange juice. The Captain arrived shortly afterwards … a huge bull of a man in full uniform. He stood at ease, placed his hands behind his back, glared at us, then proceeded to expound the value of INDEFATIGABLE.
"The values that honest men know to be true … integrity, discipline, the determination to do one's best, a wish to serve others. These are the values by which the INDEFATIGABLE has tried to live and strives to maintain, so that true INDEFATIGABLE boys the world over are able, not only to cope with life and all its complications, but are ambassadors, trying to show others by example the way we should lead our lives."
'He abruptly turned on his heel and departed, leaving us to our supper. After this we were allowed some leisure time and allotted to our bunks in one of the large rooms in the mansion and put under the care of a Leading Hand in the dormitory.'

Joe settled fairly quickly into the routine and his account continued.
'One challenge was a boy called Beagly. He didn't like me and one day after a slight mishap with a bucket of water, we started swapping punches. However, before long we were caught red-handed by the Sports Officer, Mr. Adams. "Earl, Beagly, we'll finish this tonight in the gym." The gym was a converted stone barn, sparse and cold with a bare wooden floor and a boxing ring permanently set up.

'The specific rule for a 'grudge fight' was that there were no rounds, the fight continued until one was knocked out or gave in. My second and good friend Jimmy Hughes from Leeds came armed with a white towel and a sponge and a very worn pair of boxing gloves. Mr. Adams was the referee and started the match by saying "Get stuck in!" So we did. Before long we both had nose bleeds, the inside walls of the gym were coated with whitewash and as our blood was being freely splattered everywhere, what missed the avid audience was sprayed all over those nice white walls. Egged on by my supporters, I refused to give in. So did Beagly. Eventually, battered, bruised and bleeding, we could fight no more. The bout was declared a draw. I became Beagly's respected friend. Beagly was to earn the rank of Petty Officer, Drake Division, Jimmy Hughes, Petty Officer of Raleigh and I became Petty Officer of Hood Division.

'A few of us lads were entered for the National Schoolboy Boxing Championship and I managed to do quite well, although in one bout with a Conway Boy one of my front teeth was broken off. When it came to the Welsh Finals, I managed to loose on points in a hotly disputed decision to a chap named Walsh. He, however, beat the English champion easily in his next fight and he consequently won the Great Britain Schoolboy Championship. So close, never mind!

'Another injury I received was when I had a severe kicking while playing rugby. It was very painful and turned out to be quite serious with complications. This involved taking a urine sample to the hospital in Bangor. On one of these journeys I stopped at the suspension bridge to watch the old H.M.S. CONWAY, which was ablaze below me. Eventually, I ended up in the Royal Southern Hospital in Liverpool for two weeks. I actually put on weight in the hospital, possibly due to the admirable administrations of Nurse Margaret Fenton. She was a chocolate-box beauty and took care of all my needs … mainly in the sluice room in the small hours. I fell madly in love with her. It couldn't last, of course … she was too old for me. Margaret was seventeen … I was but fifteen!

'Sunday was Church Parade. The duty bugle-boy would sound Divisions, which was the signal to line up on the parade ground. Dressed in our best uniforms, standing in three ranks in our respective Divisions, and the band with their instruments gleaming and the white caps, belts and gaiters newly blancoed, we would be inspected by the Chief Officer and the Captain. The lads that were not attending church, the sick and those of some obscure religion, were dismissed and, as the village barber always attended on Sunday mornings, those were detailed off for a haircut. The rest of us marched off in columns of threes, headed by our drum and bugle band. We took the long way round to the church, along the A4080 with every boy marching proudly to the tunes of Sousa.'

Many thanks to Joe Earl.

Fred White was just 13 years old when he arrived at Inde in 1959. Bravely he has recounted his story about running away from the Inde with another boy and ending up in Wellesley Nautical School in Blyth, Northumberland, where he stayed until he was 17 years old.

'It was around 1959 and all that I can tell from memory is that the Captain was a huge man. The only other officer that I can remember was Mugridge. He was the P.T.I. Inde was heaven compared to Wellesley.

'We ran away from INDEFATIGABLE because the Petty Officer of the dorm told us to. How I regret that looking back! We spent a night out in Snowdonia. It was late November and very cold. We were both taken to Llandudno Junction hospital for a check up and to thaw out.

'We were both drummed out when we returned to Inde. A drummer played a roll. My cap band was ripped off and thrown to the ground, silks ripped off and collar. You cannot imagine what that did to a 13-year-old boy at that time. Then we were taken indoors to the Captain's Office and received six strokes of the cane across our bums, given a rail pass and escorted off the Ship.

'At 17 I could barely read or write. Now I'm a published poet, have letters from the Queen and from Hilary Rodham Clinton. I am also an engineer dealing with automotive failures, a member of the Institute of Motor Engineers. I have travelled the world, China seven times. I have four wonderful children, not bad for a lad who from the age of four until fourteen spent his time in an orphange, pushed from pillar to post.'

That is quite a story!

The school's capacity by 1959 was increased from 123 to 136 and a recruitment campaign was to prove to be successful. A new mess hall had been completed and the old one became a classroom. Another improvement must have given great joy to the boys. We all know that Welsh water which comes down from the hills is colder than cold, and in this the lads had swum. At last the pool was to be heated and thus enabled non-swimmers to learn the art before dying of hypothermia. I suspect that it was still cold!

There is still no mention of the Captain's house.

A. Yates, 1959-63, shared his memories.
'I was only 13 years old when I arrived at the School, only a babe really. I grew up rapidly whilst there and although conditions were primitive in comparison to today, I have no memories of bullying or unpleasantness which must, I suppose, be down to the discipline imposed by the staff. I do remember being forced to plunge into the indoor pool every other day, naked and through all seasons at crack of dawn, and various methods we would employ to avoid it (rarely successful).

'I recall the Chief Officer who would distribute mail in the dining hall by standing on a chair and throwing one's letters, frisby style, at a named individual and was never known to miss.

'I remember washing and rinsing clothes in a galvanised bucket, cold water, bare feet, snowing at 5.30 a.m. and holding up white fronts for inspection.

'I remember witnessing the drumming out of an individual whose crime I do not recall. How his uniform was ceremoniously stripped from him, hat spiked, buttons cut off, uniform slashed, all done with a cutlass, then paraded up and down the ranks in disgrace, marched to the main gate, given a single ticket to his home town and 'that's yer lot mate'. He was only a child really. However, although this sort of treatment might be considered cruel or even abuse in today's climate, I am glad that I had the experience. The discipline was character building and stood me in

good stead. I went to H.M.S. ST. VINCENT after that, with the Royal
Navy, still only fifteen years old and felt that I was ahead of the race,
institutionalised and obedient and not quite so wet behind the ears.

'I retired from the Navy in 1986 after 26 years as a Chief Petty Officer.
Now I have to work for a living. I would do it all again (I think).'

In 1961 the swimming pool was enlarged and two new staff houses
completed. The following year had more news. The construction of the
fifth pair of houses for the staff was finished and they were all now in
new houses "with the exception of the Captain, a new house for whom
will be engaging our attention in the not too distant future." Mrs Irvine
was still silent!

Jonathon Pope gives us his thoughts.
'I joined INDEFATIGABLE on the 13th September, 1961 and left 18th
July, 1963. The Captain Superintendent was George Washington
Irvine, a seaman of the 'old school' who would today be considered not
only non-PC, but rough with it!

'School was divided into four divisions, Drake, Raleigh, Rodney and
Hood (colours red, blue, green and yellow). All boys were numbered,
there being about 130 - 140 at any one time. Inter-divisional rivalry
was encouraged and, depending upon the zeal of the divisional officer
instructors, could be interesting from an anthropologist's angle, if
studying tribal warfare.

'The food was pretty awful, however a goodly and an unlimited quantity
of sliced Mothers Pride stowed in a large rack at one end of the mess
deck kept us all from starvation. My friend Terry Kelly could get a
whole meal, well mixed, spread thinly into a stack of sandwiches some
ten inches tall. We didn't exactly starve but were constantly hungry, no
doubt due to the very long and physical day. The thing I did retain from
this period is the knack to eat anything (if it does not move too quickly)
and a love of bread with my meal! This has been helpful during my
years at sea.

'Laundry was done by hand with large bars of soap and lukewarm water which didn't prevent almost all boys taking a pride in having very clean, smart uniforms. Sartorial elegance was the order of the day when on parade and also when on 'liberty'. Collars and white front edgings had to have the correct shade of light blue, trousers, blouses and silks all creased correctly and sharply at the right places, caps bent and worn at the correct angle and name tags tied with an ornate (usually false) bow tie. All of this was achieved without the aid of irons or modern appliances and without attracting the attentions of any instructor who was on the lookout for non-regulation items or colours. Cleaning, polishing etc., was a constant operation, all done by hand and the decks of oak board were polished with large quantities of RONUK polish and gleamed like glass. The fire risk does not bear thinking about! Inspections were numerous and a cake was presented to the cleanest dormitory, a prize indeed!

'Bullying of a very violent or physical nature was rife; black eyes, cuts, lumps and bruises often in evidence, discipline was military with defaulters doing extra and unpleasant tasks. The ultimate was caning, which given the violent nature of some of the boys wasn't much of a deterrent, the weals and bruises even being seen as a status symbol that you could 'take it'. The boys came from all walks of life, many from backgrounds which today would entitle them to their own Social Services Team. Some came as an alternative to reform schools and others, like myself, from a middle-class upbringing. The mixture was responsible for many of the less agreeable aspects of the school, there being very little in the way of attention or interest taken in those having a 'hard time'. I could go on at more length, enough to say that I didn't particularly enjoy my time at the Inde, even though it gave me a good insight into the makeup of the male society of this country over the past thirty years.

'The educational level was not high, given the vastly-differing mental abilities of the boys. Those of us who had the capacity rose and the rest didn't. In those days more reliance was placed on physical and manual ability than education. It was after all a school for would-be seamen. Some of us, three or four every term, managed to reach an educational standard which was acceptable within the industry as evidence that we could be trained as deck cadets/apprentices. The remainder went to sea as deck/catering boys in the Merchant Navy or joined the R.N. as boy seamen.

'Sports were fives, rugby or sometimes athletics; naturally rowing (cutters) and sailing were indulged in on the Menai Strait. Smoking was prohibited and therefore taken up by all! Tailor-made fags were a real luxury, so we rolled our very own very thin ones or nicked the fag ends from the staff room ashtrays to break down and re-roll. The Captain's messenger was a plum job as he had access to the village on a daily basis and could assure himself of a steady income obtained from the supply (at a profit) of quarter ounce packets of Old Holborn or Golden Virginia. The school abounded in 'baccy' barons who were a constant source of supplies, once again at a profit. The corner shop at Llanfair P.G. must have had their tobacco brought in on an articulated lorry!

'R.N.L.I. collecting (this was close to George W's heart) consisted of two hulking boys in uniform knocking at local doors, thrusting a tin under the nose of the terrified occupant and suggesting that they give generously in what was probably to the Welsh a foreign accent, but was in fact merely broad Scouse, Glaswegian, Cockney, etc. The school band did march in the occasional Parade about Remembrance Day. We always took part in the Battle of the Atlantic Parade in Liverpool.

'Going ashore mainly consisted of a fry up in the local village café … food being the main pre-occupation. There were Pictures in Menai or Bangor. Sometimes there was a trip to Beaumaris. However, after some of our Scousers sorted out some of the local boys, we didn't get there much! Also there was the usual trying to chat up the local girls and fisticuffs with the local boys who objected to the former always on a Saturday afternoon. That was the only day that we had a 'liberty'.

'North Wales in the 1960's was not exactly noted for interesting leisure activities or its fun-loving, gregarious population. I think that they probably viewed us as those boys from THAT school, best kept away from honest chapel folk and their virginal daughters! We also suffered from being the poor relations to CONWAY, which was just up the road. We never mixed at all ... they were Officers. As far as the local countryside went, I marched over most of it, and as far as I can remember it was usually during the winter and always bloody cold with your sleeves rolled up and wet and miserable. There were spectacular views of Snowdonia from the dormitory windows (always open) and in fact we had an annual trip up Snowdon, which was a kind of vertical route-march.

'I have had a thirty-six year (so far) career at sea ... and, yes, I did reach command rank. So on reflection INDEFATIGABLE must have done me some good!'

Thank you Jonathon Pope, 1961-1963.

Charlie Claridge, 1962-1963, wanted to go to a sea training school and as other establishments had an entry only for sixteen year olds, it had to be INDEFATIGABLE. At the age of fifteen he was given his number,

112, his division was Hood and the dorm was 19 Harrison Line. His first supper was he later discovered a special treat … a slice of corned beef and a tomato.

'We got up at 0630 hrs and either went washing or swimming, changing each day. Swimming one day and washing the other, the same in the afternoon. That pool was very cold and I used to dive in and do one width as fast as possible and get my number ticked off. You only had half an hour to get up, make your bed, get dressed and undressed for swimming and drying yourself, getting dressed ready to fall in for work, clearing the school at 0700 hrs. Everyone had to clean a certain part of the school, dorm, toilets and main hall, etc.

Prize Day - *1967*

'All the decks were polished and had to be polished by hand and with blankets wrapped around your pumps. The brightwork was kept immaculate, everything was cleaned by the boys and we had to do our own washing once a week in the laundry. Although there was a cook, which is an honour to call him that, the food was cooked by the boys and all the washing up was done by the boys.

'The food left much to be desired, but we were allowed as much bread and marge as we liked as long as we did not waste it. The galley had coal or coke fires and I especially remember the jelly we used to get on Sunday afternoons. It was made with not enough jelly and left to set on the deck in the galley where the dust from the fire would land in it. In this day and age the Public Health or whatever would shut the place down, but we survived.

'During my last term there, a notice went on the notice board that me and another boy would be flying out to Montreal to join a ship there. Needless to say, we were very excited and could not wait to get away from the place. Eventually, we went to Liverpool and were given our discharge books etc. by Mr. Hobbs. Then we went down to London and joined other members of the crew and flew out to Montreal, the first time that I had been in a plane.

'Life on board ship was very easy after the Inde. I was the 'peggy', that is, getting the meals from the galley, doing the washing up and cleaning

March Past - *1962*

the seamen's mess. We were running between Canada, the States and Australia through Panama. I enjoyed it, but it was two years before I got home, arriving at Hull after going through Suez on our last trip. I had sailed all round the world.'

Charlie Claridge then went on coastal ships and having bought a book on navigation, found that to his surprise he could do the exercises and worked his way through the book. By 1968 he had enough sea-time to enable him to take his sea-going tickets in Liverpool, including the Master's Home Trade Certificate.

Yet another Inde Boy makes good.

A new thought was on the horizon in 1963. Incidentally, the Captain's house had not been forgotten ... "the matter is engaging our immediate attention". The new thought was the inevitable raising of the school leaving age to sixteen ... a challenge to be faced.

Another Old Boy puts pen to paper ... Alan McGurk.
'I had the pleasure of attending during 1963 - 1964, not long after losing my parents. During the time that I was there, the Scousers were definitely the ruling class and, as a young lad from the North-East, I had to be careful. A couple of mates at the time were Pete Williams (Liverpool) and Peter Swann (Pocklington, near York). I remember the Royal visit and the size of the Duke of Edinburgh's nose at close quarters stays with me! I can't remember what he said, if indeed he did speak to me. I also remember Captains Irvine and Wade ... a very ruddy faced man.

'I had nearly completed my training and had been assigned a ship, the RUAHINE. I think it was a N.Z.S.C. ship, but I decided to join the Fleet Air Arm on Pete William's recommendation. Pete Swann took the ship and used to send me postcards from Tahiti and other exotic stops, whilst I was training at Shotley Gate. The experience of the Inde helped me sail through training at GANGES. I remained in the R.N. until 1986, then started work in civil aviation where I am still working.'

Clive Ellis 1963-1964, wrote for the Inde Magazine and these are some snippets.

'I remember getting on a coach with twenty or so other lads in INDEFATIGABLE uniforms to travel to the school with very mixed feelings. The boys in uniform were telling us horror stories about the school and the food, hauntings, etc. We new boys were worried.

'I remember on one occasion a new boy came down to the old boys' dorm area and was caught. We decided to toss him in a blanket. On the third throw someone shouted that Davo was coming so we all dropped the blanket. Down came the new boy on the bare floor and broke his leg or his arm.

'The lad named me as a perpetrator and I was hauled up in front of Captain Wade. He asked me for names and honestly and truly I could not recall them. The Captain did not believe me. He told the whole school that it must stop and complimented me for my loyalty to the other lads!

'We now reside in Sydney, Australia, and I run a small International Freight Forwarding business. We have three grown up children.'

The Centenary Year was celebrated in 1964 and the Captain-Superintendent, Captain G.W. Irvine gave his thoughts to the Liverpool Daily Post.

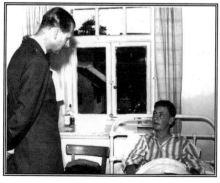

'The honour bestowed upon the school by the Duke of Edinburgh in graciously consenting to visit us on this notable occasion has given us all, not only joy, but added inspiration to further our effort in training efficient seamen and good citizens.

'My best wishes go to past and present boys of INDEFATIGABLE wherever they may be. I also compliment the many boys who have risen to command their own ships or who have succeeded to positions of responsibility in the Merchant and Royal Navies.

'May our long traditions of service, loyalty and self-discipline ever continue.'

Many young men were to find their way into the Royal Navy for service on deck and were drafted direct to H.M.S. GANGES or H.M.S. ST. VINCENT for the Royal Marines, after passing examinations by Royal Navy examiners each month.

The school was divided into four Divisions - Drake, Raleigh, Rodney and Hood - each under the charge of a Divisonal Officer. There were six forms, sub-divided into A and B streams, and after an initial two-week period of kitting out, marching, physical training, boating instruction and general routine, new boys were drafted into their respective forms according to academic ability, age and knowledge. They all received a sound comprehensive education up to G.C.E. level.

Peter Roberts, 1964-1966, adds to the story.
'Greetings from New Zealand. I was surprised to read that some of the former trainees disliked being at Inde. I personally can say that the training has been of great benefit to me. I went to Inde as a green, wet-behind-the-ears, boy with basically no idea what went on in the real world. But I soon learned that your Mam was not there to pick up after you and do for you the things you were too idle to do. I have in all honesty a very fond memory of my time in Inde and some of the lads there. It was a great shame that the old school had to close.

'It helped me, not only when I was at sea, but in recent years. I was a Sea Cadet Officer with the New Zealand cadet forces. I was the Training Officer and Boats Officer, and being on the other side of the coin, I now sympathise with the Officers of the Inde.'

The Centenary of Inde was celebrated in 1964. In the May a letter was received from Buckingham Palace.

'During the hundred years existence of the Indefatigble and National Sea Training School for Boys there have been many great changes in conditions of service at sea, and progress has brought about a complete technical revolution. This will go on, but the human qualities needed in the men who go to sea will remain the same.

'The School has always been succesful in fostering a sense of discipline, humanity and loyalty in the boys it has trained and I hope that this tradition will long continue.

'I send my very best wishes to all past and present boys and instructors and to all those who have helped to manage the School, for the celebration of its centenary. I hope it will continue its good work far into the future.

Philip.'

It was with pride that the Chairmen throughout the hundred years were thanked.

Mr. James J. Bibby	1864 - 1890
Mr. Frank Bibby, C.B.E.	1890 - 1913
Mr. Arthur W. Bibby	1913 - 1931
Sir A. Harold Bibby, Bart., D.S.O., D.L, LL.D.	1931 - 1958
Mr. Derek J. Bibby, M.C. M.A.	1958 to date.

The Centenary Brochure carried much information about the school, but it reserved a special page which was read with pride by all of us involved with seafarers in Liverpool. In 1964 there were eight Old Boys of Inde who had been or were serving in Harrison Line.

Captain R.W.C. Baldwin, Assistant Marine Superintendent, joined the Firm as 3rd Officer, 3.12.28. Ashore 1.7.56. At present resident Marine Superintendent in the West Indies, based in Trinidad. "He was known as 'Butch Baldwin' and was always 'chipping'. Once, off Beira, he fell into the sea. The cry went up "Get the mate." The reply was "It is the so and so mate!" Incidentally, our Ron could not swim!"

Captain W.S. Eustance, O.B.E., joined the Firm as 3rd Officer, 26.6.28. First Command 3.12.53. Now in command of M.V. DALESMAN. Received O.B.E. for services to Belize, British Honduras, at time of hurricane 'Hattie' in October 1961 whilst in command of M.V. TACTICIAN.

Captain C.A.V. Daly, Cargo Superintendent, joined the Firm as Cadet,

16.2.28. Ashore 1.10.49. At present attached to Head Office, Liverpool, as Assistant Cargo Superintendent. "He was torpedoed and badly injured during the war."

Captain C.S.S. Boam, joined the Firm as Cadet, 18.8.27. First command 7.2.56. Has recently taken over command of Company's new M.V. INVENTOR. "Charlie Boam was to write plays for B.B.C. Radio. Apparently, he played a 'silent piano' and demanded absolute silence whilst he was playing!"

Captain R.P. Jones, joined the Firm as Cadet, 19.5.37. First command 19.10.59. At present in command of M.V. ARBITRATOR. "Known as R.P, he was a firebrand and was to become the Marine Superintendent at Manchester, where he ruled with the proverbial rod of iron."

Captain F.L. Cobb, Cargo Superintendent, joined the Firm as Cadet, 12.7.39. Ashore 12.3.57. At present attached to Company's London Office as Assistant Cargo Superintendent. "Ken Cobb sailed with a tank of tropical fish. Before handing over command, he would leave detailed instructions on how they should be fed. He became the Cargo Instructor. Incidentally, his son also joined T. & J."

Captain J. Richardson, Assistant Marine Superintendent, joined the Firm as Cadet, 2.9.20. Ashore, 1.9.55. At present attached to Head Office, Liverpool as Assistant Marine Superintendent. "His nickname was 'Pug-nose' and he ever wore a Homburg hat. When he sailed out of Brunsick Dock, the dockers called him the Mayor of Brunswick. Apparently, he whistled as he walked."

Captain Harry Traynor, Second Officer, joined the firm as a Deck boy in 1940. Promoted to Master in 1968. His nickname was 'Frank Sinatra' and his favourite instruction was "Do it my way!" For the record, the details were provided by Harry Traynor ... blame him!

The capacity of the school was maintained at 140 in 1964, but there was uncertainty ahead. A major threat was the opening in 1966 of a magnificent National Sea Training School at Gravesend with its obvious attraction to young men. This together with the expected raising of the school leaving age made the future uncertain for INDEFATIGABLE. Major capital expenditure had to be shelved. A decision was taken that "the Captain's House was to be improved rather than build a new one."

Captain G.W. Irvine was officially to retire at the end of the Summer Term, 1965, but for medical reasons was unfortunately compelled to hand over command to Captain W. Wade at the end of the Spring Term. Captain Irvine had steered INDEFATIGABLE through many problems and successes for some fifteen years. There had been much reorganisation of plant and upgrading of education during his years of office and both he and Mrs. Irvine deserved the complete gratitude of all concerned with the future well-being of INDEFATIGABLE.

The modernisation of the Captain's House was successfully completed in 1965, but another problem arose immediately. Dry rot had broken out in the School and the repairs were costly with more to come. By the next year that cost hit £19,000.

By this time Gravesend was in full operation and on paper was large enough to supply the needs of the whole industry. This was a major challenge for INDEFATIGABLE. One advantage for the Inde was that the training was for a longer period than at Gravesend. There were other advantages. The School was fairly well equipped with a fleet of small boats, which included two power boats, plus 27 ft. whalers, 14 ft. G.P. sailing dinghies and two rowing fours to practise the finer skills of rowing. Steering by compass was initially taught ashore on a Steering Training Simulator after which the boys practised afloat. There was a natural harbour where the boys could swim in summer, but all tuition in swimming and life saving principles was given in the heated pool. All boys were taught to swim. The possibilities for 'outward bound' activities were legion, as opposed to the 'wilderness' of Gravesend.

R.D. Haynes, 1965-1966, tells a story in the Spring 1985 Newsletter. 'During the South Atlantic conflict, I was serving in H.M.S. HERALD. The ship had just completed a six month survey around the coast of

Oman and had arrived in the U.K. for just one week, with most of the ship's company on leave. Then we received orders to sail for the South Atlantic as a hospital ship.

'The ship had its yellow funnel painted white with red crosses, also red crosses on the hull with fixed lighting for use at night. After leaving, the ship got down in earnest to train and practise the various medical procedures that would be expected for us to carry out as the ship carried only two naval doctors. The experience gained in Northern Ireland with regard to shot wounds and bombings was invaluable. As was to prove later, we did not have to deal with these as the casualties were treated ashore at the field hospital and on board the UGANDA.

'Following an accident on board, we put into Rio de Janeiro and then had to steam at full speed to catch up with the rest of the ships making their way to the Falkland Islands. We met in a designated zone called the 'Red Cross Box' just off the coast of West Falkland. While down in The Falklands, the B.B.C. World Service was being continually jammed and, having no contact with the other R.N. ships, the people back home had a far better idea of what was happening. This was a very frustrating time, just slowly steaming up and down. The boredom was broken when the ship was detailed to search for a ditched aircraft. We spent three days doing this, but did not find anything.

'All our injured troops were transferred to Montevideo for onward flight back to U.K. These trips to Montevideo took fourteen days and some were very rough, which did not go down well with the troops, having to contend with injuries and feeling sea sick. Having taken the last troop back to Monte, we received the long-awaited signal to proceed back to U.K.

'The ship arrived back three weeks later, anchoring off Spit Head and taking on the Port Admiral before proceeding into Portsmouth harbour. The ship's welcome was very emotional. I do not think that there were many that did not feel so.'

Nigel Firman, 1967-1968, 24 Drake Division, adds his thoughts.

'H.M.S. GANGES was a doddle after the Inde! Rugby with P.T.I. Mr. Williams and the slaughter once a term against CONWAY. We had to row there and back in those 32 ft. cutters - no wonder we were knackered!

'Seamanship was Mr. Curtess. The band was run by the Deputy Head, Mr. Wade. I think. He was a very old man. The only live-in teacher was Mr. Bond, who had his room next to our dorm, which was over the sick bay. During my last three months, I used to work for him, carrying out special duties in the stores a few afternoons a week.

'The Cane! I only received it once. There were four of us. Harry Chong was the ring leader. He was a Scouser from an orphanage and he had heard 'through the grapevine' that there was a girls' school on the other side of the covered railway bridge. So off we went - alas, no school! But there was the cane on return in front of the whole school.

'I left Inde a far better and stronger person, even though at the time a lot of the disciplinary actions that were taken were hard to understand, especially at fourteen years of age. For children of thirteen years plus and not much of a home life, it was home and had a great impact on my future in the Royal Navy as a clearance diver and in bomb mine disposal.'

Yet again Inde had done its job.

In 1967, the postponing of the raising of the school leaving age to 1973 gave a little more breathing space as it would dramatically affect the teaching curriculum. At this time, the conditions of service in the Merchant Navy were also under review. As the industry itself was unsure of the future, it was difficult to plan ahead. General Purpose ratings were becoming the vogue on many ships and this demanded classroom space and equipment as Engineering was possibly to enter the syllabus. This advance in training facilities and other improvements would cost tens of thousands of pounds, but was fully justified.

Mr. R.N. Hatfield was the Secretary of the INDEFATIGABLE National

Sea Training School for Boys which had its Head Office in the Liverpool Sailors' Home. He wrote an article in October 1968 for the Liverpool Daily Post.

'The School-ship is now recognised by the Department of Education and Science as a 'Direct Grant Nautical School' of which only two remain in the country. The School has kept a full complement of 140 boys coming from all over Britain and some from overseas. All are found employment with reputable shipping companies at the end of a year's minimum course.

'In 1864 the first Chairman was Mr. James J. Bibby of the Bibby Line and the chairmanship has been passed continuously from father to son, the present Chairman, Mr. Derek J. Bibby, M.C., M.A., succeeding his father, Major Sir A. Harold Bibby, Bt., D.S.O., D.L., LLD., in 1958. This link of 104 years in command must be unique in the country - if not the world.'

By 1969, engineering training had been instituted.

The Committee still believed that the industry would require in future years boys from INDEFATIGABLE and that the Rochdale proposal that all should be trained at Gravesend did not take fully into account the unique standing of INDEFATIGABLE. In preparation for the future, more residential staff were employed, two more staff houses were built … the Annual Report noted that running costs were rising at an alarming rate. The exact future role of the School should be known in a couple of years.

Stephen B. Gibbons started keeping his diary on January 1st, 1969. As happens to most of us, he started well and then became somewhat spasmodic. Here are just some excerpts.

January 1st   Today is only fifteen days until I go to a Naval School in Anglesey in Wales, the T.S. INDEFATIGABLE.

January 5th   This morning, Sunday, I got up at half past nine. There had been a plane crash not a mile away. Fifty people were killed. They were mainly Indians. The plane took the top off an oak tree and crashed in a farm field. He was landing at Gatwick. I had a roast dinner at half past one. I then watched tele. Had tea about six.

January 14th   Today I stayed in bed until twelve and then I bought plimsolls, sweets and polish. The rest of the time I packed for tomorrow. Went to bed at seven.

January 15th   Today I woke at half past three and rose at four. I had breakfast, dressed and said Goodbye to Mum and went with Dad to get the 5.20 train. Arrived at London 50 minutes later. Underground to Euston and caught the 7.20 to Liverpool. We arrived at Liverpool at 10.20. After arriving at the the Sailors' Home I went before the Committee, had dinner, said Goodbye to Dad and we were off to T.S. Inde.

January 16th   Today was my first day at the T.S. Indefatogable. I am Boy No. 13, Drake Division, Dorm eleven. Today we were issued with kit.'

The next entries until January 25th merely say 'Settling in.'

January 26th   Homesick.
January 27th   Homesick.
January 28th   Getting over it.
January 29th   Nearly over it.
January 30th   Homesick again.
January 31st   Normal!
February 1st   Today I woke up at 0630, washed, dressed and made my bed. After Reveille, when the rest got up, my mate and I polished our boots. At 0730 I went down to Assembly and after some jobs had breakfast at 0800 (cornflakes, eggs and bacon and bread and marmalade). Leave. I walked to Bangor. Rang Mum. Saw film The Detective, which I did not enjoy.'

Thereafter the diary continues with normal routine and young Stephen had obviously settled in well. We shall peep at just one more entry.

July 1st   *Prince of Wales investiture. We went (30 of us) to the Ferodo Works and had a seat in the Forces section. I saw the Queen, Duke of Edinburgh, Prince Charles, Princess Margaret, Princess Anne, Lord Mountbatten, Duke and Duchess of Kent and loads of other VIPs. It was great. This sort of thing only happens once in a lifetime. I also saw the Queen's mother. There was a flypast consisting of nine Phantoms and four Lightning escorts. There were soldiers everywhere and police too. The security was very high in standard. We left at twenty to six.'*

It was good to sample Stephen's jottings.

The full complement of 140 boys was maintained in 1970 and in spite of the fact that Gravesend, which was run by the industry itself, was such a threat to the employment of Inde boys, the quality of training enabled them to be absorbed into the Royal and Merchant Navies. Happily the eventual raising of the school leaving age was to have little adverse effect. The closure of Ganges meant that the Royal Navy's natural supply of entrants might now be met by INDEFATIGABLE.

It was noted that over £120,000 had been spent over the past three or four years, but the School was fully booked up to September 1974, and whilst the state of finances was basically sound, the annual deficit was growing.

Chapter 8
The Final Decades

1972 was a water-shed when Mr. Derek J. Bibby, who had served on the board for twenty-five years, announced his retirement. He had been Chairman for his final fifteen years on the Board. Since the inception of the school in 1864, the Chairman had always been elected from the Bibby family. Derek now became President in place of his father, Major Sir A. Harold Bibby, who consented to become a Patron. Sadly the year showed a heavy deficit on the profit and loss side.

1972 was possibly the year that marked the 'wind of change' for INDEFATIGABLE. It is difficult to differentiate between a 'knee jerk' reaction to challenges and forward planning. When that difference is evident, it is generally too late to meet the challenge. Other national sea training schools were to founder for similar reasons. The Inde was to remain until 1995.

Happily once again in 1972 the school kept its full complement of 140 boys, 6 masters and 4 instructors. The demand for places was not slackening and was again fully booked up to September 1973.

In October 1973, ARETHUSA announced its closure and INDEFATIGABLE offered to continue their sea training. The offer was accepted and this meant that from September 1974 INDEFATIGABLE would be the only residential nautical school catering for boys of school age in the country.

Occupancy in 1975 was at full capacity of 140 boys, but the battle with inflation continued. The year's working loss was £21,805 and would have been £30,000 if the Liverpool Sailors' Home had taken its management fee of £3,000 and if the Home had not made a donation of £5,000.

Perhaps 1975 was the most important and memorable year in the history of the School ... this was the judgement of the Governors. In the November, word was received from the Welsh Education Office that the School would not be affected by the Government scheme to phase out Direct Grant Grammar Schools. It was also stated that there was no present intention of stopping the Grant to INDEFATIGABLE.

It is worth noting the financial state at this time

From the 1st April, 1968, to the 31st March, 1975, the School incurred each year an excess of expenditure over income and the total of those seven years of loss amounted to £93,000. The same period saw the book value of the investments reduced from £204,000 in 1968 to £61,000 in 1975 and the market value from £253,000 to £61,000. Clearly this situation could not be allowed to continue without endangering the future of the School.

The figures show that during those seven years, 980 boys were educated at an average loss of some £95 per student per year. Whilst fees were increased, there were generous donations received, in particular from King George's Fund for Sailors and the Liverpool Sailors' Home. This was the sort of benefaction which made it possible for a boy to be fed, clothed and housed for thirty-eight weeks of the year at a cost to parents or the Local Education Authorities of £4.80 per week, and to be educated and trained for a further £15.40 per week.

Whilst the nautical side was of great importance, the academic side had been strengthened year by year. In 1974/75, 82% of those boys eligible were entered for CSE Examinations, of whom 77% obtained passes in various grades. This compared quite favourably with the National average.

Captain W. Wade, the Captain Headmaster for eleven years, retired at the end of 1976, having been associated with the School initially as an Instructor and subsequently as Chief Officer since 1961. That was the same year that I made contact with INDEFATIGABLE. Captain Wade made a considerable contribution during his years in charge and his wartime experience added to his expertise in producing healthy and disciplined boys who were eagerly sought by both the Royal and Merchant Navies. There had been many changes ... a new Science and Engineering Block, houses for additional staff, a new Ablution Block and a new Leisure Centre. Above all this, Captain Wade had coped with the problems associated with the raising of the school leaving age.

His successor was Captain R.T. Youngman, B.A., who assumed command in January 1977. Captain Youngman was educated at CONWAY and started his career with New Zealand Shipping Company, and at one time had been responsible for the full time instruction of their apprentices. After leaving the sea, he taught at a school in New Zealand and subsequently in two schools in England. His first move was to increase the intake of boys from 140 to 150. This was achieved.

Ronald Savory recalls a group of ten lads who sneaked out one evening into Llanfair P.G. to greet trogs in the village. Whilst they were out, there was a roll call and just as they were about to jump the trogs in a bus shelter the teachers and police turned up! The ten of them took off in different directions. Ronald and his mate, Hilton, ended up in Bangor. Some lads were expelled. The result? Never have those urinals gleamed as much. Apparently half the Anglesey police force were on full alert as it had been reported that one of the locals was sporting a shotgun.

The death of two visiting chaplains was noted. In November 1977, the Reverend Canon Victor Jones, B.A., passed on having been attached to the School since 1950. His successor at the Church of St Mary was the Reverend G.M. Hughes, B.A., in his first post following his chaplaincy in the Royal Navy. Another old friend of mine, who died in 1978 at the age of 92, was the Reverend Frank Davies. Frank had been a Chaplain in the Mersey Mission to Seamen and had been seconded to

INDEFATIGABLE in the 1920's. He became a Vicar in Wallasey and finally at Frankby and retained his interest in the School throughout his career.

During 1977 the academic side continued to expand. Geography was re-introduced into the timetable for all boys and became an examination subject in 1979. Some boys studied History to CSE level as a voluntary activity. In fact more boys than ever sat CSE and GCE examinations.

David Hazel, 1979-1981, writes in the Spring Newsletter, 1984.
'We've been on patrol in the South Atlantic for four days, moving from one whaling station to another. So far we've been ashore at Leith, Husink, and today into Gritviken which is the so-called capital. The whaling stations have all been deserted for over eighteen years and are now 'ghost towns'. Most things have been left as they were and it is quite a sight to walk through them. Also in most of the harbours lay some of the old steam whalers, half-sunken but still fascinating. The wildlife is sometimes different as well. It is lovely to see penguins and seals in their natural surroundings, although they are very snappy.

'We leave again for The Falklands tomorrow for another seven weeks before heading for home - this time via the West Indies, U.S.A. and Bermuda. I'm looking forward to that.'

For the ten years prior to 1980 the school was fully booked and demand for places looked well set for the future. However, it must be noted ominously that without the continuing financial support from King George's Fund and the Liverpool Sailors' Home the establishment would have had great difficulty in surviving. There really was a battle for survival. So much equipment was provided automatically in the maintained sector that was denied to the private sector. Survival was not easy. An estimated bill for extra fire precautions amounted to £10,000. There was no way round this, even though the syllabus taught fire drills and safety drills for the future careers of the young men.

The boys were taught discipline and self-discipline as a normal expectancy. This was firmly contrary to shoreside thinking where indiscipline was beginning to be accepted as natural and respect for home or school authority was quickly diminishing. INDEFATIGABLE fostered tolerance, firmness and understanding.

Of the 94 boys who left at the end of the Summer Term 1980, 92 had sat external examinations, 47 were accepted into the Royal Navy (2 as Marines), 22 went into the Merchant Navy as Deck Boys and 1 applied for a Police Cadetship, 7 applied for Merchant Navy Catering Department, 5 continued in further education and 3 entered shore employment. Only 7 out of 94 were not placed in employment by the School and they did not ask for any help in obtaining it.

There was a terrible tragedy when Mrs Pauline Youngman, the wife of the Captain Headmaster, was killed in a road accident as a pedestrian. She had played a considerable part in the activities of the School, caring for boys with bouts of home sickness and going the extra mile with those who found the going hard.

Mr. R.N. Hatfield, Secretary of the Liverpool Sailors' Home and of the School had a very serious operation in 1977 and had never really recovered. The daily journeys for twenty years from Liverpool to Anglesey were too exhausting so he retired early on health grounds in March 1980. Ray was a good friend to myself and to all on board. He was succeeded by another friend of mine, Mr. Les Ridyard.

Two Drascombe Long Boats were purchased in 1980 at a total cost of £5,000. They were paid for by King George's Fund and by an anonymous donor. They were ideal craft to encourage the boys to handle boats under sail.

Problems with buildings always cost money. The swimming pool was housed in an extension to the main building, and its roof had deteriorated to such an extent that for safety reasons the pool could only be used when there was no strong wind. In addition there was some subsidence. It was serious because the pool was used for life- saving instruction and survival at sea. Once again, the Liverpool Sailors' Home Trust came to the rescue with a grant of £40,000. One suspects that the boys never really understood or even knew that INDEFATIGABLE depended upon the goodwill and kindness of so many benefactors.

Each year, the School was inspected by a Naval Officer on behalf of the Commander in Chief Naval Home Command. In 1980, that inspector was Captain R.G. Fry, R.N. "INDEFATIGABLE continues to be most successful in preparing a boy for his chosen career by advancing his academic achievement and forming his character, even though some boys spend only a year at the School. The small Staff's obvious enthusiasm and dedication shine through, and they are fully stretched. They and the Captain Headmaster are to be congratulated for the fine results achieved. This was a Very Good Inspection."

The Second Sea Lord, Admiral Sir Desmond Cassidi, who had been unable to officiate at Prize Day in either 1981 or 1982, made an appointment early in 1982 to visit the School on the 26th of May. That

he was able to keep this visit, in spite of the fact that it was in the middle of the Falklands crisis, gave much pleasure to the Staff and to the boys. He expressed his thanks ... "I was impressed by all that I saw - by the boys and the obvious spirit of the School."

A letter received in INDEFATIGABLE on 20the June, 1982, after the Falklands campaign, is a sound testimony to the discipline and training.

"Dear Captain,

I would like to thank you and INDEFATIGABLE for the training that I received in life-raft tuition.

I was aboard H.M.S. COVENTRY when she was tragically hit in the Falkland Islands. I felt that the training helped a great deal in my survival and for this I am very grateful. I used to wonder what the point was for going through everything as thorough, but now the reason for it is clear.

I know that my last days in School were never wasted and I am ever thankful for them.

Yours sincerely,
Mark W. (1979 - 80)"

The School kept no Roll of Honour to mark those Old Boys who gave their lives in the service of their country, either on sea, land or air. Two Old Boys are known to have lost their lives in The Falklands.
R.D. Griffin, 1975-1976 ... serving with the Royal Marines.
J.D. Stroud, 1977-1978 .... serving in H.M.S. GLAMORGAN.
I suspect that the Honours Roll would be long and that it is now too late for it to be created. Again, it is too late to record the names of those who have ben awarded medals for bravery over the years. The life of INDEFATIGABLE spans many wars.

The policy of restricting entry to 14 year-old boys for two years and 15 year-olds for one year came under review. If the School entered 13 year-old boys for three years, it was felt that a higher standard of academic achievement must be attained. To this end an extra staff member was engaged. All of this was implemented in 1982.

Soon after he joined the staff as schoolmaster in 1977, Patrick Purser, himself an old CONWAY boy, realised that there was something missing. Incidentally, it must be noted that CONWAY provided many staff members for Inde and greatly enhanced the academic standing of the School. The missing factor was that there was no organisation to which the boys, leaving the INDEFATIGABLE, could belong to enable them to keep in touch with their 'alma mater', and conversely allow the School to keep in touch with their future careers. Finally, after a sceptic response from the Governors, and apathy from the School staff Patrick Purser was given permission to try! Thus, in 1983, with a personal loan of £100 from Bob Youngman, the Captain Headmaster, the INDEFATIGABLE Old boys Association was born. Publicity in the local Liverpool press, on local radio and in nautical magazines, and slowly, very slowly members were recruited. The aims of the Association were very clear:
1. To enable Old Boys to keep in touch with one another.
2. To assist the School in any way possible.
Alas, as we shall see later this second main aim is no longer applicable; but between 1983 and the School's forced closure in 1995, many thousands of pounds had been raised by the Old Boys, not only to fund projects at the School, but also to provide an annual bursary to assist a boy's fees.

The first Old Boys Newsletter was produced in the Autumn of 1983, and in Pat Purser's editorial we read: 'So much has changed over the last century, and hopefully we will continue to change as the school adapts itself to the 21st Century. No organisation can stand still. It must continue to adapt and change to new circumstances and the new requirements of our modern society.' Pat Purser's contribution to this story is invaluable ... so much has been 'lifted' by me from the Newsletters. His wise observations about life in INDEFATIGABLE are well noted. A typical Purser piece of advice to me, as the author, deserves to be recorded. 'Your book doesn't want to be made up solely of anecdotal experiences by the inmates! I tend to find that the 'boys' love to dwell on how 'hard' it was in their days; I feel one has to use a 'pinch of salt' when reading them! Though what they say is probably a much embellished 'truth', we must try and judge by the standards prevailing at the time. We all like to think we were 'tougher' than today's kids. Life was different, that's all. And we accepted it. In a similar way, it is no good castigating Nelson for allowing flogging in his ships. In those days, it was the norm, both afloat and ashore. I'm sure future generations will have a lot to say about our moral behaviour!'

Thank you, Pat Purser. We hear you!

Captain W. Wade, who retired as Captain Superintendent in 1977, wished the Old Boys Newsletter and Association well and added a few thoughts.
'You left us knowing that you were expected to live up to those precious 'three Rs' - Respect - Response - Reliability. We were very fortunate once in being able to invite to Prize Day, Captain W. Bramhill, who was then Master of a passenger cross-channel ship, and himself an Old Boy of INDEFATIGABLE. His old school number was 77 and the reigning 77 was invited to meet him and look after the good Captain for the rest of the day!

'Whether your fortunes, after leaving INDEFATIGABLE, afforded you a career at sea, where, for example, a V.I.P. visiting the Middle East sought comfort in a T. & J. Harrison ship anchored in the Roads, who was greeted on board by the Chief Officer (ex-Inde), introduced to the Captain (ex-Inde), served refreshments by the Chief Steward (ex-Inde) or whether you have climbed some other ladder, I am sure you will have been glad that at one time you were part of INDEFATIGABLE.'

By 1983 it was becoming obvious that INDEFATIGABLE was changing into a public school offering general education within a nautical discipline. Without this change of attitude the future could only be bleak because the shipping industry had ceased to employ boys in any appreciable numbers. However, the School remained full with half of the boys entering the armed services ... the Royal Navy, the Army, the Royal Air Force and the Royal Marines. Not one boy was employed by the Merchant Navy.

1983 was an exceptional year for sport with numerous football, rugby and cricket matches being played against local teams. Orienteering was popular and, with the aid of the Conway Trust, canoeing. Two boys represented Gwynedd County in rugby and one played for North Wales Under 18's. Several boys played hockey with Bangor Clubs.

Mr. Alan Brown, who had served on the Committee since 1958 and had been Chairman for ten years, retired. The new Chairman was Mr. Richard E. Hutson. Dick Hutson had been responsible as Principal in Liverpool for the 'Blue Funnel' cadets and had operated from Aulis, the residential hostel in Riversdale Road in Liverpool. I used to visit Aulis and shared the evening meal with the cadets most Thursday evenings.

By this time, the School was beginning to experience difficulties with recruitment, but with help from the Liverpool Sailors' Home promising £10,000 a year for five years and £30,000 from the Wolfson Foundation, the Bursary Fund was much strengthened. With this help, the recovery was almost immediate and the Autumn Term in 1985 commenced with a full School with fifteen boys benefitting from the Bursary Fund. By this time half of the School's complement comprised lads starting at the age of thirteen.

An Old Boy, Richard Armstrong, aged 88, joined INDEFATIGABLE in 1908 and chatted to Pat Purser for the Newsletter in 1984. "I did not spend all my life at sea, but after the Great War I joined the Mersey Docks and Harbour Company, serving eventually as Piermaster in various parts of the dock complex." During the conversation he sang a little ditty, "Inde boys eat spottom and tack, CONWAY boys drink skilly." Incidentally, Mrs. Armstrong was the daughter of one of INDEFATIGABLE's previous Captains and at that time was still going well at the age of 91.

A few lines appeared in the Liverpool Daily Post dated 12th July, 1984.

HISTORY IS MADE AFTER 120 YEARS

'Old boys of the once-famous Liverpool training ship, INDEFATIGABLE, last Tuesday held their first reunion dinner in the 120-year history of the School. It was the occasion of the Annual Prize Giving. The Second Lord of the Admiralty was the guest of honour.'

It was with sadness that we learned of the death of another Inde boy, Captain William Eustance, in May 1986. He had probably been at INDEFATIGABLE from 1919 to 1920. He had risen to Senior Captain in Harrison Line, spending fifty years at sea. He was torpedoed off the Bahamas and badly wounded when his ship was bombed in the Mediterranean. In 1962 he was awarded the O.B.E. after playing a prominent part in relief work when Belize, then the capital of British Honduras, was hit by hurricane Hattie. During my time with the Mersey Mission to Seamen he was a tower of strength and information in the College of the Sea Library at Kingston House, guiding many a young officer through his 'tickets'. He gave of his time entirely voluntarily. INDEFATIGABLE has produced superb characters and professional seamen and many personal friends. Bill had died in a Southport Hospital at the age of 81 and I had the privilege of conducting his funeral service.

A.D. Eady, 1943-1944, was the Catering Officer on board M.V. AUTHOR ... Autumn 1986 Newsletter.
'When Author sailed from Liverpool on 28the May, 1986, we had taken on board a casket containing the ashes of the late Captain Eustance, O.B.E. On Sunday, 1st June, Captain R. Bell, Master of AUTHOR, held a brief but moving service on the after deck before committing the ashes to the deep. For the record, on AUTHOR there were two ex-Inde boys, myself and Stephen Jeffrey, who was serving as Fourth Engineer on board.'

John Tranmer, History Teacher, 1981-1986, remembers Peter Burrell. Here are a few extracts from the article produced in Newsletter 29.
'Peter had spent most of his life before Inde in the Army and had specialised as a P.T. Instructor. He had an insatiable appetite for

Peter Burrell

1973 - 1995

learning ... photography, fly fishing, and target shooting were just a few .. and loved to share his newly acquired skills.

'He was a hard task master and demanded high standards, but always gave extra time to those in need.

'What of the notorious keys? Peter believed in swift justice. A flick on the buttocks from the leather thong attached to his keys and the matter was sorted out on the spot. More serious transgressions, e.g. a leading hand who failed to clean the 'abbo block' properly, would lead to the dreaded key end. Approximately ten keys at the end of a metre-long thong, swirled with enthusiasm and aimed with deadly accuracy would bring a tear to the eyes of even the toughest Inde boy. And, the experience left a lasting impression, both literally and metaphorically as I recall seeing more than one boy emerge from the showers with the clear imprint of a Yale key on his bottom!

'It would be true to say the Inde has featured its fair share of unique characters, none more so than Peter Burrell.'

He was missed greatly and truly loved by all ... except maybe one or two.

Captain R.T. Youngman, B.A., had been at the helm for ten years. It had not been easy, as the change from the traditional ratings training had given way to a more conventional academic curriculum required by the new educational standards demanded by the government. He had worked tirelessly to implement the changes needed by reducing the emphasis on practical seamanship, taught by instructors, and increasing it on academic studies taught by qualified teachers. This in turn meant higher salaries to be paid and thus higher school fees. At the same time, he had to keep a wary eye on the need to preserve viable numbers on the School's books. A difficult juggling act! By 1986 he felt he had had enough and sought early retirement from the Governors.

The staff of INDEFATIGABLE approached the Governors to appoint an academic headmaster in order to break the traditional link associated with the title Captain Headmaster, but it would be a further three years before such a radical step could be taken. In the meantime, the Governors approached Captain Terry Beggs to succeed Captain Youngman towards the end of 1986.

Captain Beggs, M.Sc, Extra Master, had served at sea in the Blue Funnel Line before advancing into nautical education and training. He had been Principal at Aulis, in charge of the Blue Funnel Cadets, until in 1986 the Company, with only six ships remaining, closed their operations. I had worked well alongside Terry Beggs for a number of years and knew his impressive record of experience in education and marine training. It was a good appointment.

Captain Beggs, as Captain Headmaster of INDEFATIGABLE, endeavoured to broaden the boys' opportunities through improvement in academic resources, the fabric of the school, outdoor pursuits and the boys eventual employment or further education. Such development, however, had to be achieved in parallel with the ethos and character of the School, not at their expense.

In 1989 the Governors decided to appoint Peter White to the new post of Head of Academic Studies, but, as Captain Beggs had already decided to resign, for personal reasons, Mr. White's appointment was up-graded to that of Headmaster.

Mr. P.D. White, B.Sc., from the minor public school, Bedstone College, where he had been serving as Boarding House Master, Head of Maths and Sixth Form Tutor for the past seven years. An added 'bonus' he brought to the job was the fact that 40 per cent of the college pupils were from service families. Aged 36, and single, Mr. White knew the area well in that he was educated at Colwyn Bay High School and obtained his honours degree in mathematics at Bangor University.

During the year, 1986, the major administrative affairs of the School were transferred from Liverpool to Anglesey and following this move, Mr K.R. Edmonson, the Administrator, and Mr. L.R. Ridyard, the Secretary, retired from office. They had worked long and hard for the School. Mr. L. Dodd was appointed Secretary in place of Mr. Ridyard and the Bursar Mr. E.J. Chiverell took on extra administrative duties in the School.

There was much improvement of the fabric in 1986 with the addition of five new classrooms, computer facilities and an outdoor pursuits centre. The library and catering facilities were upgraded. The workshop was re-equipped and a technical drawing room created.

During the year, forty-five boys left. Fourteen went into the Royal Navy, fourteen into the Army, five into the Royal Air Force, five into the Merchant Navy, three into further education and four into other jobs or training.

The Editorial in Autumn 1988 Newsletter indicated the problems that faced the Inde.
'INDEFATIGABLE, in a way, is still a 'ship at sea'. She has weathered many storms in the past, and today is meeting squalls of a type she has never encountered before. What are they?
1.   Falling numbers of young men in the country.
2.   A decrease of manpower in the three Armed Services, and the Merchant Navy ... our traditional outlets.
3.   A demand for higher standards from the Royal Navy.
4.   An increasing demand from industry for young people with a sound academic education.
5.   Lack of sufficient applicants to join INDEFATIGABLE, therefore little or no selection, therefore lower academic standards than one would wish.

6.   New restrictions on the M.O.D. Boarding School Grant for Service children, which also now includes a parental contribution of 10% (at the moment).
For all these reasons, a determined 'Marketing exercise' is underway.'

The uniqueness of the school was emphasised, not to mention the very reasonable fees (currently, approximately £3,000 a year). Various thoughts emerged. The present age spread was 13 to 16 and should be broadened to 11 to 16. A greater concentration on the education from 11 to 14 would enable boys to be literate, numerate and confident to tackle G.C.S.E. courses when they join the main school at 14. This would mean the provision of a totally separate Junior Complex. The aim was to be a good school for the average boy with a better chance of achieving G.C.S.E. success. It was a daunting vision for the future of the school, demanding a fundamental change of attitude towards the aspirations of parents seeking a boarding education for their sons. It was vital to realise that INDEFATIGABLE could produce a small, unique community, which could not be found in large comprehensive schools or in the concentrated atmosphere of more expensive boarding schools.

It is not true to say that Snowdon over-shadowed INDEFATIGABLE, but like a shadow it was always there ... apart from the odd bit of Welsh impenetrable mist. It was, however, an ever-present challenge. Howard Trillo of the History Department makes a contribution which will bring back many a memory for the Inde boys. (Taken from the 125the Birthday Edition Newsletter.)

' "Not the most spectacular route, nor the most difficult, but certainly one of the most interesting" ... such is my verdict on the Watkin Path, which leads from the valley of Nantgwynant, just above Beddgelert, to the summit of Snowdon, 3,560 feet above sea level. I usually try to avoid Snowdon in the summer as the peak acts as the proverbial 'honey-pot' for the swarms of tourists, all would-be Chris Boningtons, who do their best to spoil the peace and solitude of the mountain experience. However, mid-June saw me organising a trip onto the hill, with "Y Wyddfa" the much-demanded goal by the 'team' of mountaineers (ten

boys who insisted on taking the 'old man of the mountains' as their mascot - Mr. Purser, that is).

'The Watkin Path ascends gradually into the valley of Cwm Llan, and as we climbed, the landmarks came and went: attractive waterfalls and pools, ideal for 'teasing' boys who want to stop after only fifteen minutes walking; the Gladstone Rock, where the great 19the Century Prime Minister addressed the quarry workers and their families in the election tour of the 1880's; the group of houses and work buildings of the quarry itself, set below the head of the valley, just where the path gets steeper - but if you're lucky, as we were, you now have a view of your destination to spur you on.

'Elements remembered from that June day include the heat, the frequent encouragement needed for some of the boys, the extensive view to the north from the col below the final summit pyramid, and, of course, the summit itself, where I was asked for directions to the 'Snowdon Horseshoe' (a lengthy and technically-difficult mountaineering route)

... by an elderly couple wearing shorts and plimsoles!

'Despite several faint-hearts halfway up, everyone (I think) enjoyed the trip and everyone got to the top (one boy had attempted, and failed, twice before, and at least one other was frightened of heights - see next article!). Although limbs were aching, more than one person was rushing the last few yards to the swimming pools passed earlier in the day ... and the phrase "This one's deeper and with a better waterfall" seemed to be repeated continuously as mountaineers became acquatic explorers for a while.'

But what did the boys think about that 'not most difficult' route? Chris Alderton (fifth year) gives his version of 'Mr. Trillo's Agony Walk'

'We finished our breakfast and went up to the Outdoor Activities Store, to get our boots on and collect the other equipment needed for the walk. We then jumped into the School mini-bus and 'pedalled' our way to Pont Bethania, the chosen starting point of our walk up Snowdon. We didn't bother to lock the mini-bus because nobody would nick it!

'Before we started off, Mr. Trillo dished out the suntan lotion, but we hadn't even done a mile before people started complaining about the heat. Then Piesse-Mills highlighted the walk with a nose bleed.

'As we were walking up the path we had quite a view: the mountains, the trees, the waterfalls and plunge pools, and the skinny-dippers! It was at this point that we had our first ten minute break ... twenty minutes later we set off again. Within a short time we had lost sight of Wood, Hicks and Selby, but we caught up with them at some old ruins which used to be the miners' huts. By the time we reached these huts, we could see the summit of Snowdon clearly.

'We carried on walking until we reached a large rock, where we had some lunch. Finishing my own lunch, I went ahead to see if we could find Mr. Purser, Wood and Co. It was when I caught up with them that I saw Long John Silver in his second life ... as a one-legged seagull! It was only a little way from here that the final four-hundred-foot climb started. This was the bit I didn't like because the path was steep, we could see all the way down, and I don't like heights!

'When we got to the top, Mr. Trillo broke open his piggy bank and bought us all an ice lolly, and a beer for Mr. Purser. Oh yes, Mr. Trillo was also off the orange juice. We had a couple of photos taken, then it was back down. When we got back to the pools we all had a swim ... all, that is, except Mr. Purser. We finally got back to school pretty tired out.

'One word of advice, next time you are asked to go on an 'easy' walk with Mr. Trillo and Mr. Purser ... say 'No' ... OR YOU'LL REGRET IT!'

Outward Bound activities were ever on the school map and were an important part of life in Inde. There was a three-year Outward Activity and Seamanship course. The boys devoted half a day each week and the emphasis was on 'Learning and Fun'. The Lord Derby O.A. Challenge Cup was coveted by each Division. There were six challenging events.

1.	Mountain Run	Snowdonia
2	Canoe Races	Menai Straits
3	Tent Pitching speed test	School Grounds
4	Assault Course	School Grounds
5	Initiative Tests	School Grounds
6	Orienteering	Beddgelert Forest

The boys were out all weathers, from hill walking in 80 mph winds - hill crawling - to the only hot day of the summer on Aberfraw Beach! 1988 saw the introduction of Abseiling, which many found frightening, but fun. There was also a weekend to Towyn to visit the Joint Services Camp ... this included a trek into the mountains, a 'death slide' of 80 feet into a lake and a vertical descent into a mine shaft. Mike Ellesmore organised it and remarked, "God help us, they want to do it all over again!"

1989 was the 125the Anniversary of the School. Three prime objectives were set for the year. First to open the School to boys from the age of eleven and thus provide full secondary stage education. Secondly, the School aimed to provide a breadth of curriculum which would meet National standards. Lastly, but by no means least, to redefine and reinforce those aspects of INDEFATIGABLE way of life which contribute to the wellbeing and success of the young men in their chosen careers. Much new building and adaption of old buildings would be needed. The estimated cost of all these schemes was £300,000. The future of INDEFATIGABLE was deemed to depend upon the fulfilment of these aims.

A letter was received from the Duke of Edinburgh.

'Buckingham Palace.

INDEFATIGABLE School has a long and successful record for training boys for life at sea, but this particular type of education is just as relevant to other professions and occupations. Using the sea as a workshop, it is possible to develop qualities of character that will be of benefit to individuals throughout their careers.

'I commend the courageous decision of the Governing Body to widen and expand the entry and to improve the facilities at the school. I have no doubt that in the years to come there will be many former pupils who will be able to look back with gratitude to the start they were given by INDEFATIGABLE School.

Philip.'

A new teaching block provided five new classrooms and two new science laboratories. This meant that all academic subjects were now taught in a custom built complex, leaving the main building free for domestic enlargement and accommodation. At the same time a 'state of the art' Sports Hall, the envy of other Anglesey schools was built on the site of the old kitchen gardens, paid for by the generosity, once again, of the Liverpool Sailors' Home Trust.

The battle for survival instilled an urgency into INDEFATIGABLE.

It was obvious that the School could not stand still and survive. More changes were ahead and essential. The School was to work a six-day week in line with other boarding schools and to compensate for the extra work entailed, the length of the School Term was to be reduced. More space was required, more staff were to be enrolled for the expanded curriculum and more money was urgently needed. In order to keep the tradition and character of the School it was the intention to start a C.C.F. unit.

A new uniform was introduced. The No 8's, which was the previous working dress, had been replaced by black shoes, black trousers, blue shirt with epaulettes, school tie with the Crest and a naval pullover also bearing the INDEFATIGABLE crest. The Petty Officer and Chief Petty Officer boys had white shirts and black ties. The aim was to improve the appearance and enhance the naval aspect of the School. It was decided to keep the No. 1 uniform for ceremonial purposes.

The boys were no longer to wear school uniform when at 'liberty'. The Headmaster stated that boys were often picked upon by locals and that naval uniform invited abuse.

The Liverpool Sailors' Home Trust gave a donation of £66,443 plus their committed £10,000. The 125the Anniversary Appeal for £250,000 by March 1990 had reached £146,815, which included a further gift of £50,000 from the Liverpool Sailors' Home Trust. This was remarkable generosity and the future was built upon it. Could it continue?

The new Headmaster wrote in the Autumn 1989 Newsletter.
'There can't be many parents who haven't heard of the National

Curriculum. They might not know what it involves, but I am sure that most will have read that it is a good thing and every school should offer it.

'Where does that leave INDEFATIGABLE? The National Curriculum includes Art/Craft, Music and a Modern Language. Apart from a small amount of Art and Music done on a voluntary basis, there was none on the curriculum. A handful of boys studied either French or German, being taught in the evenings on the odd night per week. Obviously INDEFATIGABLE was not anywhere near satisfying the National Curriculum.

'Starting from the beginning of this term I have introduced Art/Craft and Music on the timetable for our younger boys. We still need a foreign language, but it is planned that this will be offered from September 1990. The demands of the G.C.S.E. course, with all the course work that this involves, dictated that I increase considerably the amount of prep that boys must do. Fourth form boys now do twice as much prep as they previously did and fifth form do more than twice as much. As the curriculum expands it will be necessary to increase it further.'

The construction of a new Junior Boys Boarding House was under way. It was planned to start the intake from September 1990, but that had to be advanced because the demand was there.

The new Headmaster ended his article with challenging words. 'Further, I am also of the view that these changes are of fundamental importance to the future of the school. It would not be going too far to say our very survival depends upon them.'

Some extracts from first year essays (eleven year olds!) on the subject of 'My First week at School' are of great interest. The year is 1990.

'... The things I like about the School are the sports, some of the work and the food. I don't like getting up early. This week I have done French, Maths, Science, Sporting Activities, History and English. I

have learned how to count up to fifteen in French ...'

Robert Rowlands

'... It's good here, but I miss home, and I see children cry because they're homesick. I like some of the teachers. I don't like a few of the teachers though. This week has been very hard, but I keep trying. I have learned a lot this week. I hope to get better at this ...'

Anthony Whitehead

'... The School is like a second home to me. The food is alright, but I don't like some of it. I find the School strange some times, because I have never been away from home without my Mum ... I don't like going to bed so early, or getting up so early ... We have learnt to be polite, very kind and very very good. My ambition is to go in the Navy as an Admiral, or go as an Admiral on the Q.E.2; so I can travel the world and give my family good support.'

Colin Kelly

From Melbourne (Oz), via e-mail and other such magic, have come the memories of Paul Martin, Inde 1989-93. His brother Alan was also on board ... 1991-95. Both were in Rodney Division.

Paul states that he was one of the first to be taken in at the age of twelve. His memories are of change and the winding down to the inevitable end. 'In many ways I feel that the true value ... the name, location and traditions and history were never fully harnessed. The School could have been a great place had it embraced the past, yet changed for the better. What stronger traditions could there have been! After reading the Old Boys memoirs over the years one thing has become increasingly apparent to me ... the impression given is that every boy who passed before you had it tougher and that every boy who joined after you had it easier. "I had it worse than you and am proud of it!"

'When I arrived at the school in '89, civvies were still locked up in a storage room all term, so we wore our No.1 uniform on liberty and we still bumpered all the floorboards with cast iron bumpers and cloths. Dorms were large and split by Divisions, we had blankets, iron beds and divisional duties. I remember polishing King Billy's back with Brasso before a parade during the depth of a Welsh winter. We were even still punished by a stint of hours under the ship's bell. We all suffered the sort of hunger that goes with very physical days and your last food of the day at 5 pm. On top of that we still had time-tabled 'dhobey' lessons dedicated to washing clothes.

'By the time I left, there were lockers in rooms, civvies on liberty, cleaners to do the floors and clothes, duvets, single beds, a chocolate vending machine, small dorms split by year and divisional duties were minimal. We even had to wear shirts, ties, shoes and V neck jumpers instead of the old No. 8s and white trainers!

'In truth, the look of the place may have changed, but School never did. Education was a dirty word to the end. Most of the boys still came from troubled backgrounds and spent most of their time either trying to prove that they could hack it or trying to do a runner. I never once heard the word 'college'. And when I reflect on the beatings that the younger boys received whilst wrapped in sheets ... always by older boys who 'had the right to do it' ... along with the well organised fights that a teacher had no chance of getting within hundred yards of without a nozzer raising the alarm, do I wonder what the point of it all was!

'Personally, I endured more than I enjoyed ... yet somehow miss the old place. At the end of the day, if I ever see old King Billy in the Maritime Museum instead of on the end of the parade ground, I am certain that it will all feel very strange.'

Thank you Paul Martin (1989-93) from Oz. Endings are invariably sad and opinions are purely subjective and judgements are based on one's immediate knowledge.

Chapter 9
The Closure of the Indefatigable

The Annual Chairman's Report in 1993 made salutary reading. Alarm bells were ringing. '1992 and 1993 proved difficult years for a number of reasons, not least the necessity for considerable capital expenditure coupled with lean years for recruitment. However, our capital expenditure has strengthened our position in respect of accommodation for eleven to sixteen year-old boarders and will allow sufficient classroom space for starting our Sixth Form.

'Over the last few years there has been a trend by Local Authorities to phase out the grants which enabled boys to attend INDEFATIGABLE.

'The Education Acts over the years have required us to alter the direction of the School and required us to offer an increased number of subjects.'

Those two basic facts were to prove to be fatal.

The decision to close the School was announced to the staff on 1st July, 1995. In truth, closure had been imminent for three years, when the staff had agreed to take a 10% cut in salaries for two full terms. The decision of Gwynedd Council in 1992 not to support boys in the School except for those already in residence had proved a further nail. The general recession in the country and cuts in defence employment did not help, and the final hurdle was the rapid decline in numbers ... the next school year would only have housed one hundred pupils, with only four for the first year and twelve for the second. There truly was no way forward.

To put it bluntly, the School had to close because there were, to use an understandable phrase, 'not enough bums on seats.' No School could possibly survive that situation. Many folk wanted to blame somebody or anybody, a natural but fruitless pastime. In truth the reasons for the ultimate closure had been well sign-posted for some thirty years.

The editorial in the 1995 Newsletter analysed the problems.

Historically the role of the School was to take in 'the destitute and orphan sons of seamen'. This obviously rather quickly had to change to taking in boys of fifteen years after they had finished their schooling. That remained for many decades, but the first real threat to the 'status quo' was the raising of the school leaving age (ROSLA) to sixteen. For the first time in the history of Inde the academic time-table became important. A laboratory and engineering workshops were built and more staff had to be employed. Other similar institutions felt the same pressure. ARETHUSA and GANGES went to the wall. Above all, help with numbers from the Naval world faded away as defence cuts were made.

INDEFATIGABLE responded by taking in thirteen year-old boys to counter the falling intake figures. This imposed another great strain upon the finances, staff and accommodation.

The savage decline of our merchant fleet almost closed what had been the natural outlet for the boys and that left the Armed Services and Industry. This meant that the academic demands were yet again increased. Boys had taken the burden of most of the domestic duties in the past, but now more classroom time was needed. The increase in domestic staff led to greater costs. The big challenge of change was now becoming evident. Was the INDEFATIGABLE to remain a Sea Training School or enter into competition with the well established, traditional boarding schools?

The maximum intake was only about 160 and this was on the edge of viability. By the mid-eighties sponsorship by local authorities was drying up. Finally in 1992 Gwynnedd Education Authority withdrew support and the M.O.D. cut back on the Services Boarding School Grant.

Nationally, boarding education was losing popularity and the schools resorted to Day Pupils and 'Co-ed' to meet the shortfall! Geographically, on Anglesey there was insufficent local population for Day Schooling and it met with negligible response; 'Co-ed' was completely non-viable.

So it was finally decided to 'go for broke'. Admission age was reduced to eleven and a sixth form established, all this to compete on a level playing field with other Independent Schools. The cost was vast and there was little time. INDEFATIGABLE was not well endowed and the modest investments were liquidated, but remarkably generous grants came from nautical charities and building plans began to materialise. Time was vital to survival. What probably ought to have been undertaken decades before was at last under way. Over the next three years a new classroom complex, accommodation blocks and a sports hall were completed in record time.

Was it too expensive, too fast and too late?

The overall plan was to increase the size of the School to nearer 200 pupils. However, numbers only trickled up to near 160, but the Junior School side trickled down and almost dried up entirely. That was the end. There were no investments to buy time. There were no finances available to meet the heavy maintenance and insurance costs and large wages and salaries bill. Inde was living well beyond her means.

For 130 years there had ever been 'fairy godmothers' which had come to the aid of Inde and kept her afloat. Even the reason for the existence of the School was in doubt ... the decline of shipping had stretched back over thirty years! The basic, cruel fact was that Inde was just another boarding school which 'couldn't make it', as the very need for its existence faded away.

The Chairman of Governors said: "On June 29th when the Board very regretfully reached the decision to close, the size of the School at the start of the next school year would have been 100, with only 4 pupils in the First Year and 12 pupils in the Second Year, and this is too low a number to enable the pupils to receive the quality of education, enjoy the social activities and receive the pastoral care which the parents and pupils are entitled to expect from a school with INDEFATIGABLE's reputation.

"The latest proposals to the Board suggest that there could be as few as 40 pupils, if the School is re-opened on the 1st September, compared with the average of 145 pupils in recent years."

The School had debts of almost one million pounds.

The closure obviously caused much pain to all those involved. Let the media tell the story as it unfolded.

The Liverpool Daily Post sported banner headlines on Monday 3rd July, 1995.

PUPIL CRISIS SINKS SCHOOL
Island bombshell as top services training college forced to shut

'Now 40 members of the staff are without a job, 120 boys are without a school, and the Anglesey economy has suffered a severe setback, say islanders.

The Chairman of Governors, Councillor Donald Stewart, of Eryrys, near Mold, said the decision to close the school was inevitable. There is a great shortage of pupils and we would have been around thirty pupils short this coming year, so the decision was unavoidable.'

The Bangor Chronicle on the 27th July.

FIGHT ON TO SAVE SCHOOL

'The Fight to save one of the area's most historic schools has been stepped up by parents and supporters. They have set up an action group and have already managed to secure a stay of execution until next month.

'To look into a viable financial future for the School, the Action Group has secured the services of lawyers, accountants, surveyors and marketing and insolvency experts to help them.

BACKING

'Teachers at the School have agreed to a thirty per cent reduction in wages to help the school survive and the group have received the backing of all the parents of present pupils and pupils who will be joining the School at the next term.

'Last Friday they met with two representatives of the School's governing board, including the chairman, in Liverpool. A spokesman for the Action Group, Michael Livingstone said: "Although a most negative viewpoint was maintained throughout by the Board, sanity prevailed for what was the only positive solution, given by the action group to the crisis. The Board subsequently advised the group that a stay of execution was to be granted until August 4th, 1995. A new management, however, realises that a purely nautical slant cannot be its main reason for continuing. It will be ready to take under its wing all those who seek a well-rounded, family-valued, general education that will meet the needs of all careers in the modern world of today and the next century. We also aim to have more integration with the local community in the future and bring in Welsh teachers."

'The secretary of the INDEFATIGABLE Old Boys' Association, Mr. Patrick Purser of Beaumaris said: "We would desperately like to see INDEFATIGABLE carry on as a school and we would welcome anything which would carry this tradition on. We are basically in a 'wait and see' situation and it is up to the Board of Governors now to accept or reject any new plans." '

The Daily Telegraph had included the same information and added: 'The curriculum includes compulsory courses in nautical skills and sea survival. Pupil numbers at the £7,500 a-year school had held steady at about 160 for the past two decades until the roll fell by 30 last year. The governors believed that demand for future places would be insufficient.'

Bangor and Anglesey Mail, 30th August, 1995.
'The Action Group have admitted defeat. Last week the governors rejected the rescue package. The chairman of governors says that keeping the School open would be impossible, because the number of pupils would have dropped to 100 by next month.

'Brian Edge, the former Maths teacher at the School who was leading the campaign to keep the School alive expressed his disappointment that the governors had rejected their proposals. Mr. Edge added that the action group may still take legal advice about the future of the School, and said that if they manage to buy the School before next year, it may open earlier for outdoor pursuits.'

The Chronicle, 5th October, 1995, carried a notice under the Insolvency Act, 1986, stating that a Liquidator had been appointed and invited Creditors should send the necessary details on or before the 31st day of December, 1995.

The Mail, Wednesday, 29th November, 1995.

SCHOOL'S FINALLY UNDER HAMMER

'More than £100,000 was raised by the auction of the contents of Anglesey's defunct INDEFATIGABLE boarding school. A packed hall was witness to the sale at the Llanfairpwll school last Tuesday, organised by Liverpool firm Edward Symmonds and Partners. The school's Old Boys' Association was among those bidding, buying the school's historic ship's bell for £1,150.'

A letter in Liverpool Daily Post, Tuesday, 5th December, 1995, gave realism to the saga.

FLYING THE FLAG

'It saddens us when we continue to hear people asking, "Will the INDEFATIGABLE School reopen?" The INDEFATIGABLE and National Sea Training School for Boys ceased to exist as a limited company on July 1st last.

'Recently the School's contents were auctioned at Plas Llanfair. When a suitable purchaser comes forward, the estate will be sold. Only then will it be possible to assess the position.

'Hopefully, there will be enough capital to settle debts, which are considerable, and to set up an INDEFATIGABLE Trust to provide grants to deserving youngsters eager to follow a maritime career.

'In this way, the ethos of the founding fathers of the Inde will be maintained and the INDEFATIGABLE flag will fly again to serve young people as has been done so successfully for 131 years.
> H. Traynor, Chairman,
> P. Purser, Secretary,
> INDEFATIGABLE Old Boys' Association.'

That really was the last word on the matter.

Liverpool Daily Post, Wednesday, 23rd October, 1996.

INDEFATIGABLE MAY REOPEN AS TOP MoD TRAINING BASE

'The famous INDEFATIGABLE School, which closed with massive debts last year, could be sold off to the Ministry of Defence as an outdoor pursuits training centre, it emerged yesterday. The MoD wants to restructure its adventure training for the armed forces and believes the Anglesey school, which was put in the hands of liquidators 16 months ago, may be ideal.

'Whether the Ministry buys the site, which has an asking price close on £500,000, depends on it securing planning permission for development work.'

The Mail, Wednesday, 27th November, 1996.

DEFENCE MINISTRY BUY OFF SCHOOL

'The INDEFATIGABLE School, which closed last year with debts of nearly £1 million, has been bought by the Ministry of Defence.'

So ended 131 years of tradition.

As the years passed, when the merchant fleet of this country sadly diminished, this really was the end for the School. Back in the 1960's the Inde, although carrying on for the sons of those with slender means, was forced to become 'a school' for the first time. Then the sponsoring of boys by Local Authorities dried up and when the Gwynedd Education Authority finally withdrew its generous sponsorship of local boys, the way ahead was bleak. The rearguard action was well fought over three decades, but the end, however painful and distressing, was inevitable.

To ensure our economic survival more than ninety per cent of our trade in this country must go by sea. We have obviously lost the historic ability to carry our own trade to look after ourselves and these days we almost completely depend upon foreign ships. Too often, third-world crews are employed at sea in order to keep us prosperous and alive. No longer are we a seagoing nation.

Not wanting to end this chapter on a sour note, and with regret and sadness, I have chosen a letter which was sent to the Newsletter, Souvenir Copy, 1995. It was written by Gerald Morgan, 1939-1940, with all the nostalgia and love that epitomises an Old Inde Boy.
'Thank you very much for your surprise letter of 20th, beautifully timed for the 54th anniversary of the day they cheered me (surprise) away from the old INDEFATIGABLE. A journey into light you might say,

only I left for grimy Newcastle where George Formby in the comic film got fired through the torpedo tube just as the bomb dropped in the street outside. The REAL torpedoes in due course, and that first voyage to the Isles of Light Ancient Antilla, ended with our passage past Anglesey, recalled by your letter with the three Cymric dragons on the 19p stamps, and two Welsh addresses including Llanfair Pwll((…llantysiliogogogoch?).

'Surprise too, at hearing from a CONWAY aboard Inde. Hostilities in the old days, although CONWAY's motor boat once gave ours a tow amongst the ice flows of horrible January, 1940. We had to lower the cutters, and the water froze on our oars! I was perhaps the only Inde boy on CONWAY, when as cox'n of the 'stinker' I once carried Captain Cochrane, V.C., to dine with Captain Goddard. I've met a few CONWAYs, a happy crowd.

'Always I've admired John Masefield - "The gull's way and the whale's way" is exactly what Inde and CONWAY trained for. The gull knows his part and watches to see if you know yours; whether you are of the stuff that can suffer and get through, come what may. "A grey mist on the sea's face … " Someone should update 'Sea Fever' for the grey convoys. Joseph Conrad, though he put his son through WORCESTER, made two CONWAYs the heroes of his story, 'The Secret Sharer'. He too knew life on ship's deck after ship's deck; like a segmented street across what he called, "the restless mirror of the infinite".

That letter just about puts in into a nutshell. That is the Inde spirit..

'And all I ask is a merry yarn from a laughing fellow-rover,
And a quiet sleep and a sweet dream when the long trick's over.'

John Masefield, 'Sea Fever'.

Chapter 10
The Indefatigable
Old Boys Association

INDEFATIGABLE is no longer in existence, except in the memories of many old and not-so-old seafarers and ex-students. The School closed in 1995. The demand for sea-going by that time had almost ceased and the original purpose was lost in the changes of time.

The Old Boys Association, founded in 1983 (or was it 1982?) still thrives, holding an annual reunion on Anglesey, and publishing a bi-annual newsletter, to enable Old Boys to keep in touch with one another. When the School closed in 1995, the chairman, Harry Traynor, and the secretary, Pat Purser, after seeing the CONWAY memorial stained glass window in a chapel at Birkenhead, were fired with the idea that Inde ought to have one too! A well known Anglesey artist, Ieuan Williams, produced the design which was subsequently approved by the Church. A local stained glass artist was commissioned to construct the window, the cost of just over £6,000 being met by the generosity of the Liverpool Sailors' Home Trust; and in 1998, before an assembly of Old Boys, the window, erected in the north transept of St. Mary's Church, used by generations of Inde boys, was dedicated by the President of the Association, Lionel Storrs, and blessed by the Vicar of the parish of Llanfair Pwll. There it stands today, a lasting memorial to all past boys of the School since its inauguration in 1864.

Another dream to be fulfilled was an erection of a memorial to all those boys who gave their lives for their country. This was to take the form of a tree planting ceremony at the national forestry project at Alwres, north of Lichfield. An S.O.S was sent to all members asking for donations. In a very short time enough money had been collected to pay for an oak sapling, a memorial plaque and an oak bench, so that in years to come relatives and friends will be able to sit in comfort beneath the spreading branches of a mighty oak and ponder upon earlier times!

Alas, the final dream of these two could not be realised. It was hoped that once the School was sold and the dust had settled, there would be enough in the kitty to create an INDEFATIGABLE Trust. The idea was to perpetuate the name and good works of the INDEFATIGABLE by providing funds for deserving youngsters to pursue a maritime career. However, far from there being monies left over, the School was bankrupt. Even members of the teaching staff were unable to claim any salaries still due to them.

Having been actively involved with the Association for so many years and with 'anno domini' setting in, Harry Traynor and Pat Purser decided to hand over the reins to younger hands. Perhaps, one day they might be able to fulfil the final dream!

What of today's Old Boys ... where are they now?

Gary Cross, 1978-79, gives us two stories. They are produced 'as is'.
'Way back in '83, I was serving in the Army in Belize. Half way through the six-month tour, I was granted R & R leave, and decided to take it in Florida. After a couple of days in the sunshine state, I took a cruise from Miami over to Nassau, Bahamas, to relax over a gin sling or two and to recharge my batteries in preparation for the second part of my tour.

'After docking in Nassau, I left the ship and proceeded towards the custom house, passport in hand, ready to chill out on a beach somewhere, anywhere, as long as I was as far away from a British serviceman as it was possible to be, of whatever ilk, soldier, sailor or airman.

'My dreams were about to be shattered. I looked ahead and saw docked in front of us, a Type 21 Frigate by the name of H.M.S. AMBUSCADE, the West Indies Guard Ship. "No problem," I thought. "Nobody has a clue who I am and I'm not about to introduce myself." I walked past the gangway of the ship, confident that I would be sipping something blue, probably with a cherry and an umbrella in the top, very, very soon. "GAZZAAA!!!"
I heard that clearly, shouted at the top of a voice, from somewhere near the top of the gangway. Thinking that I had imagined it, I casually

strolled past, thoughts turning again towards something containing angostura bitters.

"OI! CROSSY, GET YOUR ARSE UP HERE NOW!"

The same dulcet tones wafted down from above.

'Knowing there was no way to avoid an imminent pressgang, I looked up to see him, Mike White, ex British Forces school brat from Hohne, Germany, ex INDEFATIGABLE boy, now standing guard in his shining white tropicals, the pride of Her Majesty's Navy.

"I'm off duty anytime now, so get your sorry arse down to the ratings mess, and no, I won't take no for an answer!"

'My thoughts of a poncy, coconut-laced, Caribbean beverage served by a dusky bird in a grassy skirt soon vanished. In my despair, all I could see on the horizon was Lamb's Navy Rum, Carlsberg by the pallet-load, a fart-lighting competition, no eyebrows in the morning ... and one almighty headache.

'As expected, I achieved most of those things. But we had a grand time doing it, and the lads in the ratings' mess wouldn't let me put my hand in the pocket once. Me and Mike had not seen each other for five years, but it felt like only yesterday, chewing the fat, talking not only about our days at school together in Germany, but of course, reminiscing about the times we had at Inde, both good and bad. I never did make it through passport control. Mike and his mates carried me off the ship and put me back onto the cruiser, whereupon I woke up a number of hours later docked in Miami, wondering whether it had all been a dream ...'

Gary Cross tells another tale for us ... again totally unabridged.

'A quick fast forward from 1983 to 1995. By now I had left the Army, tried my hand at a number of things, but the lure of a uniform got the better of me. I exchanged the Queen's shilling for the Queen's Oath of Allegiance and was serving as a Constable with the West Midlands Police at Steelhouse Lane Police Station in Birmingham.

'Still being a probationer, I had drawn the short straw, and found myself one Saturday morning acting as the 'Striker' or Gaoler, as it is known. My main job was to assist the Custody Sergeant in sorting out the prisoners for the early turn, making sure that they were fed, watered and generally as happy as you can be, whilst banged up in a grim, smelly, sweltering lock-up.

"Go and check on our customers," the Custody Stripe growled at me sarcastically. So, with cell keys dangling from my belt, I went to check on the first, who had been arrested for a public order offence, after a tiff with his girlfriend in a city hotel. He had refused to calm down, and after a minor struggle with the 'officers of the watch' had been arrested and taken back to the nick to sober up and calm down.

'I opened the cell hatch and looked at the sorry figure stretched out on the mattress, still fast asleep.
"Wakey, wakey, breakfast is about to be served, Mr. Wakefield," I said, reading his name off the custody sheet. Just as I was about to launch into full sarcastic mode, asking him whether he had enjoyed a pleasant night's sleep at the Hotel de Steelhouse Lane, I was rendered speechless by one thought bouncing around in my head. No, it can't be, I thought, can it? This CANNOT be the same lad that made my life a misery whenever he could at the INDEFATIGABLE all those years ago. Not only my life, but anyone else's that got in the way! Can it? I was still unconvinced, as he had not recognised me, but I didn't want to make the dreadful mistake of letting the cell door shut behind me, just in case. I hastily made my excuses and beat a retreat through the cell door, grateful for an extra three inches of steel between me and the West Midland's Most Wanted.
"Sarge, the bloke in cell 17 is being a bit economical with the truth."
"Whaddyamean", he growled, still moody after walking into the hell that is Steelhouse Lane Police Station the morning after the night before.
"I mean, Sarge, that he has given false details, and that he is trying to pull the wool, if you know what I mean!"
"Oh really, and how do you know?" he enquired.

'I then spent the next five minutes telling him how the prisoner in cell

17 had made it his intention to make life a misery for not only me, but anyone else smaller than him that he could bully, whilst at Inde. I remembered his hulking shape in the corridors by the tuck shop, swaggering around, daring any nozzer to get in his way. Not daring to answer a question in History, for fear that he would grab me round the throat for being a "crawling swotty bastard".

"I guess your ship has just come in then, son", the Custody Sergeant smirked. "Go and give him the good news!"

I walked back to the cell, smiling but trembling with nervousness, those feelings never go away. I opened the hatch, and shouted out, **"Shaun Duncan, Division Drake Blue Star Line Ho!"**

(Names changed for obvious reasons.)

He looked at me, and slowly a glimmer of recognition came into his eyes … he was always a bit slow. A nervous, wolf-like grin spread across his lips, as I reminded him who I was.

"Guess you had better provide your correct details mate or the Sarge will drop another charge on you," I said.

"What's gonna happen to me?", he said with barely a noticeable tremor in his voice.

"Dunno," I said "It's down to the Sarge, but I have explained all about your previous history, so he will probably be guided by me," I said, revelling in the irony of it all, determined to keep him in suspense for as long as I could.

"Given the choice, would you charge him or caution him?" the Sarge asked, suspecting he already knew the answer.

"Caution him Sarge, and kick him out, everyone deserves a chance."

'That was the Inde spirit. Despite the tough times he gave me, he was still an ex-Inde boy, and much as I tried to hate him, I couldn't. I gave him his property back, shook his hand and wished him well, telling him that next time he would probably end up in front of the Magistrate, as the next Custody Sergeant would not be as lenient. To tell the truth it was water off the duck's back. He strode off without saying thanks or looking back. Still I thought, what goes round comes around, he will never forget that night in the cell … and neither will I.'

Thank you Gary Cross, ex Inde Drake Division, 1978-1979.

But let's go back a bit! R. Armstrong, 1909-1911, wrote a piece in the Newsletter.

'I was a member of the first O.B.A. ... Captain Dunn formed it at the Sailors' Home, Canning Place. I still have many memories of my days in the Inde. When living in Rock Ferry I went to the Ship's Prize Day. One period the Prince of Wales (the uncrowned King) was on the first INDEFATIGABLE. Words now could not express my feelings for the Friendship I have had since the formation of the Association. These days I am unable to do all that I wish, I have two sticks. Just wish I could see you all again.'

Autumn 1990 Newsletter.

Obituary

'It was with sadness that I learnt today of the death of Richard Armstrong, 1909-1911, our oldest Old Boy, on August 31st, aged 94 years.

'I was privileged to know Richard. He was our last known link with that era and he had nothing but the fondest memories as a boy in the

Inde. Richard served at sea during the first World War, with the Royal Navy; and subsequently with the Merchant Service. He was a member of the crew of the ship which took the 'boy', Peter Scott, and his mother down to New Zealand, to visit his father's grave in Antarctica.

'Soon afterwards he joined the Mersey Docks and Harbour Board, serving eventually as Piermaster in various parts of the dock complex. His wife, who was the daughter of Captain Aldous, the 'skipper' of INDEFATIGABLE's tender, the JAMES BIBBY, died five years ago aged 91.'

Joe Rourke, 1941-1942, passed away in 1995 and many old friends from the Liverpool Retired Seafarers Club were present at his funeral, together with numbers of Inde's O.B.A. We have a letter written in pencil when Joe was an Inde boy.

'Dear Mum and Dad,

Just a few lines to say I am doing fine, and you are the same. Well, Mam, I won't be able to come home for Xmas cos I am going second leave with all the other Liverpool lads, and all the boys who live far away are going first. I wrote to Dave the other day also for my Navy hat thanks for the 4 shillings and stamps. I don't think you understand about the Ration books because I meant the old book from the beginning of 1941 you know last January. I suppose I will get a letter from you tomorrow. Don't forget Mam if you send a parcel put anything you can spare and a packet of envelopes. I am sorry to trouble you but could you send me two or three stamps. I am doing fine here so don't worry over me. I hope you and pop and Danny are all right. Well there is not much to say for the present so good by from Joe.

P.S. Tell Auntie Lizzie I would like a fountain pen or something of the sort. I hope you have got my watch out of the menders.

XXXXXX'

Memories!

I was personally happy to note a small paragraph in the Spring 1982 Newsletter.

'The creation of Mersey Branch of the Association at the Seamen's Mission, Colonsay House, Crosby Road, South Crosby, has proved most rewarding. With the help of Padre Bob Evans, we have a meeting every other month. Our last meeting was more like a 'get together' - talking over old times, recalling the good times. Very thirsty work!'

In the Spring 1982 Newsletter, N. Spencer, 1980-1982, gave an excellent reason for absence from the Reunion that year.

'I am afraid I will not be able to make the Reunion due to H.M.S. BRITANNIA's programme. I joined the yacht in January 1982 after some recommendations and interviews. We sailed straight into a Force 11 gale on passage to Gibraltar. After a week I began to find my way around only to discover we had sailed straight into a civil war at Aden.

'We immediately prepared for an evacuation and all got detailed jobs. Mine was bowman of the starboard sea boat. At 1000 on Friday we received the signal to proceed with the evacuation. We were lowered into the sea and headed for what we thought was the beach. When we arrived we found a beach completely lit up by car headlamps and at least 250 people waiting on the shore. Our boat's job was to proceed to the shore and take out 15 people at a time and then transfer them to the faster motor boats waiting about 500 yards off shore. We eventually finished about 0200. We were also told to prepare to proceed inshore again at 0600.

'Come 0600 we were again lowered into the water and again proceeded to the same beach. When we arrived we carried out the same procedure as the previous night. After about an hour of this, we noticed rebel troops gathering at the far end of the beach. Also the ship noticed a long line of tanks heading towards the beach. At around 0900 a lot of fighting broke out and we seemed to be caught in the middle. At one stage a bullet skimmed the water two feet from our boat. At this point we pulled out for things to calm down. After fifteen minutes of waiting we were able to proceed back to the beach to carry on the evacuation. We carried out three more evacuations in quieter places , thank God!

'In the end we evacuated 50 nationalities, 1,081 people. Apart from a very successful operation, it was a very rewarding one. To see the relief on people's faces is an image that will remain in my mind forever. We then proceeded on Royal duty, berthing in Auckland with eight hours to spare until the Queen embarked.'

And he was an Inde boy!

C.K.T. Haygarth, 1981-1983, Spring 1988 Newsletter.
'At the moment we are just off a place called Fuzairah, near the Strait of Hormuz, where we have been mine-hunting for the past couple of days. Two days ago a French minesweeper picked up five mines in the area we are now hunting in. The situation down here isn't as bad as the press are making out. Apparently they are saying that there are mines everywhere you look, which is just not true.

'We are working in 'Defence Watches' carrying gas masks, antiflash and lifejackets around with us all the time. We also wear hard helmets between decks. When we go ashore in Dubai, the Captain asks us not to speak to the press. The situation is sensitive, so it is important to keep a low profile.'

K. Wreford, 1982-1984, Autumn 1988 Newsletter.
'After two and a half months of solid patrol, we were making our last inbound transit of the Gulf, before disappearing down to Mombasa, for a bit of a rest. Well, we arrived off Dubai to collect mail when we heard a 'Mayday' call over the 'guard', which is an open channel for all aircraft and ships. The 'Mayday' was a Cypriot tanker being attacked by Iranian gunboats. We can only assist on humanitarian grounds except if the tanker is British flagged. We sent our helo out to the tanker who was 30 miles from our position. All the helo could see was a trail of burning smoke stretching out about a mile. The Iranians had disappeared back to their homeland. Our doctor helped, but fortunately there were no casualties.

'When we were down on our way to Mombasa, the Americans and the Iranians started shooting at each other, so we had to turn back. That was unfortunate because lots of married men flew their wives over to see them. Luckily, London sent back a signal saying that we would return to Mombasa as planned. We had a good ten days of sunshine and sand.

'Now we are on our way home. At this moment we are anchored off Port Suez waiting to enter the Suez Canal. We have six days in Spain, then home on June 10th. There will be a band and families waiting on the jetty. Should be a good day!'

The Editorial in the Autumn 1990 Newsletter.
'We have another illustrious member! He makes a truly fitting and historical link with the very 'roots' of INDEFATIGABLE. I refer to Viscount Exmouth, who has very kindly consented to join our list of Honorary Members.

'Viscount Exmouth is the descendant of Captain Sir Edward Pellew of the first INDEFATIGABLE, during the Napoleonic Wars; subsequently promoted Admiral, and created the first Viscount Exmouth of Canonteign.'

That Newsletter also stated that the long awaited Honours Board was nearly completed. The inscription was noted.

Presented to the INDEFATIGABLE School by the Old Boys Association both to commemorate the School's 125th Anniversary, and to act as a memorial to all Old Boys, Known and Unknown, who have given their lives in the Service of their Country.

As you stand and read,
Listen, and hear us say,
'For your Tomorrow,
We gave our Today.'

The Board was mounted that year in the Lower Corridor of the Main School. Many thanks are due to Nick Carter, one-time teacher and Honorary Old Boy, who obtained the timber and carried out all the carpentry work. He also made the glass fronted case to protect the gold leaf inscription.

The Liverpool Daily Post on the 11th July, 1997, included an important article.
'A memorable figurehead has finally come to rest in the Merseyside Maritime Museum. It was in a sorry state after being battered for years by seas and all weathers. Former members of INDEFATIGABLE came to the rescue and restored it.

'The wooden figurehead was carved for H.M.S. INDEFATIGABLE in 1848 in the image of the Duke of Clarence (later, King William IV). The figurehead was moved in 1944 to Plas Llanfair.'

Old Boys of the school, Harry Traynor, Alf Eady, Jack Harrison, Ron Phillips, Jim Clark, Joe Rourke and woodcarver Dave Williams, took three years to complete the painstaking task of restoring their school's symbol. Expert advice was afforded by Richard Hunter, a national authority on figureheads and their restoration. His guidance was invaluable and he never underestimated the perseverance, ingenuity and dogged determination of British seamen determined to preserve their Inde roots! Three years!

It was no easy task. Captain Harry Traynor has given us the details. The figurehead had been transported to the workshops of Messrs T. & J. Harrison. It took four months for it to dry out and that resulted in splitting and the opening of the laminated seams, showing the method of construction of these figures ... planks of pine bolted together longitudinally. When it had been cut from the bows of the ship, 'King William' was probably taller. Concrete had been poured into its base to give him the stability to rest on PHAETON's poop deck. During the next period of its life, 1914-1941, moisture would have been absorbed off the wet deck and rotting had set in.

On the 9th January, 1995, it was dry enough for work to commence. The shoulders were separated from the main body and that revealed a large block of soft wood for the middle section into which the head had been set. The remainder of the body and separate carvings had then been laminated on to this central core and it was all held together by long iron bolts through the body ... and they had rusted away. By this time the 'Sailor King' was a sorry sight.

The concrete had long since disappeared and the paint had to be removed with much care. What was left was thoroughly soaked in a 'preserver' and fungicide! The work intensified. Cascamite glue made sound joints, reinforcing the brass screws and plastic coated steel bolts which held the laminates together. Woodfiller was an unacceptable word.

The work was finally completed and King William now sits proudly in our Maritime Museum.

David Searle, Boy 97 Hood Division, 1955-1956, gives us his thoughts in Newsletter 29.
'During October of 2000 my wife and I decided to visit Anglesey and pay a visit to the old Inde. I had been saying for years that one day I would return to see my old haunts. It is sad that the School has now gone, and I am grateful to Lt. Col. Nicholls, Joint Services Mountain Training School, for inviting me and my wife to tour Inde and for the extreme courtesy which we received while we were there.

'The main building had not changed and I recognised many other buildings. The walled garden and the greenhouse behind the mast, where I used to help the gardener grow tomato plants, had now been developed. It was strange somehow to see cars parked on the sacred parade ground. My tour through the building was nostalgic, to say the least. I half expected to bump into Chief Clifford 'making his rounds' and the daunting prospect of being detailed to peel spuds outside the galley, clean out the sump, or at worst receive 'cuts' (corporal punishment) in the old library. I never experienced the latter ... many did!

'I managed a peep into the messhall and was quite amused to see that it now had a bar. I can always remember the portrait of Lord Nelson (was it?) and a revolver belonging to him in a glass case in the reception hall. The swimming pool was most impressive and heated, unlike when I swam there! I can remember that we were detailed to perform our band practice around the pool, away from the rest of the School because of the awful noise that we made.

'Outside I came across Nozzer's Rock, something I had completely forgotten about. We used to have a crafty smoke behind it from time to time. We walked the shores of Menai and saw the jetty and beach, where I spent many hours messing about with boats. In the summer we swam in Menai, it was cold but compulsory, and if you didn't have swimming trunks, you went in naked. The winter months were the worst, and I can still remember young lads sitting in the cutter, crying with the cold.

'After visiting the School, we found our way to St. Mary's Church, where as a boy I was confirmed. Unfortunately, the church was locked and we were unable to go inside and see the window, which I understand is dedicated to the Inde.

'When I left Inde as a boy, I went on to join the Royal Navy, where I served aboard H.M.S PALLISTER with the fisheries Protection Squadron in Iceland. Then I was in H.M.S ULSTER in the West Indies and South America at the time of the Cuban crisis. There were several trips back to the West Indies in H.M.S. URCHIN with the Dartmouth Training Squadron. My days in the Navy ended in the late '60's' aboard the old aircraft carrier, ARK ROYAL.

'I have never forgotten my time at the School, it was a tough place in those days, but I'm sure that it helped me with life.'

Ian Gibson, Boy 67, Raleigh Division, 1965-1966.
'Joining the Inde was a sudden shock to a young schoolboy who had never been further than to watch Chelsea play at home. I arrived at the Sailors' Home in Liverpool, with a small grip and the clothes I stood up in to await my fate. How did I come to be there? Well, with a shock of ginger hair and a tendency to fight anything and anyone at the drop of a hat, my parents quite logically thought I would turn out to be a hooligan. They decided that I needed discipline and what better place than the Inde! Looking back if I were my son, I would have done the same thing. But where the hell did they find INDEFATIGABLE?

'I remember the good times and the hard. I remember joining the band, not that I could play an instrument, but just to get out to the Fairs and Istedfords (?) or whatever the Welsh call them! Mr. Snape, the bandmaster, used to cringe and used to dread me being the duty bugler. I ended up on the drums.

'The instructors were the finest ... Mr. Gauge, Davies, Curtis, Crux, Dixie Dean our Divisional Officer, T. Davies, Jones, Keighley, Snape, Bond and Captain Wade. I remember them with fondest memories, they could be hard, but they had a human side ... most of them!

'After Inde I joined the Marines and spent two years in Singapore with 40 Commando R.M. Much followed ... Australia, Canada, New Guinea and in 1969 I was back with 41 Commando. I married my Teresa and the honeymoon week was shattered by the Ireland situation and I found myself standing in the Shankhill Road. That was my second day as a married man!'

Ian spent sixteen years with the Royal Marines and then transferred to the Prison Service as a Physical Training Officer. He represented Great Britain in the Quadrathlon World Championships in 1993 in Ibiza and came back with a Gold Medal in the team event.

Yet another Inde boy!

When the news of the closure of INDEFATIGABLE went around the world, a letter arrived from Australia from a Mrs. Purkis.
'My father, the late Andrew Galbraith, was placed in the care of Inde. He was born at 2, Thomaston Street, Kirkdale, Liverpool on 11th December, 1878; the son of a then licenced victualler, who died two months later. At the age of seven, on the death of his mother, Andrew was orphaned.

'I have in my possession a bible, prayer book and his indentures - all from this period of his life in INDEFATIGABLE. He was first at sea under sail, and I believe held a Master's ticket in sail. He served three years in the United States Navy during America's war against Spain. After this period he was at sea (steam), and eventually left the sea for good, in Melbourne, in 1911. He married in Sydney in 1916 and did not return to the U.K. He had two children, and died in 1969, aged 90.'

Her father's School records were sent to Mrs. Purkis.
Andrew Galbraith Reid.
Admitted: 19th December, 1892.
Age, 14, Height, 4 feet seven and a half inches; Weight 82 lbs.
Where from: Seamens Orphanage (father and mother dead).
Relative: Aunt; Miss Austin, 9, Marshall Street, Wellington Road, Toxteth.
Date leaving: 12th February, 1895. For Cardiff to join ship Deva as Boy - 10 shillings a month. William Just & Co.
Character on leaving: Very Good.
Height, 5 feet 1 inch,

Weight, 105 lbs.
9th April, 1896 - Received news of this boy having been left in Mauritius with fever.
17th May, 1896 - Visited ship after return home.

Newsletter 1998, J.A. Harrison, 1941-1942.
Captain Harry Traynor and Alf Eady, one time Chairman and Vice-Chairman of the O.B.A. spent much time aboard KIWI 1 in Albert Dock, giving instructions to some of the old Inde lads, who turned up for work in refurbishing the newly-acquired craft. Harry, as ever, had to be very patient. They all were to spend part of their time at the business end of a chipping hammer and paint brush and had to help with the rewiring. Other tasks were to swing the lamp and have a good laugh.

But here is the real story. The volunteers were all pensioners of uncertain age ... the boss was Harry Traynor, better known as Misa Captain Harry, Alf Eady was i/c the galley, Alec Sinclair, ex-Harrison

was the Chief Engineer, the Bosun was Jack Harrison, the Deckhands were Jim Clark, Tom Roberts and Steve Denton and the owner was Pat Moran. She was designed in New Zealand as one of the KIWI Class, 52ft 6inches by 13ft beam with a service speed of 10 knots and a range of 400 miles at full speed. Captain Harry Traynor takes up the story.

Incidentally, the ship's name is INDEFATIGABLE ... of course!

'On the Friday we mustered at Albert Dock for the bus to take us to Devonport ... a clapped out old banger, which was well past its scrap-by date. The driver had painted it red with a black nose for this special job ... it should have been black with a red nose!

'Pat Moran told us that he had two boats to bring to Liverpool, but only one navigator, me! The other boat was to follow in my wake, with a very good Greek restaurant owner in charge. The remainder of his crew consisted of soldiers from the King's Liverpool Regiment, who knew nothing about navigation but claimed to be very good at fishing.

'My orders were to proceed to Sam's Bar in Tithebarn Street to collect the seven stalwarts, plus kit and bedding, 14 lifejackets, 14 bedrolls, 14 bags of personal effects, 7 fishing rods, 3 cwt. of best coal for the galley fires, food for 14 men for 7 days, fire extinguishers and an anchor. We hitched a trailer.

'Finally loaded up, we were a shipowners dream, full and down with no space wasted. I must also add that we had to bring our own pots, pans and eating irons, plus our very own Elsan toilet ... just like the good old days. At 0900 hours in the pouring rain we departed Sam's Bar and staggered towards the Mersey Tunnel, the A41 and all places South, praying that the police would not stop us and run us all in for over-loading. Before we got to Eastham we discovered that the roof was leaking, right on Alf Eady's head; he was half buried in pots, pans and toilet rolls and was unable to move. He just contented himself with uttering foul expletives from time to time and we ignored him.

'After three long hours, the driver let us into a secret that the radiator was leaking and that, if he did not get water soon, the engine would seize. We stopped every few hours until we approached Exeter. Here the driver made an emergency turn into Sainsbury's car park; there was a long queue of cars, but the driver shouted that the radiator was dry and shouted "We're Scousers" to which the lady raised her hat and called us in.

'Next day we had a mammoth breakfast and prepared the vessel for sea. All outfacing windows were boarded over and hatch covers into the hull had to be secured; these had been open for a year and were rust-welded open. My merry men soon put them right and by late evening, the boat was ready for departure on the early tide next morning.

'Sunday 21st September dawned bright and sunny, the barometer steady, light Easterly breeze and the forecast was good. I decided to leave at 0900, about one hour before high water, to enable the boat to cross a 1.5 metre patch over the 'Bridge', a short cut South of Drakes Island, thereby saving a couple of miles of harbour steaming.'

Meantime all was not too well on the other vessel as the soldiery had decided to go fishing. They had also no kit, rations or anything on board. There was a slight delay. The story continues.

'The boats were rolling heavily. At 1500 our consort called on the radio, "Misa Captain Harry, all my men are in bed seasick, what to do?" "Turn 'em out!", was my advice, being a considerate old-sailorman.

'Lands End was rounded at 0300 and at 0430 we had Cape Cornwall abeam, so we set course to cross the Bristol Channel. Shortly after this our consort was again on the radio, "Misa Captain Harry, do you have any cigarettes to spare?" With the boats rolling so heavily I had no intention of going anywhere near him. I replied that we were all non-smokers. Quiet reigned for another hour, then, "Misa Captain Harry, what time we get into port today?" I informed him that the next port was Liverpool, some 48 hours away. "That's okay by me", he replied.

'Silence descended on our radio channel if only for a short while, then,

"Misa Captain Harry, we have no food or water left, can you give me some? I will come alongside and you can pass the food." The boats were now rolling violently and no way was I having him near me. I told him to wait until my men had made up some watertight parcels, then I would tell him when we were ready. This took a couple of hours. At last I told him to come under my stern and we would pass a line to him. Simple you may think. Not so. Our hungry duck commenced his approach from dead astern. The range decreased, 50ft, 20 ft, 10ft. Then I noticed a sharp increase in his bow wave. He had put his engine control the wrong way. I slammed mine to full ahead and reached for the Rennies! Go away, go away, I pleaded or words to that effect. Our Greek Restaurater thought it a huge joke, he not being a Harrison man! Eventually, through the good offices of Alf Eady, the food and water was transferred, though I swear I saw tears in Alf's eyes!

'Clinging on for dear life we wended our way towards the Welsh coast. I felt content. I had sorted things out. Liverpool here I come.

'Later in the afternoon I noticed our consort dropping astern. What now, I mused. I called him and was told he had engine trouble and would I put our engineer aboard his boat. "No way", I replied. "Why not?", said he. I had to explain that the boats were doing everything except turn turtle and out gallant engineer, Jock Sinclair, was 70 years of age, although he was at that moment jammed into the corner of the wheelhouse. He would give advice over the radio which he did and, by remote control, soon had the other vessel under way.

'Once more the air waves fell silent, but not for long. Shortly after midnight came the cry, "Misa Captain Harry, we are exhausted, we must have rest." I decided to make for the nearest port, Milford Haven, to let them rest. The old fogeys on my boat were as fit as fiddles, but I had been on the bridge for 44 hours and my legs were feeling like lead. I was not sorry to be going in.

'I called Milford Haven and explained the situation, requesting a Pilot on arrival. The brotherhood of the sea came to the fore; they said it would be very expensive to take a Pilot and to avoid this cost they would send out the Pilot Boat to lead us in free of charge.'

They were secure alongside at 0700.

'The soldiers, who had been bedridden since Plymouth, made a miraculous recovery and were on their way home to Liverpool by 0730. They had had enough. I mustered my troops and gave them the opportunity to pack up and go home, but they were made of sterner stuff and were ready to continue to Liverpool. I decided that we should sleep until midday, have a shower and a good meal and sail at 1500. We kept to this schedule.

'It was a perfect day so I went inside Skokholm and Skomer Island, our draft being only six feet; thence through Ramsey Sound to bring St. David's Head abeam, where I set course for Badsey Sound and Braich y Pwll; thence North for the South Stack, after we went inside the Skerries and made our way to the Liverpool Bar. The vessel entered Canning Half Tide dock at 1930 and, after waiting for the docks to level, we berthed in the Albert Dock at 2230 and rang F.W.E.

'We had been 3 days 9 hours on passage - a distance of 390 miles, giving an average speed of 4.81 knots with fuel consumption of 82 gallons of diesel.

'The Kingsmen had requested that we display their regimental banner along the shipsides when we entered the Mersey. This I was pleased to do. Dressed overall wearing the INDEFATIGABLE O.B.A. flag at the masthead and the regimental banners on our sides, we entered the channel. On passing the Liverpool Pilot boat, I overheard them reporting a strange Pilot boat, dressed up like a fairground and full of old men! I just could not resist calling them and telling them that we were the King's Regiment returning from the Crimean War!'

Thank you Misa Captain Harry … that was truly splendid.

The Daily Post on the 2nd June, 1999 carried an article written by David Greenwood.

IMMORTALISED IN GLASS, THE INDEFATIGABLE SPIRIT

'The name of a school which trained generations of seafarers is to live on in stained glass. For the first time this weekend, Old Boys of the INDEFATIGABLE will be able to inspect a memorial window which has been given pride of place at St Mary's Church at Llanfairpwll in Anglesey.

'On Sunday morning up to fifty former pupils, who are expected to gather for the INDEFATIGABLE Old Boys Association annual meeting in Anglesey, will take a nostalgic stroll down memory lane for a morning service at the church.

'Mr Patrick Purser, a one-time geography teacher at the school and the Association chairman, and ex-master mariner, Captain Harry Traynor from Helsby, stated that it was a dream come true. "We wanted the window to tell the INDEFATIGABLE story and that has been achieved superbly well."

'The window was created by Neil Willis, formerly of Beaumaris, and is based on paintings by Menai Bridge artist, Ieuan Williams.'

Pat Purser had published a letter in the Inde Newsletter, dated March, 27th, 2001.

'VALE

First, I would like to thank you all for the very generous response to our appeal for an 'Inde spot' at the National Memorial Arboretum. As I write, donations continue to arrive and we have virtually covered all expenses! Thank you. It was a grand gesture to remember your old 'comrades-in-arms', as well as those boys who have passed through INDEFATIGABLE over the years.

'I came to Inde as a schoolmaster in 1977 and it wasn't long before I saw a need for an Old Boys Association, which could benefit the School enormously. After repeated requests I was finally given permission to start such an organisation on my own and with a personal budget loan from the then Captain Headmaster, Bob Youngman. I retired in 1991 but continued to act as Secretary, Treasurer and Editor until after the

School closed in 1995. Throughout the years, the Association has grown from a mere handful to over two hundred, under the able leadership of successive Chairmen, notably the longest serving, Harry Traynor, whose unstinted efforts and enthusiasm have contributed towards many notable achievements - school bursaries and the figurehead restoration immediately come to mind - but there were other projects which he helped bring to fruition. Thank you, Harry!

'I typed and printed out the very first O.B.A. Newsletter on the School duplicating machine in the Autumn of 1983 and in my editorial I gave a resume of the Inde's history. We little thought then of its closure some twelve years hence! I finished by saying that over her history INDEFATIGABLE's golden principles had always been - " to try and teach boys to love and care for their neighbours, to strengthen their characters, to make them self-reliant, honest and industrious; so that they are well equiped to go out and meet life 'head-on' with a cheerful smile on their lips and determination in their hearts." I honestly tried to follow those precepts during my fourteen years teaching at the School. The work was hard and demanding, but as time went on I grew to love and respect the boys in my charge. Of course, there were 'rotten apples'; is there any cross section of society which won't have them? But, what sterling fellows you all are!

'The time has now come for the Old Guard to bow out from control and let younger blood take the helm. What direction your Association will take, now that its lynch pin - the School - has gone, I don't know. It is up to you to see that it all continues, as a primary aim, to serve and help others, very much as the Founding Fathers of Inde wanted for you Old Boys, and your predecessors. So let us continue to carry the INDEFATIGABLE motto in our hearts as we severally face the future … Deo Adjuvante.

Pat Purser, as ever, has used the right words.

Friendships and memories of 'the Inde' will remain to the end.

Other Titles by Bob Evans

HMS Eaglet £12.00

The Centenary of the Royal Naval Reserves in 2004 is the perfect excuse for a 'jolly'... the saga of HMS Eaglet. This book is proof that history can be informative, uplifting and full of fun. The only excuse for the nautical nonsense is that it actually happened. We travel from sail to steam, the trenches in France to Gallipoli, the Battle of the Atlantic to Iraq ... and this is the story of people who were there. Bob Evans is firmly part of it all and has added yet another interlocking piece to the jigsaw of Liverpool's proud maritime history. This is the story of the Royal Navy in the Northwest.

Soft back 362 pp - A5 - Illustrated - ISBN 1 901231 38 0

The Way to Liverpool £5.00

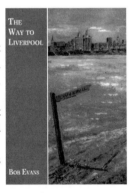

This book is fun with laughter and tears, wit and wisdom, and tells the true story of life in the valleys of South Wales with magnolia, mice and a colliery with no coal to be seen. From suburban Cardiff to an up-market Cathedral in Llandaff, we meet all sorts and conditions of humanity and another mouse. Then Bob Evans came to Liverpool and this autobiography is about that journey.

Soft back 159 pp - A5 - Illustrated - ISBN 1 901231 14 3

Dog Collar in the Docks £7.00

This book is much more than an autobiography. It is an encounter with almost thirty years of Ships and Seafarers in Liverpool at a time when this great port was adapting itself to the changes and challenges of the tail end of the Twentieth Century. The people are real, the pain and laughter compelling, the story is a good read. Bob Evans is part of that story. His ministry at the Mersey Mission to Seamen and the Royal Naval Reserve placed him at the forefront of waterfront life, as his 'dog collar' seems to open every door.

Softback - 219pp - A5 - ISBN: 0 907768 76 8

Mersey Mariners £7.00

The story of seafarers from the last two centuries. From sail to steam, boarding houses and crimps, extortion, poverty, the unforgiving sea; all these are vividly described. The courage of the men, the mix of nationalities and races and the cheapness of life all add colour to the scene. Against all this is the remarkable saga of the charities and welfare organisations that were set up to combat the problems. That story continues. Bob Evans is firmly part of that history and brings it alive for us in this compelling read.

Softback - 285pp - A5 - ISBN: 1 901231 05 4

The Training Ships of Liverpool £7.00

The basic aim was the training of young lads. H.M.S. Conway was the officers' training ship and lay a little south of Rock Ferry Pier. The Akbar, a Protestant reformatory vessel, sat between Eastham and Rock Ferry. Next in line was Indefatigable, an old sailing frigate, housing orphaned sons of seamen of good standing. Life was really tough, but the great hardships of the reformatory ships were better than the streets of Liverpool. Bob Evans is again firmly part of this history. It is the story of Liverpool seafaring.

Softback - 205pp - A5 - ISBN: 0 901231 31 3

The Indefatigable